The Legal Guide For Practicing Psychotherapy In Colorado

2012 Edition

Denis K. Lane, M.A., J.D.

BRADFORD PUBLISHING COMPANY
Denver, Colorado

Disclaimer

This book, *The Legal Guide for Practicing Psychotherapy in Colorado, 2012 Edition,* is intended to provide general information with regard to the subject matter covered. It is not meant to provide legal opinions or to offer advice, nor to serve as a substitute for advice by licensed, legal, or other professionals. This book is sold with the understanding that Bradford Publishing Company and the author, by virtue of its publication, are not engaged in rendering legal or other professional services to the reader.

Bradford Publishing Company and the author do not warrant that the information contained in this book is complete or accurate, and do not assume and hereby disclaim any liability to any person for any loss or damage caused by errors, inaccuracies, omissions, or usage of this book.

Laws, and interpretations of those laws, change frequently and the subject matter of this book can have important legal consequences. It is the responsibility of the user of this book to know if the information contained in it is applicable to his or her situation, and if necessary, to consult legal, tax, or other counsel.

ISBN: 978-1-932779-75-2

Bradford Publishing Company
1743 Wazee Street, Denver, Colorado 80202
www.bradfordpublishing.com

About The Author

The original author of this book, Louie Larimer, has entrusted to **Denis Lane** the privilege of keeping this book updated so that it continues to serve as a valuable resource for mental health professionals. Denis Lane has been practicing law since 1976 in Oklahoma, the District of Columbia, and Colorado. Mr. Lane has practiced mental health law since 1978, when he was assigned to represent the District of Columbia in mental health commitments and to represent St. Elizabeth's Hospital in landmark litigation involving the rights of adolescents committed to psychiatric facilities.

Since that time, Mr. Lane has handled both routine and complex issues involved in 72-hour holds, short-term commitments, long-term commitments, and court approval of electro-convulsive treatment. He has also advised and represented hundreds of mental health professionals in malpractice actions and Grievance Board matters. In addition, he consults with mental health professionals on legal and ethical issues related to subpoenas for production of documents in court, reporting child abuse, and the business aspects of the practice of psychotherapy.

As part of his law practice, Mr. Lane conducts audits of programs at mental health facilities to ensure compliance with Colorado statutes and ethical provisions. Mr. Lane is also the author of the *Lawyer's Corner* articles published quarterly in the newsletter of the Colorado Association of Marriage & Family Therapists.

The **Center for Professional Studies,** which previously published this book, provides workshops and seminars on malpractice avoidance, ethical issues, legal standards, record-keeping practices, and testifying in court.

Acknowledgments

Louie Larimer first conceived of the need for this resource for mental health professionals, and labored over the first volume of the *Legal Guide to the Practice of Psychotherapy in Colorado.* Since its initial publication in 1992, this book has been a standard for psychotherapists to use in identifying ethical issues and complying with the legal standards established by the Colorado Legislature for the practice of psychotherapy.

Louie Larimer's contributions to psychotherapists and to the mental health profession itself are enormous. He has advocated the adoption and application of laws that reflect standard ethical practices in the field. Where he perceived a lack of clarity in the law and a need for interpretation of legal guidelines, he sought changes and clarity from the legislature and from the mental health boards. I appreciate the training provided to me by Louie Larimer, his mentoring, and the challenge to carry on his legacy.

Thanks to all of the mental health professionals who continue to submit questions and seek consultation on the difficult issues in the day-to-day practice of psychotherapy, and who inspire a great deal of the discussion and analysis of the ethical issues contained in this work.

This book is dedicated to Toni Zimmerman, M.A., LMFT; Sharon K. Anderson, Ph.D.; and all the professors, educators, and supervisors who teach graduate students and clinicians the legal and ethical standards of their profession. Their work is truly a labor of love.

Contents

CHAPTER 1: COLORADO JUDICIAL SYSTEM ... 1
- 1.01 Judicial Districts ... 1
- 1.02 County Courts ... 1
- 1.03 Small Claims ... 2
- 1.04 District Courts ... 3
- 1.05 Colorado Court of Appeals ... 4
- 1.06 Colorado Supreme Court ... 5
- 1.07 Municipal Courts ... 5
- 1.08 Federal Courts ... 6
- 1.09 Players and Roles ... 7

CHAPTER 2: CONFIDENTIALITY ... 15

PART I: DUTY OF CONFIDENTIALITY ... 15
- 2.01 Sources of Confidentiality ... 15
- 2.02 Colorado Confidentiality Statute ... 17
- 2.03 Common Law ... 19
- 2.04 Ethical Duties ... 21
- 2.05 Federal Privacy Statutes ... 22
- 2.06 Statutory Privilege ... 22
- 2.07 Physician-Patient Privilege ... 23
- 2.08 Therapist-Client Privilege ... 24
- 2.09 HIV/AIDS Reporting ... 26

PART II: EXCEPTIONS TO CONFIDENTIALITY ... 27
- 2.10 Mandatory Reporting of Child Abuse or Neglect ... 27
- 2.11 Criminal Prosecutions for Child Abuse ... 33
- 2.12 Duty to Warn ... 34
- 2.13 Duty to Report a Crime ... 37
- 2.14 Duty to Report Mistreatment of an At-Risk Adult/Elder Abuse ... 38
- 2.15 Waiver by Client ... 40
- 2.16 Care and Treatment of the Mentally Ill ... 41
- 2.17 Treating Adolescents ... 42
- 2.18 Federal Law Regarding Confidentiality ... 43

PART III: PRACTICE POINTERS ... 44
- 2.19 Releasing Files and Records ... 44
- 2.20 Office Management ... 45
- 2.21 Responding to Subpoenas and Requests for Client Records ... 46
- 2.22 HIPAA Business Practices ... 53
- 2.23 HIPAA Standards Concerning Authorizations to Disclose Confidential Healthcare Information ... 57
- 2.24 Preparing a Professional Will: Protecting Clients and Their Treatment Information After a Therapist's Retirement, Disability, or Death ... 59

CHAPTER 3: TESTIFYING AS AN EXPERT . . . 65
3.01 Expert Witness Testimony . . . 65
3.02 Offered Testimony Must Be Helpful . . . 65
3.03 Qualifying as an Expert . . . 67
3.04 Types of Testimony . . . 68
3.05 Basis of Testimony . . . 68
3.06 Disclosure of Underlying Facts or Data . . . 69
3.07 Being Retained . . . 70
3.08 Preparing a Report . . . 71
3.09 Deposition Practice . . . 72
3.10 Preparation for Trial . . . 75
3.11 On the Witness Stand . . . 76
3.12 Your Rights as a Witness . . . 78
3.13 Immunity . . . 79
3.14 Testifying Is Fun . . . 80
CHAPTER 4: MALPRACTICE AND PROFESSIONAL LIABILITY . . . 81
4.01 Negligence . . . 81
4.02 Specific Types of Negligence . . . 84
4.03 A Word of Caution . . . 85
4.04 Duty to Warn and Protect . . . 87
4.05 Invasion of Privacy . . . 92
4.06 Outrageous Conduct . . . 92
4.07 Sexual Relations with a Client . . . 93
4.08 Failure to Report Child Abuse . . . 94
4.09 Insurance Fraud . . . 95
4.10 Billing Practices . . . 97
4.11 Responding to a Lawsuit . . . 98
4.12 Malpractice Insurance . . . 99
4.13 Malpractice Prevention . . . 100
4.14 Informed Consent . . . 104
4.15 Litigation Trends and Controversies . . . 106
4.16 Maintaining Client Records . . . 110
4.17 Pastoral Counseling/Spiritual Counseling . . . 116
4.18 Legal Standards for Forensic Evaluations . . . 119
4.19 College and University Counseling Programs: Best Practices . . . 123
4.20 Testifying in Divorce Litigation: Prevention of Foreseeable Risks . . . 124
CHAPTER 5: RESTRICTION OF CLIENT LIBERTIES . . . 127
5.01 Guardianship . . . 127
5.02 Conservatorship . . . 136
5.03 Restraining Orders . . . 137
5.04 Involuntary Mental Health Commitments . . . 143
5.05 Care and Treatment of a Minor . . . 154

5.06	Treatment of Alcoholics	157
5.07	Care and Treatment of the Developmentally Disabled	161
5.08	Criminal Insanity	165
5.09	The Role of the Psychotherapist	169
CHAPTER 6: LICENSING CONSIDERATIONS		171
6.01	Licensed Professionals	171
6.02	Mandatory Disclosure of Information	175
6.03	Non-Disclosure of Confidential Communications	179
6.04	Grievance Procedures	180
6.05	Rules of the Mental Health Boards	181
6.06	Standards for Clinical Supervision	186
6.07	Prohibited Activities	191
6.08	Unauthorized Practice	193
6.09	Professional Service Corporations	194
6.10	Psychiatrists	195
6.11	Addiction Counselors	200
6.12	Psychiatric Technicians	201
6.13	The Michael Skolnik Medical Transparency Act of 2010	203
6.14	Statutory Requirement for Continuing Professional Development	206
6.15	Technology in Counseling	208
CHAPTER 7: BUSINESS ASPECTS		213
7.01	Government Employment	213
7.02	Nonprofit Corporations	213
7.03	Business Entities	214
7.04	Sole Proprietorship	214
7.05	Partnerships	216
7.06	Corporations for Profit	219
7.07	Employees or Independent Contractors	223
7.08	Employment Law	227
7.09	Workers' Compensation	230
7.10	Employer Payroll Taxes	230
7.11	Employee Withholdings	231
7.12	Insurance	231
7.13	Use of Professionals	232
7.14	Billing Standards and Billing Practices	232
CHAPTER 8: STANDARDS FOR DOMESTIC EVALUATIONS AND FOR DOMESTIC VIOLENCE TREATMENT PROVIDERS		239
8.01	Allocation of Parental Responsibilities	239
8.02	Parenting Time	243
8.03	Standard of Care for Testifying in Domestic Cases	244
8.04	Standards for Child and Family Investigators	244
8.05	Access to Treatment Information	250
8.06	Parenting Coordinators	251

8.07 Decision-Makers 254
8.08 Recent Caselaw Concerning Domestic Evaluations 255
8.09 Limitations on Testimony by Mental Health Clinicians in Domestic Actions: Practical and Ethical Considerations for Attorneys 256
8.10 Approved Domestic Violence Treatment Providers 260
8.11 Compliance with DVOMB Standards by Approved Treatment Providers 262
8.12 Recordkeeping Practices for DVOMB Approved Treatment Providers 267
8.13 Potential Parental Alienation and the Best Interests of Children 268
FORMS 271
TABLES OF AUTHORITIES 297
INDEX 305

CHAPTER 1: COLORADO JUDICIAL SYSTEM

1.01 Judicial Districts

The State of Colorado is divided into 22 judicial districts. Each judicial district encompasses at least one county and in some cases two or more counties. For example, the Fourth Judicial District provides judicial services for Teller and El Paso Counties, while the Second Judicial District services only the City and County of Denver.

Within each judicial district there is a County Court and a District Court. These two courts are responsible for deciding cases that arise under appropriate federal and state law.

1.02 County Courts

The County Court is a court with limited jurisdiction. It may only hear and decide certain types of cases. Specifically, the County Court is limited to the following types of cases:

1. Civil actions in which the debt, damage, or value of the personal property claimed does not exceed $15,000;
2. Criminal actions that constitute misdemeanors or petty offenses;
3. Change of name proceedings;
4. Domestic abuse proceedings under Article 4 of Title 14, C.R.S.; and
5. Actions for the issuance of restraining orders to prevent assaults and threatened bodily harm.

In light of the foregoing limitations, the County Court has no jurisdiction to hear and decide the following types of cases:

1. Probate matters;
2. Matters of mental health, including commitment, restoration to competence, and the appointment of conservators, except when a County Court Judge is appointed by a District Judge as a Magistrate to hear such matters;
3. Matters of divorce, legal separation, and annulment;

4. Matters affecting children, including custody, support, guardianship, adoption, dependency, or delinquency;
5. Matters affecting boundaries of title to real property; and
6. Felony criminal cases.

Since the County Court has no jurisdiction to hear the foregoing types of cases, they are handled by the District Courts, which are described in section 1.04 of this book. Because most expert witness testimony offered by psychotherapists typically involves matters of mental health, divorce, custody, adoption, etc., such testimony is most often heard in the District Court.

Although each judicial district has one County Court, there are usually several County Court Judges in each judicial district. These judges are appointed by the Governor for an initial term of two years and thereafter are placed before the general public for retention every four years.

Matters before the County Court are typically heard within a relatively short time frame, ranging from two to six months. The rules of procedure are not as cumbersome as in the District Court and do not allow extensive discovery, such as the right to depositions and written interrogatories before trial. There is a right to a trial by jury in the County Court.

1.03 Small Claims

In order to provide public access to the courts, the Colorado Legislature has established a Small Claims Division within the County Court. Like the County Court, the Small Claims Court is a court of limited jurisdiction.

To qualify for Small Claims treatment, the following conditions must be met:

1. The controversy must be a civil matter (as opposed to a criminal matter); and
2. The monetary amount involved cannot exceed $7,500.

Each litigant presents his or her case in a manner remarkably like that popularized by Judge Wapner in *The People's Court.* A small claims case is heard within a relatively quick time frame. There are few rules of procedure, and the rules of evidence are greatly relaxed.

1.04 District Courts

There is a District Court within each judicial district. This court is a court of general jurisdiction; it is not limited as to the types of cases it may hear. Although a District Court may hear and decide cases in which the County Court has jurisdiction, it will be reluctant to do so, since the County Court was established so that the District Court could concentrate on actions of a more serious nature, e.g., criminal actions that are felonies, juvenile cases, probate, mental health, divorce, and civil cases in which the amount in controversy exceeds $15,000.

The Colorado Rules of Procedure and the Colorado Rules of Evidence are strictly followed. A typical District Court case could take as long as two years to get to trial. There is a right to a jury trial in certain cases.

Like the County Court, there are several District Court Judges who preside in the same District. They are appointed by the Governor for an initial two-year term and are placed before the public for retention every four years thereafter.

The District Court in some districts is divided into specialty courts that handle similar types of cases. For example, it is common to find in many large districts the following types of specialty courts: Divorce, Juvenile, Probate, Civil, and Criminal. The specialty courts are presided over by a District Court Judge who hears only those particular types of cases. The rationale for such an arrangement is that there are certain economies of scale that occur through specialization. Not all District Courts embrace this belief. In those districts where specialization has not been adopted, the District Court Judges hear and decide the entire spectrum of cases.

There are certain types of cases that involve routine legal and factual issues and are voluminous in number. Divorce, probate, and juvenile cases fall into this category. In order to process the sheer volume of these cases, the District Courts are permitted to employ Magistrates who work under the supervision of a District Court Judge and are given limited authority to handle these routine matters. The Magistrates are lawyers who are appointed by the Chief Judge for each judicial district.

The District Courts generally have an Office of Dispute Resolution that conducts alternative dispute resolution (ADR) of civil cases, domestic litigation, and dependency and neglect actions. This Office provides dispute resolution at a reasonable cost for litigants, who may otherwise be embroiled in lengthy, expensive litigation. ADR enables parties to resolve both domestic conflicts and civil suits in an efficient, cost-effective process.

1.05 Colorado Court of Appeals

The County and District Courts are trial courts. Evidence is introduced and witnesses testify in a trial setting. There may or may not be a jury, depending on the type of case and the desires of the litigants.

A decision of the County Court may be appealed to the District Court, which will determine whether or not the County Court Judge erred in his or her application of the law. This review will be made by a single District Court Judge. If it is determined that an error of law was made, the case may be returned to the County Court for retrial or it may simply be decided by the District Court Judge based upon the evidence presented at the trial.

A litigant may appeal the decision of a District Court to the Colorado Court of Appeals. This appeal is a matter of right and cannot be denied. The Court of Appeals is comprised of judges appointed by the Governor for an initial term of eight years. Thereafter, each Judge of the Court of Appeals is periodically placed before the public for retention.

The Court of Appeals is located in Denver. It is organized into divisions of three judges. Each division hears and decides cases that come before it. There is no trial. The divisions simply review the written transcript of the proceeding before the District Court, study the legal briefs submitted, and listen to the oral arguments of the attorneys to determine whether there was an error of law in the lower court proceeding. This decision is the result of a majority vote of the three-judge division.

If the division determines there was no error, the lower court decision is affirmed. If the division determines there was an error, the lower court decision is reversed and remanded for trial. In some cases, the Court of Appeals corrects the error itself without remanding the case for retrial.

A written opinion of the decision is prepared by one of the judges, and the opinion becomes a part of the common law of the State of Colorado, until or unless it is reversed by the Colorado Supreme Court.

1.06 Colorado Supreme Court

The Colorado Supreme Court is the highest court in the State and it is the court of last resort for most litigants. Unless the appeal involves some interpretation of a federal statute or a constitutional issue, there is no other appellate remedy.

Except for a few narrow circumstances, there is no automatic mandatory right of appeal to the Colorado Supreme Court. The Colorado Supreme Court exercises its discretion as to which cases it will review. A litigant seeking to appeal a Court of Appeals decision files for a *writ of certiorari.* If the Colorado Supreme Court decides that the legal issues are of statewide importance, or if the case would help to clarify the law in Colorado, it may elect to hear the case and grant the request for a writ of certiorari. The writ is an instruction to the Colorado Court of Appeals to forward the case to the Colorado Supreme Court. If the court elects to refrain from hearing the case, the writ is denied and the appeal is over.

The Colorado Supreme Court sits in Denver. It is comprised of seven Supreme Court Justices who are appointed by the Governor and who are placed before the public for retention at the expiration of their initial term. The Colorado Supreme Court does not sit in divisions like the Colorado Court of Appeals. Each case is presented to all of the Justices at the same time. Each Justice has one vote. The vote of the majority becomes the decision of the Court.

Like the Colorado Court of Appeals, the Colorado Supreme Court reviews the trial court record of proceedings, reviews the legal briefs prepared by the attorneys, and listens to oral arguments. There is no direct taking of evidence. Once a decision is reached, a written opinion is prepared and published. The decisions of the Colorado Supreme Court become law and are binding upon the appellate and trial courts in the State.

1.07 Municipal Courts

Municipal Courts are established by various city charters and ordinances. Because municipal entities (cities) promulgate laws known as ordinances, there must be a court in which disputes involving such ordinances can be heard. Accordingly, cities and towns have established local municipal or city courts.

These courts are limited to hearing petty offenses, such as building and zoning violations, minor traffic offenses, minor neighborhood domestic disputes, and dog-at-large cases. These are offenses against the municipality and do not usually involve mental health issues. Hence, the testimony of a psychotherapist is typically not required.

1.08 Federal Courts

The laws of the United States of America require a judicial forum for cases involving federal issues. Accordingly, a federal court system has been established for the purpose of resolving certain civil and criminal cases arising under the statutes and the Constitution of the United States.

The federal court system is organized into various federal districts, which roughly correspond to the geographical boundaries of the 50 states and the territories of the United States. Each District has one Federal District Court. This court is a trial court having specific jurisdiction over cases involving the United States Constitution, federal statutes, rules and regulations, and certain civil cases between citizens of different states, provided the amount in controversy is in excess of $75,000.

There is at least one United States Federal District Court Judge in each federal district. Each Federal District Court Judge is appointed by the President for life.

Like the state court system, the federal court system has created specialty courts to hear and decide cases involving a specialized area of the law. Tax, Admiralty, Patent, and Claims are examples of federal specialty courts.

Appeals of the decisions of the Federal District Courts and the specialty courts are handled by the United States Circuit Court of Appeals. The Circuit Court of Appeals operates in a manner similar to the Colorado Court of Appeals.

The United States Supreme Court is the highest court in the United States. There are nine United States Supreme Court Justices. The court operates in a manner similar to the Colorado Supreme Court, except it interprets and construes federal statutory law and constitutional issues as opposed to state law issues.

The potential for expert witness testimony from a psychotherapist is more limited in the federal system than in state courts because—except in federal criminal prosecutions—federal court cases generally do not involve mental health issues. Also, there are no divorce, child custody, adoption, or other such cases in federal court, which typically require expert witness testimony from a psychotherapist.

1.09 Players and Roles

The smooth and efficient operation of the Colorado judicial system depends upon a variety of people to perform specific duties and fulfill carefully defined obligations.

In order to meaningfully contribute to the judicial system, a psychotherapist must have a clear understanding of who these people are and what roles are expected of them. Although most people have a vague idea of the key players in the judicial system, many do not fully comprehend the specific functions of each. Frequently, this lack of knowledge results in a breakdown in communication, unnecessary frustration, and an inability to effectively serve the psychotherapist's client.

The following paragraphs outline the role of the key players in the judicial system.

Arbitrator. An arbitrator is a person selected by the parties to a dispute to hear the positions and arguments of both sides and then render a decision that is binding upon both parties. Both parties typically share the arbitrator's fee. Arbitration is a voluntary alternative to a judicial resolution of a controversy. It is generally less expensive and less time-consuming than litigation.

Attorney. An attorney is a person trained in the law to act as an advocate for his or her client.

Attorney General. The Attorney General is a statewide elected official who is responsible for representing the State of Colorado in its various legal matters. Most of the day-to-day legal representation is performed by Assistant Attorney Generals who are appointed by the Attorney General.

Bailiff. A bailiff works for a trial judge and assists the judge in maintaining courtroom order and performing other routine duties necessary for the smooth functioning of the court when it is in session. When a jury has been selected, the bailiff is responsible for escorting the jury and taking care of their personal needs while they are in service to the court. Some judges are hiring recent law school graduates as bailiffs and using them as aides in their legal research.

A bailiff usually has a close personal relationship with the Judge and the Judge's clerk. Consequently, most seasoned attorneys are careful to cultivate good working relationships with the bailiffs, since bailiffs can exercise much control over the simple administrative details of the court's operation.

Bondsman. A bondsman is a person who charges a fee for posting a bond as a condition for the pretrial release of a criminal defendant. The bond is forfeited if the criminal defendant fails to appear for trial or other legal proceedings.

CASA Volunteer. "CASA" refers to "court-appointed special advocates." CASA volunteers advocate the best interests of children in domestic cases. CASA volunteers are appointed by a judge or magistrate whenever, in the opinion of the court, a child who may be affected by such action requires services that a CASA volunteer can provide.

A CASA volunteer's duties include the following:

1. To conduct an independent investigation regarding the best interests of the child, which will provide factual information to the court regarding the child and the child's family;
2. To determine an appropriate treatment plan, designed to render the respondent in a dependency and neglect action fit to provide adequate parenting to the child, considering the child's needs; and if an appropriate treatment plan has been created, to determine whether appropriate services are being provided to the child and family according to the plan;
3. To make recommendations consistent with the best interests of the child regarding placement, visitation, and appropriate services for the child and family, unless otherwise ordered by the court; and
4. To prepare a written report addressing the recommendations made in the best interests of the child.

A CASA volunteer must maintain the confidentiality of information relating to any case to which the CASA volunteer has access, and shall not disclose such information to any person other than the court and parties to the action.

Child and Family Investigator. The District Court Judges who handle domestic relations cases have been appointing both therapists and attorneys as special advocates pursuant to the provisions of C.R.S. § 14-10-116. The name "special advocate" was changed to "child and family investigator" in 2005 by the General Assembly, but the investigator's duties remain the same, as described in C.R.S. § 14-10-116.5. Although the courts have been appointing therapists in this role because of their ability to resolve conflicts and to work in stressful situations, an individual who is appointed a special advocate is not engaged in the practice of psychotherapy. According to C.R.S. § 14-10-116.5, an investigator "shall investigate, report, and make recommendations [regarding] ... the best interests" of a child whose parents are involved in domestic litigation. These professionals, therefore, conduct investigations by interviewing family members, parents, children, family friends, and associated professionals in order to make recommendations to the court concerning the allocation of parental responsibilities or regarding parenting time. This provides an invaluable service to the court, helping judges to resolve factual disputes and to make the difficult decisions involved in domestic cases. Guidelines have been published which discuss the scope of a child and family investigator's duties. The investigation conducted must include, at a minimum, the following:

1. A meeting with each parent and the children;
2. Observing the interaction between the children and the parent;
3. Evaluating the home itself;
4. Meeting with and observing the children;
5. Interviewing the children, if they are old enough;
6. Reviewing court files and relevant reports, records, school records, and other documents;
7. Interviewing the parents; and
8. Interviewing teachers and other associated professionals.

Child and family investigators recommend to the court, when needed, psychological evaluations of the parents or children.

This is a new field, and the role of the investigator varies from one judicial district to another. If a therapist is interested in this work, he or she should identify the district judges or magistrates in his or her locality who handle domestic cases, and provide the following: a professional resume; a letter to the judge, expressing interest in having his or her name added to the appointment list maintained by the court; and a brief summary of his or her qualifications. If the local judicial district has a Judicial Administrator, that is the individual whom the therapist should contact to express interest in accepting appointments as an investigator. Fees should be charged on a sliding scale, depending upon the family income.

Court Clerk. Each Judge has one or two clerks who process the court's paperwork. The court clerk controls the court's docket and has vital information about the status of all cases. Most clerks are frequently overworked and are under constant pressure. They should be treated with courtesy and the utmost care, since they can make things smooth or difficult. A psychotherapist should not hesitate to leave detailed messages with the clerk if there is a need to communicate with the Judge.

Court Reporter. A court reporter is responsible for stenographically recording the trial proceedings as they occur. Court reporters listen to testimony, and through the use of a mechanical coding system, preserve the testimony. There are two types of court reporters. The first type is a state employee working as part of a Judge's courtroom staff. The second type is a freelance reporter who works independently and is hired by attorneys to record and transcribe depositions and other proceedings.

Conservator. A conservator is a person appointed by the court to take charge of and manage another person's financial affairs. There must be a finding by the court that the person to be protected by a conservator no longer has the capacity to handle his or her own financial affairs. A conservator's powers are limited to financial matters and do not encompass other aspects of a protected person's life. Matters such as consent to medical treatment, residency, etc., are handled by a guardian. A conservator's authority is evidenced by the court's issuance of a document known as "Letters of Conservatorship," which should be presented if a question arises as to a conservator's authority. A psychotherapist should never discuss a client's case with a conservator unless a copy of the Letters of Conservatorship is obtained.

Decision-Maker. A decision-maker is either a legal or mental health professional, appointed by the court in a domestic case to resolve parenting issues or to implement a parenting plan.

District Attorney. Each judicial district in the state has an elected official known as the District Attorney. This person is responsible for prosecuting criminal cases on behalf of the State. The District Attorney performs this function by appointing Deputy District Attorneys. Deputy District Attorneys are the individuals most psychotherapists will encounter in criminal proceedings.

Expert Witness. An expert witness is a person found by the court to have special knowledge, skills, education, experience, or training in a particular field. An expert witness is allowed to render opinion testimony. An expert witness receives compensation for his or her testimony from the party calling the expert at trial. Usually a psychotherapist called to testify in court is testifying as an expert witness.

Guardian. A guardian is appointed by the court to take responsibility for the non-financial affairs of a person who has been found by the court to be incapable of making life decisions for himself or herself. The guardian makes decisions that are binding upon the incapacitated person. A guardian may or may not also be given the powers of a conservator. A guardian is generally a family relative or close personal friend of the incapacitated person. The appointment as guardian is evidenced by the court's issuance of a document known as "Letters of Guardianship," which should be presented if a question arises as to a guardian's authority. A psychotherapist should never discuss a client's case with a guardian without first obtaining a copy of the Letters of Guardianship.

Guardian ad litem. A guardian ad litem or G.A.L. is usually an attorney who has been appointed by the court to represent the interests of a minor or an incapacitated person during a legal proceeding. A guardian ad litem is typically appointed in cases involving custody or visitation issues. The guardian ad litem conducts an independent investigation and makes a recommendation to the court regarding the appropriateness of the request before the court. The guardian ad litem has no power or authority over the minor or protected person. A guardian ad litem's appointment is evidenced by a written court order. A psychotherapist should never discuss a client's condition with a guardian ad litem unless a copy of the court order appointing the guardian ad litem for the client is obtained or the therapist has been authorized by the client to release information to the guardian ad litem. A psychotherapist should not hesitate to request a copy of the order. A guardian ad litem does not have the authority to authorize the release of therapy records.

C.R.S. § 19-3-203(2) states: "The guardian ad litem shall be provided with all reports relevant to a case submitted to or made by any agency or person pursuant to [the Children's Code]." The duties of a guardian ad litem are set forth in C.R.S. § 19-3-202(3).

Investigator. There are private investigators and there are public investigators. A private investigator is hired by an attorney to assist in the factual preparation of a litigant's case. The investigator will locate and interview witnesses and take witness statements. A public investigator performs the same functions, except his or her employer is a government body such as the District Attorney's or Public Defender's Office. A psychotherapist should never speak to any investigator without written consent from his or her client. Additionally, it is recommended that another person be present when the interview occurs and that this person take detailed notes of the substance of the conversation. Investigators have a habit of hearing only what they are seeking to find in a witness.

Judge. A judge presides over a legal proceeding by ensuring that the Rules of Procedure, Rules of Evidence, and substantive law are applied to a case. A judge will determine the outcome of a proceeding when there is no jury.

Jury. A jury is comprised of citizens drawn from the judicial district. The jury determines guilt or innocence in a criminal case, and whether or not a person is liable in a civil case.

Lay Witness. A lay witness has personal firsthand knowledge about an event and is called to relate that knowledge at trial.

Legal Aid. A legal aid office is an organization that provides free legal representation to indigent individuals in civil matters.

Magistrate. A magistrate is a lawyer who is appointed by the chief judge of a judicial district to exercise limited judicial authority over routine legal matters, such as temporary orders in a divorce, juvenile matters, and probate. Magistrates work under the supervision of a

District Court Judge. Prior to 1991, they were referred to as Referees or Commissioners.

Mediator. A mediator is a third party selected by the parties to a dispute who is asked to meet with the parties and assist them in reaching an agreement. The mediator has no power to force an agreement upon the parties. He or she simply acts as a facilitator of communication and suggests possible alternatives to the controversy. Mediation is now required as a condition precedent to obtaining a court date in selected judicial districts. Additionally, some divorce litigants are now using trained psychotherapists as mediators to assist them in the resolution of custody and visitation issues.

Parenting Coordinator. A qualified professional may be appointed by the court in a domestic case as a parenting coordinator to assist the court in resolving disputes involving parenting or to assist the parties in learning appropriate parenting skills.

Parole Officer. A parole officer supervises and monitors a convict's fulfillment of those conditions under which an early release from prison was allowed.

Police. A law enforcement officer is hired to enforce a city's ordinances. His or her jurisdiction is generally limited to the geographical boundaries of the city.

Probation Officer. A probation officer supervises and monitors a person's fulfillment of those conditions imposed as an alternative to jail or confinement in criminal cases.

Process Server. A process server charges a fee for delivering subpoenas, summonses, complaints, and other court orders.

Public Defender. A public defender is hired by the State to provide free legal representation to indigent people who are charged with crimes.

CHAPTER 2: CONFIDENTIALITY

This chapter outlines Colorado law pertaining to the duty of confidentiality. Specifically, it sets forth the circumstances under which communications between client and therapist are considered confidential, and therefore not subject to disclosure to third parties by a psychotherapist. Conversely, it also describes those instances where a communication is not privileged, and disclosure by a psychotherapist to a third party is required.

PART I: DUTY OF CONFIDENTIALITY

2.01 Sources of Confidentiality

Most psychotherapists know that they have a duty to maintain client confidentiality. They know that they have an obligation not to disclose to third parties things that are discussed in therapy, or other aspects of the therapeutic process, such as diagnosis, prognosis, recommendations, test results, etc. Few, however, are able identify the sources from which the duty arises.

There are three primary sources of the duty of confidentiality: statutes, common law, and ethical codes.

In Colorado, the legislature has created a specific statutory duty of confidentiality that applies to psychotherapists, C.R.S. § 12-43-218. There are also federal statutes that apply in certain situations where federal money is involved. These are discussed in section 2.05 of this book.

Prior to the enactment of the statutes referred to above, the duty of confidentiality arose from the common law or case law. Most notably, the personal right of privacy created the obligation for psychotherapists to maintain confidentiality. This common-law duty still exists.

Professional associations have developed detailed codes of conduct or ethical duties that contain specific confidentiality mandates. Compliance with the codes is not required as a matter of state law.

However, the codes reflect the professional standard of care for therapists and therefore, as a practical matter, must be followed in order to avoid a negligence or malpractice action. Psychotherapists should obtain a current copy of the applicable code of conduct from their respective professional association, and become familiar with its requirements.

The current addresses for the professional associations for LPCs, LMFTs, LCSWs, Licensed Psychologists, and other professionals, are as follows:

Psychologists
Colorado Psychological Association
7995 E. Prentice Ave., Ste. 100
Greenwood Village, Colorado 80111
www.coloradopsych.org
(303) 692-9303

Social Workers
National Association of Social Workers – Colorado Chapter
3600 S. Yosemite, Suite 370
Denver, Colorado 80237
www.naswco.org
(303) 753-8890

Colorado Society for Clinical Social Workers
931 14th Street
Denver, Colorado 80202
(303) 893-5711

Marriage and Family Therapists
Colorado Association for Marriage and Family Therapy
1420 Abilene Drive
Broomfield, Colorado 80020
www.coamft.org
(888) 458-1713

American Association for Marriage and Family Therapy
112 S. Alfred Street
Alexandria, Virginia 22314-3061
www.aamft.org
(703) 838-9808

Non-Licensed Psychotherapists
Colorado Association of Psychotherapists
P. O. Box 101926
Denver, Colorado 80250
www.cap-psychotherapists.com
(303) 480-5733

Psychiatrists/Physicians
Colorado Medical Society
7351 Lowry Boulevard
Denver, Colorado 80230
www.cms.org
(720) 859-1001

Nurses
Colorado Nurses Association
1221 S. Clarkson Street, #205
Denver, Colorado 80210
www.nurses-co.org
(303) 757-7483

American Association of Christian Counselors
P. O. Box 739
Forest, Virginia 24551
www.aacc.net
(434) 525-9470 / (800) 526-8673

2.02 Colorado Confidentiality Statute

C.R.S. § 12-43-218(1) provides that licensed psychologists, clinical social workers, marriage and family therapists, licensed professional counselors, certified school psychologists, and registered psychotherapists shall not disclose, without the consent of the client, any confidential communications made by the client, or any advice given, in the course of professional employment; nor shall such persons' employees or associates, whether clerical or professional, disclose any knowledge of confidential communications acquired in such capacity; nor shall any person who has participated in any therapy conducted under the supervision of such persons, including group therapy sessions, disclose any knowledge gained during the course of therapy without the consent of the person to whom the knowledge relates.

The duty of non-disclosure and confidentiality applies to the following:

1. Certified school psychologists who practice psychotherapy and who are licensed in Colorado;
2. Licensed clinical social workers, psychologists, professional counselors, and marriage and family therapists, all of whom are licensed pursuant to Title 12, Article 43 of the Colorado Revised Statutes (hereinafter referred to as "licensed psychotherapists" or "licensees");
3. Registered psychotherapists;
4. Employees and associates of certified school psychologists or psychotherapists; and
5. Those who have participated in any therapy, including group therapy, conducted under the supervision of any licensed or registered psychotherapist.

Mental health professionals must undertake specific steps to inform employees, associates (e.g., secretaries, receptionists, billing clerks), and group members of the duty of confidentiality. The author strongly recommends that a signed statement be obtained from each of the foregoing classes of people acknowledging that the duty of confidentiality has been explained and will be followed.

C.R.S. § 12-43-218(2) provides that the duty of non-disclosure and confidentiality *does not* apply when:

1. A lawsuit or complaint has been filed against a licensee, registered psychotherapist, certified school psychologist, or licensed psychotherapist by a client in connection with the client's care and treatment.
2. A licensee, licensed or certified school psychologist, registrant, or registered psychotherapist was in consultation with a physician, registered professional nurse, licensee, licensed or certified school psychologist, registrant, or registered psychotherapist against whom a suit or complaint is filed, based on the case out of which said suit or complaint arises.
3. A review of services of a psychologist is conducted by any one of the following: (a) the duly authorized Board of Registered Psychotherapists; (b) the governing board of a licensed hospital; or (c) a professional review committee established pursuant to

C.R.S. § 12-43-203(11), if the client has signed a release authorizing such review.

C.R.S. § 12-43-218(4) provides that the duty of non-disclosure and confidentiality for licensed psychologists does not apply to delinquency cases or to criminal proceedings, where issues have been raised in a criminal case concerning the defendant's sanity, competency, or impaired mental condition.

C.R.S. § 12-43-218(5) provides that nothing shall be deemed to prohibit any other disclosure required by law. This means that other required disclosures, such as those described in Part II of this chapter, titled "Exceptions to Confidentiality," will be honored.

One of the most frequent grievances filed against psychotherapists is breach of confidentiality. In many cases, the psychotherapist has simply forgotten or inadvertently disclosed information to third parties. Unfortunately, memory lapses and inadvertent mistakes are not defenses. Psychotherapists must refrain from casual discussions concerning clients with colleagues, family members, friends, and other persons, particularly attorneys.

It is important to note that the duty of confidentiality does not cease upon the death of a client. Psychotherapists must refrain from releasing information about a deceased client, unless disclosure is authorized by the representative of the client's estate or is ordered by the court. This problem is a difficult one, particularly when family members and the personal representative of the deceased are demanding information. If this should occur, retain an attorney so that you can be advised of the most current law on this matter.

2.03 Common Law

In addition to the duty of non-disclosure found in C.R.S. § 12-43-218, a psychotherapist has a common-law duty to refrain from disclosing private facts or private information about a client acquired in the course of treatment. This duty exists under a legal theory known as "Invasion of Privacy." Under this theory, the common law allows a client to recover damages from a psychotherapist who discloses confidential information pertaining to a client, if such disclosure is found to be objectionable. In today's litigious environment, virtually any unauthorized disclosure would be found to violate a client's expectation of privacy.

The common law also imposes a duty of non-disclosure and confidentiality under a legal theory known as "Outrageous Conduct" or "Intentional Infliction of Emotional Distress." Under this theory, a disclosure of a private fact or private information by a psychotherapist to a third party would subject the psychotherapist to a claim for money damages if such disclosure was found by a judge or jury to be shocking to the sensibilities of the community. It is not difficult to imagine that a jury or judge would feel particularly outraged by such a breach of confidentiality.

Court decisions, which constitute the common law applicable to psychotherapists, establish precedents whereby treatment information is recognized as confidential or is ruled to be privileged. In *Jaffee v. Redmond,* 518 U.S. 1, 116 S. Ct. 1923 (1996), the United States Supreme Court ruled for the first time that federal courts must recognize the psychotherapist-client privilege. Federal courts had long recognized the doctor-patient, psychiatrist-patient, or psychologist-client privilege, as well as the attorney-client privilege. However, until the Supreme Court's decision in *Jaffee,* federal courts had generally rejected a psychotherapist-client privilege. In practical terms, this meant that before 1996 a psychotherapist could be compelled to testify concerning information gained during treatment.

In deciding that federal courts must recognize the psychotherapist-client privilege, the Supreme Court ruled that this privilege serves important public interests, because mental health therapists' ability to help their clients depends upon the clients' "willingness and ability to talk freely." The Court noted that it is difficult, if not impossible, for therapists to function without being able to assure clients that information provided in treatment will be confidential. In extending this "evidentiary privilege" to clients of psychotherapists, the Supreme Court recognized that confidentiality is necessary in order to establish the rapport between therapist and client needed to promote effective therapy. This in turn promotes the improvement of mental health on a national scale.

In discussing its rationale for this ruling, the Supreme Court recognized that clinical social workers and other psychotherapists "provide a significant amount of mental health treatment" to clients who "could not afford the assistance of a psychiatrist." Thus, the United States Supreme Court recognized what many mental health professionals already knew: that they provide the bulk of the day-to-day counseling services to the people in this country.

The Supreme Court's decision in *Jaffee v. Redmond* did note that exceptions to this privilege would exist. These exceptions are discussed in Part II of this chapter.

The State of Colorado had already adopted a law prior to this decision recognizing a *licensed* psychotherapist-client privilege. In 1998, the Colorado Legislature enacted Public Law 98-1072, which amended the privilege statute in Colorado, C.R.S. § 13-90-107, to include a privilege between registered psychotherapists and clients. In so doing, the Colorado Legislature recognized that registered psychotherapists in this state provide significant mental health services to their clients, and thereby promote the improvement of mental health within this state.

2.04 Ethical Duties

Most professional associations and credentialing authorities have adopted specific guidelines or standards that require confidentiality and impose a duty of non-disclosure of information acquired in the course of treatment of a client. These ethical standards should be consulted and followed by any psychotherapist who is a member of an association having developed such codes.

For example, the American Association for Marriage and Family Therapists (AAMFT) has issued a code of ethics on topics such as advertising, professional competence, responsibility to clients, and confidentiality. The AAMFT Code of Ethics Principle II, concerning confidentiality, states, "Marriage and family therapists have unique confidentiality concerns because the client in a therapeutic relationship may be more than one person. Therapists respect and guard the confidences of each individual client."

The AAMFT Code of Ethics discusses the problem that confronts a therapist providing counseling services to a family, when one member of the family wants to release confidential information concerning that therapy. The AAMFT Code [section 2.2] requires:

> When providing couple, family or group treatment, the therapist does not disclose information outside the treatment context without a written authorization from each individual

> competent to execute a waiver. In the context of couple, family or group treatment, the therapist may not reveal any individual's confidences to others in the client unit without the prior written permission of that individual.

The American Counseling Association, the American Psychological Association, and the National Association of Social Workers have all adopted provisions safeguarding confidentiality, similar to those of the AAMFT.

2.05 Federal Privacy Statutes

There are various federal privacy statutes that impose detailed duties of confidentiality and non-disclosure upon certain classes of people and agencies that are involved in programs funded by the federal government. These acts include the following:

1. Privacy Act of 1974, which applies to governmental entities; and
2. Family Educational Rights and Privacy Act (Public Law 90-247), which applies to all educational agencies or institutions to which funds are made available under any federal program for which the U.S. Commissioner of Education has administrative responsibility.

If a psychotherapist works in an agency where these statutes apply, copies of the statutes should be obtained and studied in detail.

2.06 Statutory Privilege

There is much confusion in the psychotherapy community with respect to the concept of "privilege" or "privileged communication." It is important to distinguish and understand the difference between "privilege" and the "duty of confidentiality." The two concepts are distinct and the differences must be understood in order to adequately protect clients.

A good starting point is to note that the duty of confidentiality is imposed upon those persons set forth in the statute, C.R.S. § 12-43-218: psychotherapists, employees, associates, and those participating in group therapy.

When a lawsuit occurs, the therapist's duty of confidentiality often conflicts with a party's constitutional due process rights to confront witnesses and to present evidence. In order to resolve this dilemma and balance the rights of all parties, the legislature enacted a statute, C.R.S. § 13-90-107, to reflect its view that there are particular relationships in which it is the policy of the law to encourage confidence and to preserve it inviolate. C.R.S. § 13-90-107 recognizes that certain relationships are confidential in nature and people in these relationships may not be forced to disclose confidential communications made to them.

C.R.S. § 13-90-107 sets forth the special privileges recognized by the legislature.

1. Spousal (husband-wife) privilege;
2. Attorney-Client privilege;
3. Clergy Member/Minister/Priest/Rabbi-Penitent privilege;
4. Physician/Surgeon/Registered Professional Nurse-Patient privilege;
5. Public Officer privilege;
6. Certified Public Accountant-Client privilege;
7. Psychotherapist (Psychologist, Professional Counselor, Social Worker, Marriage and Family Therapist, Unlicensed Psychotherapist, and Licensed Addiction Counselor)-Client privilege;
8. Qualified Interpreter;
9. Confidential Intermediary;
10. Environmental Audit report; and
11. Victim's Advocate-Victim of domestic abuse or sexual assault privilege.

Each privilege is carefully defined and the exceptions, if any, are specifically described in the statute. Sections 2.06 to 2.08 of this book address the issues relevant to psychotherapists.

2.07 Physician-Patient Privilege

The physician-patient privilege is set forth in C.R.S. § 13-90-107(1)(d). It provides that a physician, surgeon, or registered professional nurse shall not be examined without the consent of the patient as to any information acquired in attending to the patient that was necessary to prescribe or act for the patient.

Although psychiatrists are not specifically mentioned in the statute, they are licensed physicians under the Colorado Medical Practices

Act, and are therefore within the definition of the privilege. *Bond v. District Court of County of Denver*, 682 P.2d 33 (Colo. 1984). Although no cases are on record, it would appear that a licensed psychiatric nurse would fall under the protective provisions of this statute.

The statute sets forth numerous exceptions in which the privilege does not apply. Most of these exceptions involve a professional malpractice claim against a physician or cases where there is a medical review board or committee examining a physician's conduct. In such cases, client communications can be disclosed to the parties outlined in the exception.

C.R.S. § 13-90-107(3) states that the physician-patient privilege does not apply to a physician eligible to testify concerning a criminal defendant's mental condition pursuant to C.R.S. § 16-8-103.6, which provides for an express waiver of the privilege when a defendant places his or her mental condition at issue by pleading not guilty by reason of insanity or impaired mental condition. This statutory waiver includes any claim of confidentiality arising from communications made by the defendant to a physician in the course of any examination or treatment for such mental condition for the purpose of any trial or hearing on the issue of such mental condition.

C.R.S. § 13-90-107(1)(d)(VI) states that the physician-patient privilege does not apply to civil actions against a physician as a result of his or her consultation for medical care or genetic counseling or screening pursuant to C.R.S. § 13-64-502.

There are several other exceptions to the physician-patient privilege. They are described in Part II of this chapter, entitled "Exceptions to Confidentiality."

2.08 Therapist-Client Privilege

C.R.S. § 13-90-107(1)(g) describes the privilege that applies to licensed psychotherapists:

> A licensed psychologist, professional counselor, marriage and family therapist, social worker, registered psychotherapist, or licensed addiction counselor shall not be examined without the consent of such licensee's or registered psychotherapist's client as to any communication made by the client to such licensee or registered psychotherapist or such licensee's or reg-

> istered psychotherapist's advice given thereon in the course of professional employment; nor shall any secretary, stenographer, or clerk employed by a licensed psychologist, professional counselor, marriage and family therapist, social worker, registered psychotherapist, or licensed addiction counselor be examined without the consent of the employer of such secretary, stenographer, or clerk concerning any fact, the knowledge of which such employee has acquired in such capacity; nor shall any person who has participated in any psychotherapy, conducted under the supervision of a person authorized by law to conduct such therapy, including but not limited to group therapy sessions, be examined concerning any knowledge gained during the course of such therapy without the consent of the person to whom the testimony sought relates.

This statute is much broader than the physician-patient privilege for psychiatrists. For example, not only are communications made by a client to a psychotherapist considered privileged, but the privilege also extends to the following classes of people:

1. The psychotherapist's secretary, stenographer, or clerk; and
2. Those persons who participated in the psychotherapy under the supervision of a person authorized by law to conduct such therapy, e.g., group therapy clients, psychological assistants, interns, or supervisees.

Like the physician-patient privilege, C.R.S. § 13-90-107(3) states that the psychotherapist-client privilege does not apply to a psychotherapist eligible to testify concerning a criminal defendant's mental condition pursuant to C.R.S. § 16-8-103.6, which provides for an express waiver of the privilege when a defendant places his or her mental condition at issue by pleading not guilty by reason of insanity or impaired mental condition. This statutory waiver includes any claim of confidentiality arising from communications made by the defendant to a psychotherapist in the course of an examination or treatment for such mental condition for the purpose of any trial or hearing on the issue of such mental condition.

There are several other exceptions to the licensed psychotherapist privilege. They are described in Part II of this chapter, titled "Exceptions to Confidentiality."

2.09 HIV/AIDS Reporting

A little-known Colorado statute requires HIV reporting in specific circumstances. C.R.S. § 25-4-1402, provides:

> (1) Every attending physician in this state shall make a report to the state department of public health and environment or local department of health … on every individual known by said physician to have a diagnosis of AIDS, HIV-related illness, or HIV infection, including death from HIV infection.
>
> (2) All other persons treating a case of HIV infection in hospitals, clinics, sanitariums, penal institutions, and other private or public institutions shall make a report to the state department of public health … on every individual having a diagnosis of AIDS, HIV-related illness, or HIV infection, including death from HIV infection.

This statute also provides that compliance with the statute "shall not constitute libel or slander or a violation of the right of privacy or privileged communication." In addition, any person who complies in good faith with this reporting requirement "shall be immune from civil and criminal liability."

The American Counseling Association Code of Ethics, Section B.2.b, entitled "Contagious, Life-Threatening Diseases," provides:

> When clients disclose that they have a disease commonly known to be both communicable and life-threatening, counselors may be justified in disclosing information to identifiable third parties, if they are known to be at demonstrable and high risk of contracting the disease. Prior to making a disclosure, counselors confirm that there is such a diagnosis and assess the intent of clients to inform the third parties about their disease or to engage in any behaviors that may be harmful to an identifiable third party.

Because of the controversy and the privacy concerns surrounding HIV/AIDS, therapists need to comply with basic informed consent principles before disclosing any confidential information regarding a client who has tested positive for HIV/AIDS, unless the statute quoted above applies. If the statute applies, then treatment providers must comply with it.

PART II: EXCEPTIONS TO CONFIDENTIALITY

2.10 Mandatory Reporting of Child Abuse or Neglect

In 2010 the Colorado Legislature amended C.R.S. § 19-3-304(1) in order to clarify whether a mandated reporter of child abuse is required to make a report in a situation where the alleged victim of suspected abuse is over the age of eighteen. C.R.S. § 19-3-304(1)(a) now provides that any mandated reporter of child abuse who has reasonable cause to know or suspect that a child has been subjected to abuse or neglect or who has observed the child being subjected to circumstances or conditions that would reasonably result in abuse or neglect shall immediately report or cause a report to be made concerning the suspected abuse to the county department of human services or local law enforcement agency; however, this reporting requirement, amended in 2010, shall not apply if the person who is required to report does not learn of the suspected abuse or neglect until after the alleged victim of the suspected abuse or neglect is eighteen years of age or older, unless the perpetrator of the suspected abuse or neglect: (1) has subjected another child currently under eighteen years of age to abuse or neglect; or (2) is currently in a position of trust as defined in C.R.S. § 18-3-401(3.5) with regard to any child currently under eighteen years of age.

This amended statute has now dealt with the previously unanswered question concerning whether therapists were required to report suspected abuse or neglect of persons who are now adults. Now, in answering the question, "Am I required to report suspected abuse or neglect, previously unreported, of a victim who is now over the age of eighteen," the answer is that the therapist is not required to report the situation unless the perpetrator has committed suspected abuse or neglect of another child currently under eighteen years of age or is currently in a position of trust over a child currently under eighteen years of age.

Those persons who are required by C.R.S. § 19-3-304(2) to report child abuse or neglect are:

1. Physicians or surgeons;
2. Child health associates;
3. Medical examiners or coroners;
4. Dentists;
5. Osteopaths;

6. Optometrists;
7. Chiropractors;
8. Chiropodists or podiatrists;
9. Registered or licensed practical nurses;
10. Hospital personnel;
11. Christian Science practitioners;
12. Public or private school officials or employees;
13. Social workers and workers in any facility licensed or certified pursuant to C.R.S. § 26-6-101 et seq. (including child care centers, child care providers, family child care homes, foster care homes, and others listed in C.R.S. § 26-6-102).
14. Mental health professionals, defined in C.R.S. § 19-1-103(77) as a person licensed to practice medicine or psychology in the State of Colorado, or any person on the staff of a facility designated by the executive director of the Department of Human Services for 72-hour treatment and evaluation who has been authorized by the facility to do mental health pre-screenings and who is under the supervision of a person licensed to practice medicine or psychology in Colorado;
15. Dental hygienists;
16. Psychologists;
17. Physical therapists;
18. Veterinarians;
19. Peace officers;
20. Pharmacists;
21. Commercial film and photographic print processors;
22. Firefighters;
23. Victim's advocates, defined in C.R.S. § 13-90-107(1)(k)(II) as "a person at a battered women's shelter or rape crisis organization or a comparable community-based advocacy program for victims of domestic violence or sexual assault …." This does not include an advocate employed by any law enforcement agency.
24. Licensed professional counselors;
25. Licensed marriage and family therapists; and
26. Registered psychotherapists;

27. Clergy members.
28. Registered dietitians who hold certificates through the commission on dietetic registration and who are otherwise prohibited by 7 CFR 246.26 from making a report absent a state law requiring the release of this information;
29. Workers in the state department of human services;
30. Juvenile parole and probation officers;
31. Child and family investigators, as described in section 14-10-116.5, C.R.S.; and
32. Officers and agents of the state bureau of animal protection, and animal control officers.

According to the provisions of C.R.S. § 19-3-304(3), a person not on the above list may make a report of child abuse or neglect, and such a person is entitled to immunity from any civil liability pursuant to the provisions of C.R.S. § 19-3-309, assuming that the report is made in good faith. This means that the person making the report has information, either based on firsthand observations or secondhand information received from other persons, which forms the basis for a suspicion that child abuse or neglect has occurred.

When confronted with a potential child abuse or neglect reporting problem, a psychotherapist must be aware of the following definition of child abuse or neglect, which appears at C.R.S. § 19-1-103(1)(a).

Child abuse or neglect means an act or omission in one of the following categories, which threatens the health or welfare of a child:

1. Any case in which a child exhibits evidence of skin bruising, bleeding, malnutrition, failure to thrive, burns, fracture of any bone, subdural hematoma, soft tissue swelling, or death, and either: such condition or death is not justifiably explained; the history given concerning such condition is at variance with the degree or type of such condition or death; or the circumstances indicate that such condition may or may not be the product of an accidental occurrence.
2. Any case in which a child is subjected to sexual assault, molestation, sexual exploitation, prostitution, incest or "unlawful sexual behavior" as defined in C.R.S. § 16-22-102(9).

3. Any case in which a child is in need of services because the child's parents, legal guardian, or custodian fails to take the same actions to provide adequate food, clothing, shelter, medical care, or supervision that a prudent parent would take. The requirement of this subparagraph shall be subject to the provisions of C.R.S. § 19-3-103 (regarding treatment through a recognized method of religious healing).
4. Any case in which a child is subjected to emotional abuse. Emotional abuse means an identifiable and substantial impairment of the child's intellectual or psychological functioning or development of a substantial risk of impairment to the child's intellectual or psychological functioning or development.
5. Any act or omission described in C.R.S. § 19-3-102(1)(a), C.R.S. § 19-3-102(1)(b), or C.R.S. § 19-3-102(1)(c), which includes the abandonment of a child, allowing another person to mistreat or abuse a child, the lack of proper parental care for the child, or a child's environment that is injurious to his or her welfare.

C.R.S. § 19-3-103 provides that no child who, in lieu of medical treatment, is under treatment solely by spiritual means through prayer in accordance with a recognized method of religious belief shall, for that reason alone, be considered to have been neglected. However, the statute goes on to provide that the religious beliefs of the parent, guardian, or legal custodian shall not limit the medical access of a child in a life threatening situation or when the condition will result in a serious handicap or disability. When confronted with such a situation, a psychotherapist should file a report rather than refrain from doing so.

As noted above, C.R.S. § 19-3-309 grants immunity to those persons who have made a report of child abuse or neglect, thereby protecting the reporting person from civil and criminal liability as well as termination of employment that otherwise might result from making a report. Such immunity is not extended to the perpetrator, complicator, co-conspirator, or accessory. Additionally, immunity does not apply if a court of competent jurisdiction determines that a reporting person's behavior was willful, wanton, and malicious. *Montoya v. Bebensee,* 761 P.2d 285 (Colo. App. 1988).

C.R.S. § 19-3-304(4) provides that any person who willfully fails to report child abuse or neglect, or who knowingly makes a false report, shall be civilly liable for damages and commits a class 3 misdemeanor criminal offense.

C.R.S. § 19-3-305 provides that any person who is required to make a report of child abuse or neglect, or who has reasonable cause to suspect that a child died as a result of child abuse or neglect, must immediately report such fact to the police and to the medical examiner.

When making a child abuse or neglect report, an issue arises as to what should be disclosed to the authorities. C.R.S. § 19-3-307 states that such report shall include the following:

1. The name, address, sex, age, and race of the child;
2. The name and address of the person responsible for the suspected child abuse or neglect;
3. The nature of the child's injuries and any evidence of any previous cases of abuse involving the child or the child's siblings;
4. The name and address of any person responsible for the suspected abuse or neglect;
5. The family composition;
6. The source of the report and the name, address, and occupation of the person making the report;
7. Any action taken by the reporting source; and
8. Any other information the reporting source believes may be helpful in the investigation.

The statute requires that any oral report be followed by a written report. The statute also provides that the written report may be admitted as evidence in any proceeding relating to child abuse or neglect.

As a practice guide, it is recommended that psychotherapists limit their disclosures to the foregoing items and refrain from other disclosures of client communications.

C.R.S. § 19-3-311 constitutes an exception to the statutory privileges of C.R.S. § 13-90-107, i.e., physician-patient and psychotherapist-client. It does so by providing that these privileges are not grounds for excluding from evidence any client communications that are the basis for the report, or any discussion of future misconduct, or any past misconduct that could be the basis for any report. C.R.S. § 19-3-311 similarly abrogates the duty of non-disclosure and confidentiality set forth in C.R.S. § 12-43-218, which applies to psychotherapists and their clients.

It is important to recognize that C.R.S. § 19-3-311 is not a total denial of these privileges, since it appears that only those communications relating to the basis of the report are admissible in court. Therefore, communications unrelated to child abuse or neglect are still privileged. A psychotherapist should be cautious of what he or she reports and should not allow other communications unrelated to child abuse or neglect to be disclosed without a court order.

Emotional Abuse. Under the Colorado Children's Code, emotional abuse is defined in C.R.S. § 19-1-103(1)(a) as abuse that causes "an identifiable and substantial impairment of the child's intellectual or psychological functioning or development or a substantial risk of impairment to the child's intellectual or psychological functioning or development." This is a difficult standard to prove, which is why DHS caseworkers are reluctant to take a report of emotional abuse, and why we rarely see a case prosecuted that involves emotional abuse. While lack of self esteem is a significant loss in a child's personality development, does it constitute a "substantial impairment" of a child's intellectual or psychological functioning? If a child withdraws socially and is isolated because of low self esteem, does this demonstrate that a child's intellectual or psychological functioning or development has been substantially impaired? What signs and symptoms or diagnostic criteria demonstrate that a child has been subjected to a substantial impairment of intellectual or psychological functioning or development, resulting from emotional abuse? Therapists should discuss these questions in consultation with one another, so that you have a good understanding of situations in which you would be required to report emotional abuse.

Obviously, just because a parent has yelled at a child and has hurt the child's feelings does not mean that you must report a case of emotional abuse. However, in those cases where your professional judgment causes you to suspect that the statutory standard for emotional abuse has been met, it must be reported. As in all other reports of suspected abuse or neglect to Child Protective Services or to law enforcement, make certain that you document your chart carefully; and follow up by providing a written report concerning the suspected abuse to the person who took the report. This is required by the Colorado Children's Code whenever you make a report of suspected child abuse or neglect.

Colorado Criminal Statutes Regarding Sexual Assaults on Children. C.R.S. § 18-3-405 prohibits sexual assault on a child and provides, in part: "Any actor who knowingly subjects another not his or her spouse to any sexual contact commits sexual assault on a child if the victim is less than fifteen years of age and the actor is at least four years older than the victim." Applying this statute, a child who is 14 years of age could consent to relations with a 17-year-old, but not with an 18-year-old, who would then be four years older.

C.R.S. § 18-3-402 also defines sexual assault to include a situation where "the victim is at least fifteen years of age, but less than seventeen years of age and the actor is at least ten years older than the victim and is not the spouse of the victim." Applying this statute, a 16-year-old can consent to relations with a 25-year-old; but it is a crime when the victim is 16 years old and the actor is 26 years old.

2.11 Criminal Prosecutions for Child Abuse

C.R.S. § 18-6-401(4) provides that no person who reports child abuse will be subjected to criminal or civil liability.

In criminal prosecutions for child abuse, C.R.S. § 18-6-401(3) provides that the statutory privilege between a patient and physician shall not be available for excluding or refusing testimony. Thus, a physician or psychiatrist who is treating a person accused of child abuse may be forced to testify regarding the communications made by the patient in the course of the treatment. Inexplicably, C.R.S. § 18-6-401(3) does not appear to limit the psychotherapist-client privilege, which appears to be intact in this instance.

C.R.S. § 18-6-401(3) provides that the statutory privilege between the victim of child abuse and his or her physician shall not be available for excluding or refusing testimony in any prosecution for an act of child abuse. Hence, a psychiatrist who is treating a victim of child abuse may be forced to testify as to communications made by the victim in the course of treatment. Here again, C.R.S. § 18-6-401(3) inexplicably does not limit the statutory privilege existing between the victim and a treating licensed professional.

2.12 Duty to Warn

C.R.S. § 13-21-117 sets forth those circumstances in which a physician, social worker, psychiatric nurse, psychologist, mental health professional, mental health hospital, or community mental health facility has an affirmative duty to warn a third party of a mental health patient's violent behavior.

This statute specifically provides that such persons will be held civilly liable for the failure to warn or protect a third party where a patient has communicated to a psychotherapist a serious threat of imminent physical violence against a specific person or persons.

When there is a duty to warn and protect under the statute, the duty can be discharged by:

1. Making reasonable and timely efforts to notify any person or persons specifically threatened, as well as notifying an appropriate law enforcement agency; and
2. Taking other appropriate action, including, but not limited to, hospitalizing the patient.

The statute does not define what constitutes reasonable and timely notice. It is likely that this will be construed by the Colorado courts to mean notice that is reasonable under the specific circumstances.

The statute also fails to describe what constitutes "other appropriate action," other than hospitalizing the patient. This would include, for example, testifying in court in an action by the potential victim to obtain a restraining order against the patient who made the threat.

The statute does provide for immunity when a therapist has discharged the duty to warn and protect. Thus, an appropriate warning and other action to protect against imminent violence shall not be grounds for the imposition of civil damages or professional discipline. Hence, in those cases falling under the statute, a mental health worker cannot rely upon any privilege or duty of non-disclosure to remain silent. Some affirmative action is required.

The statute does not define "mental health professional"; however, the common meaning of this term includes all practitioners of "psychotherapy," as that term is defined in the Mental Health Act at C.R.S. § 12-43-201(9):

> "Psychotherapy" means the treatment, diagnosis, testing, assessment, or counseling in a professional relationship to assist individuals or groups to alleviate mental disorders, understand unconscious or conscious motivation, resolve emotional, relationship, or attitudinal conflicts, or modify behaviors which interfere with effective emotional, social, or intellectual functioning. Psychotherapy follows a planned procedure of intervention which takes place on a regular basis, over a period of time, or in the cases of testing, assessment, and brief psychotherapy, it can be a single intervention.

Mental health therapists who know they have a duty to initiate a 72-hour hold evaluation for a client who is dangerous to self or others as the result of a mental disorder have a duty to warn of any serious threat of imminent physical violence made against another person.

Therapists must record in the client's records all information concerning the threat made by the client, all action taken by the therapist to comply with the duty to warn, and all information communicated to the potential victim and to law enforcement.

See section 4.04 of this book for further information on C.R.S. § 13-21-117.

Practical Problems:

Scenario 1. You have an adult female client who is depressed and extremely anxious. During the process of counseling her for marital difficulties, you learn that she is in an abusive relationship, and has been the victim of a long history of domestic violence.

Your client sees you after a particularly brutal battering has occurred. She tells you, "I am going to get a gun, and if my husband ever gets drunk and starts to beat me like that again, I am going to shoot him."

Are you required, under the "duty to warn and protect" statute, to warn the husband of her intent? After reading the statute, several thoughts occur to you. Has your client confided to you a serious threat of imminent physical violence against a specific person? If you do warn him, is he likely to become enraged and retaliate against your client? Is the threat of violence made by your client sufficiently "imminent" so that you are required to report it to law enforcement authorities and also to your client's husband?

Most people would not sympathize with your client's husband. However, sympathy is not a factor to be considered in weighing whether you have a duty to warn pursuant to the statute. Judges, attorneys, therapists, and law enforcement officers would probably differ in their interpretation of this statute and in their answers to the questions raised by this problem. Always seek competent legal advice in such situations or consult with a supervisor concerning any question regarding whether a duty to warn exists.

Scenario 2. You have an adult male client who is having problems coping with marital difficulties. His wife is having an affair with the manager of a convenience store. In a fit of rage, your client confides to you that his wife's paramour raises show dogs and has a sports car that is his pride and joy. Your client is enraged at the thought of his wife riding around in the passenger seat of that sports car. Your client thinks that it would be therapeutic for him to express his feelings by taking a baseball bat to the sports car, and perhaps to the boyfriend's show dogs.

Are you required to warn and protect? Has your client made a threat of imminent physical violence against a specified person? Is it likely that after demolishing the sports car with a baseball bat, your client will go after its owner? Is it likely that while attacking the sports car, its owner will hear the commotion, go outside to investigate, and confront your enraged client? Although a volatile situation, this scenario does not meet the statutory criteria that give rise to a duty to warn. The actual threats of violence made by the client involve an automobile and animals. Because the threat does not concern imminent physical violence against a person, it does not give rise to the statutory duty to warn imposed by C.R.S. § 13-21-117.

Scenario 3. Your client tells you he is HIV positive and has no intention of telling his sexual partner of his condition and intends to engage in unprotected sex. Do you have a duty to warn and protect the unknowing partner? The inquiry must focus on whether or not the client made an imminent threat of serious physical violence. If you are confronted with such a dilemma, consult your attorney or a clinical supervisor for specific guidance.

These problems illustrate the difficulty of applying the statute. An easy solution to the dilemma is to provide advance notice to your client of your obligation to warn and protect prior to engaging in therapy, and to obtain your client's written acknowledgment and waiver of confidentiality to these types of disclosures.

2.13 Duty to Report a Crime

C.R.S. § 18-8-115, provides as follows:

> It is the duty of every corporation or person who has reasonable grounds to believe that a crime has been committed to report promptly the suspected crime to law enforcement authorities. Notwithstanding any other provision of the law to the contrary, a corporation or person may disclose information concerning a suspected crime to other persons or corporations for the purpose of giving notice of the possibility that other such criminal conduct may be attempted which may affect the persons or corporations notified. When acting in good faith, such corporation or person shall be immune from any civil liability for such reporting or disclosure. This duty shall exist notwithstanding any other provision of the law to the contrary; except that this section shall not require disclosure of any communication privileged by law.

Applying this statute, licensed mental health professionals and registered psychotherapists have no duty to report a crime that occurred in the past or one that is imminent, unless it (1) involves child abuse or neglect; (2) falls under the physical violence exception of the "duty to warn and protect" statute; or (3) a therapist has a duty to initiate a 72-hour hold evaluation because a client is an imminent danger to others as a result of a mental disorder.

This area is one where a psychotherapist should give advance notice of the possibility of disclosure and obtain a client's written acknowledgment and a waiver of confidentiality prior to commencing therapy.

As stated in the statute, a person who discloses information concerning a suspected crime to law enforcement or to an intended victim, when acting in good faith, will be immune from civil liability. "Good faith" immunity means that the reporting person must have a factual basis for his or her suspicions that a crime has occurred, whether that factual basis results from personal observations, statements by the victim, or statements made by the suspected perpetrator.

2.14 Duty to Report Mistreatment of an At-Risk Adult/Elder Abuse

During the past couple of decades, most states have enacted laws protecting the elderly from abuse. In Colorado, C.R.S. § 26-3.1-102 was enacted in 1991 to prevent elder abuse, as well as the abuse of developmentally disabled persons and other adults who are at risk to be abused.

An "at-risk adult" means an individual who is 18 years of age or older who is susceptible to mistreatment, "because the individual is unable to perform or obtain services necessary for the individual's health, safety or welfare" or who "lacks sufficient understanding or capacity to make or communicate responsible decisions concerning the individual's person or affairs." The definition of an at-risk adult is similar to the definition of a person who is "gravely disabled" under C.R.S. § 27-65-102.

C.R.S. § 26-3.1-102 lists those who are subject to the reporting provisions pertaining to at-risk adults. The reporting provisions apply to the following persons:

1. Physicians, surgeons, physician's assistants, or osteopaths;
2. Medical examiners or coroners;
3. Registered nurses or licensed practical nurses;
4. Hospital and nursing home personnel;
5. *Psychologists and other mental health professionals;*
6. *Social work practitioners;*
7. Dentists;
8. Law enforcement officials;
9. Court-appointed guardians and conservators;
10. Fire protection personnel;
11. Pharmacists;
12. Community centered board staff;
13. Personnel of banks, savings and loan associations, credit unions, and other lending or financial institutions;
14. State and local long-term care ombudsmen; and

15. Any caretaker, staff member, employee, volunteer, or consultant for any licensed care facility.

C.R.S. § 26-3.1-102 provides that any person specified above, who has observed the mistreatment of an at-risk adult or who has reasonable cause to believe that an at-risk adult has been mistreated, should make an immediate oral report of abuse to a local law enforcement agency within 24 hours, followed by a written report within 48 hours.

Note that the use of the term "should" is not mandatory and therefore does not require a report.

The term "mistreatment" as used in this statute is similar to the term "abuse" as used in the statutes pertaining to child abuse. "Mistreatment" is defined as "an act or omission which threatens the health, safety, or welfare of an at-risk adult," or "which exposes the adult to a situation or condition that poses an imminent risk of death, serious bodily injury, or bodily injury to that adult."

Mistreatment includes the following:

1. Infliction of physical pain or injury, as demonstrated by multiple skin bruising, bleeding, malnutrition, dehydration, burns, bone fractures, subdural hematoma, soft tissue swelling or suffocation;
2. Abuse that occurs where unreasonable confinement or restraint is imposed;
3. Subjection of an at-risk adult to nonconsensual sexual conduct or contact; or
4. Exploitation of an at-risk adult through the illegal or improper use of such person's resources for another person's profit or advantage.

The information that is to be provided in a report concerning abuse of an at-risk adult includes:

1. The name and address of the at-risk adult;
2. The name and address of the at-risk adult's caretaker;
3. The age, if known, of such at-risk adult;
4. The nature and extent of the at-risk adult's injury;
5. The nature and extent of the condition that will result in mistreatment; and

6. Any other pertinent information.

The statute provides that reports concerning the mistreatment of an at-risk adult "shall be confidential and shall not be public information." This statute does contain a provision granting immunity from any civil or criminal liability for the making of such a report, so long as it is made in good faith.

While the people specified above "are urged" to make a report, the statute does not contain language that such is mandatory. If a psychotherapist feels compelled to make such a report, the prior written consent of the client must be obtained. This can be accomplished by obtaining from the client, prior to commencement of treatment, a written acknowledgment and waiver of confidentiality should at-risk reporting issues arise in the course of therapy.

2.15 Waiver by Client

The statutory privileges and duties of non-disclosure and confidentiality can be waived by a client in three ways:

1. The client's express waiver by the execution and delivery of a signed and dated waiver or authorization to release information. You should require that any such release be notarized and contain an original signature. A client who has signed an authorization to release information or records may limit the scope of information to be disclosed and may revoke the authorization at any time. (Practice pointer: Your form for release of information must disclose to the person signing it: "You may revoke this authorization at any time.")
2. The client's commencement of a lawsuit against a therapist or the initiation of a complaint by a client to the Board of Registered Psychotherapists or to a Licensing Board. In such a situation, therapists must be able to defend themselves by disclosing information to their attorneys, to the Board involved, and to their professional liability insurance carriers.
3. When the communication is made in the presence of a third party who does not enjoy the statutory privilege or who does not have the duty of non-disclosure and confidentiality. The reason for this rule is that the communication is deemed to be outside the therapeutic relationship if made in the presence of someone whom the law deems non-essential to that relationship.

Client waiver solves the problems of breaching confidentiality in the following circumstances: (1) child abuse; (2) "duty to warn" cases; (3) harm to self or others; (4) at-risk adults; and (5) reporting of crimes. If a therapist notifies the client of the possibility of disclosing information in these circumstances, prior to commencing therapy, and obtains a written acknowledgment and waiver of confidentiality in these circumstances, most of the problems outlined above are eliminated.

2.16 Care and Treatment of the Mentally Ill

The information and records prepared in the course of rendering services to individuals under any provision of C.R.S. §§ 27-65-101, *et seq.*, "Care and Treatment of Persons with Mental Illness," are confidential and privileged. According to C.R.S. § 27-65-121, such records and information are subject to disclosure only in the following circumstances:

1. In communications between qualified professional personnel in the provision of services or appropriate referrals; e.g., treatment team staffings or treatment plan review by an interdisciplinary team.
2. When the recipient of services designates persons to whom the information or records may be released.
3. To make claims for aid, insurance, or medical assistance.
4. For research purposes, provided all identifying information has been expunged and the researchers have signed a confidentiality oath.
5. To the courts as necessary.
6. To persons authorized by the courts after notice and hearing to the person to whom the records pertain.
7. To adult family members (spouse, parent, adult child, adult sibling) with respect to the location and fact of admission of a person with a mental illness receiving care and treatment, unless the treating professional decides after an interview with the person with a mental illness that such disclosure would not be in the best interest of the person with a mental illness.
8. To adult family members actively participating in the care and treatment of a person with a mental illness with respect to the following: the diagnosis, the prognosis, the need for hospitalization and anticipated stay, the discharge plan, the medication

administered and side effects, and the short-term and long-term treatment goals.

9. In accordance with state and federal law to the agency designated pursuant to the federal "Protection and Advocacy for Mentally Ill Individuals Act," 42 U.S.C. § 10801, *et seq.*, as the governor's protection and advocacy system for Colorado.
10. To a parent concerning his or her minor child.

Such information may be released only if the treating professional determines that: (1) the mentally ill person is capable of making a rational decision regarding his or her interests; (2) the mentally ill person consents to such release; and (3) the treating professional believes it would be in the best interest of the mentally ill person to so release the information. If the mentally ill person is determined to be capable of making rational decisions regarding his or her interest and objects to the release, the information will not be disclosed. If the treating professional determines that the mentally ill person is incapable of making a rational decision regarding his or her interests and the patient objects to the release, the treating professional may disclose the information if that would be in the best interests of the mentally ill person. These decisions are subject to administrative review.

2.17 Treating Adolescents

Many therapists who treat children under the age of 18 are tempted to keep information from parents. In the absence of a specific written agreement from the parents to withhold information, these therapists are risking a malpractice action. As part of the initial intake, the better practice is to address the issue of whether or not information disclosed by a child will be withheld from the parents. The resolution should be documented in writing and signed by all parties. In the disclosure statement signed by a parent or legal guardian, giving consent for treatment of an adolescent over the age of 15, therapists may include a provision whereby the person giving informed consent for treatment agrees that the therapist will determine what information, in his or her professional judgment, is appropriate to be shared with the parents concerning treatment issues, and what information, in the discretion of the therapist, will remain confidential between the adolescent and the therapist.

C.R.S. § 27-65-103 provides that a minor who is 15 years of age or older "may consent to receive mental health services to be rendered by a facility or a professional person." A "facility" means a public hospital, a licensed private hospital, a community mental health center or clinic, or a residential treatment facility. A "professional person," to whom a 15-year-old may consent to receive mental health services, is "a person licensed to practice medicine in this state or a psychologist licensed to practice in this state."

C.R.S. § 27-65-103(2) provides that the "person rendering mental health services to a minor may, with or without the consent of the minor, advise the parent or legal guardian of the minor of the services given or needed."

See section 5.05 of this book for additional information about the treatment of juveniles.

2.18 Federal Law Regarding Confidentiality

By statute, patients in federal mental health programs or facilities have the right to confidentiality. This right is protected by 42 U.S.C. § 9501, which does not distinguish between communications made by a patient to a licensed, as opposed to an unlicensed, therapist. Under this statute, communications made by a patient in the course of a professional relationship are confidential, as are patient records.

In 1996, as discussed in section 2.03 of this book, the U.S. Supreme Court for the first time recognized a psychotherapist-client privilege. In *Jaffee v. Redmond,* the Supreme Court reviewed a federal district court's ruling, which ordered a licensed clinical social worker in Illinois to turn over notes of her counseling sessions with her client, Mary Lee Redmond. Redmond was a former police officer who had killed a man in the line of duty, and was sued in a federal civil action for wrongful death and for allegedly violating the decedent's constitutional rights by using excessive force.

After the traumatic incident in which she killed the decedent, Redmond received extensive counseling from a licensed clinical social worker. The plaintiff sought the notes of those counseling sessions for use in cross-examining Redmond. The issue presented to the U.S. Supreme Court was whether it is appropriate for federal courts to recognize a "psychotherapist privilege."

The Supreme Court held that significant public interests compelled recognition of a psychotherapist-client privilege. The Court eloquently expressed its rationale, ruling that effective psychotherapy depends upon an atmosphere of confidence and trust, and that the mere possibility of disclosure of confidential communications may impair the development of the relationship necessary for successful treatment. Federal courts had already recognized a privilege that applied to treatment by psychiatrists and psychologists. The Supreme Court reasoned that the same rationale for recognizing the privilege for treatment by psychiatrists and psychologists applies with equal force to clinical social workers.

The Court's decision noted that the clients of social workers "often include the poor and those of modest means who could not afford the assistance of a psychiatrist or psychologist." The Court then concluded, "Drawing a distinction between the counseling provided by costly psychotherapists and the counseling provided by more readily accessible social workers serves no discernible public purpose." Thus, the Court ruled that the conversations between Redmond and her therapist and the notes taken during their counseling sessions were protected from compelled disclosure.

PART III: PRACTICE POINTERS

2.19 Releasing Files and Records

The Problem. Occasionally, clients request copies of their files, test reports, and progress notes. Some therapists feel uncomfortable allowing clients to have access to this information. For others, allowing access is not a problem.

Health Care Facility Records. C.R.S. § 25-1-801 requires health care facilities to allow a patient or a patient's designated representative to inspect, at reasonable times and upon reasonable notice, the patient's medical records. However, records pertaining to mental health problems may be withheld from a patient. A summary of records pertaining to a patient's mental health problems may, upon written, signed, and dated request, be made available to the patient or his or her designated representative following termination of the treatment program.

The health care facility must note all requests by patients for inspection of their medical records, including the time and date of the patient's request, and the time and date of inspection. The patient must acknowledge the fact of inspection by dating and signing the record file.

Following a patient's discharge from a health care facility, the health care facility must furnish to the patient copies of a patient's records upon receipt of a written authorization/request dated and signed by the patient, and upon receipt of the reasonable costs of making such records available.

Records of Individual Health Care Providers. C.R.S. § 25-1-802 requires chiropodists, podiatrists, chiropractors, dentists, medical doctors, osteopathic doctors, nurses, optometrists, audiologists, acupuncturists, direct-entry midwives, and physical therapists who are licensed under Title 12 of the Colorado Revised Statutes to make available to a patient that patient's records upon receipt of a written authorization for inspection of records. However, records pertaining to a client's mental health problems maintained by a psychotherapist need not be made available to a patient. Instead, a summary of records concerning mental health problems may, upon request and signed and dated authorization, be made available to the patient or a designated representative.

All requests by patients for inspection of their records must be noted with the time and date of the patient's request, and the time and date of inspection must be noted by the health care provider. The patient is required to acknowledge the fact of inspection by dating and signing the record file.

2.20 Office Management

To assure that a client's confidentiality is protected and to comply with HIPAA Standards, a psychotherapist should undertake the following steps within the office:

1. Written policies and procedures should be developed and distributed to all staff members concerning client confidentiality.
2. All staff members should receive training on client confidentiality and sign a written statement acknowledging their duty and obligation to maintain client confidentiality.
3. Client confidentiality should be the topic of discussion with appropriate frequency at staff meetings.
4. Client files should be stored in locked filing cabinets with access limited to certain persons and checked out only to authorized persons. A record of who has the file should be maintained at all times.

5. Client information should only be released after receipt of a court order or signed release from the client specifying the information to be released and to whom such information may be given.
6. A written record should be maintained in the client file, identifying the date of any release of client information, the person receiving the information, and the specific information released.
7. Any release of client information should be stamped "Private and Confidential" and should be accompanied by a statement that outlines that the released information may not be released by the recipient.
8. All staff members should be advised that detailed messages about a client should not be left on any answering machine and that conversations about clients should not occur over any radio medium such as portable or cellular telephones.
9. Staff discussions about clients should not occur in public areas of the office such as the restroom or lunchroom.
10. Staff should not send faxes containing sensitive information unless a reasonable precaution is made to ensure that the confidentiality of the information is maintained.
11. Staff should not discuss confidential matters on a cellular telephone.
12. A client's informed consent to treatment should be obtained in writing prior to commencing treatment. The consent should include disclosures concerning exceptions to confidentiality addressed in section 6.02 of this book.

2.21 Responding to Subpoenas and Requests for Client Records

HIPAA practices have created confusion regarding the appropriate response by mental health professionals to requests for treatment records. While HIPAA practices require that patients have access to their medical records, an exception exists for "psychotherapy notes." In addition, state laws, which require medical professionals to turn over a copy of all client records when authorized by a signed, dated request for records by a client, generally contain exceptions for psychiatric, psychological, and mental health records. Therapists, therefore, need to make themselves aware of state laws concerning the access to therapists' notes and records that clients are entitled to receive. This information can often be obtained from licensing board representatives, local professional associations, or attorneys specializing in health care law.

Responding to Subpoenas. Whenever a therapist receives a subpoena for testimony or a subpoena *duces tecum* requiring the production of treatment records, an informed consent process should begin. In this process, contact the client to determine if he or she consents to courtroom testimony and will give written authorization for disclosure of confidential information to the judge, attorneys, and all others present in court. Similarly, when a therapist receives a subpoena *duces tecum* for production of treatment records, the therapist needs to contact the client involved to determine if the client is willing to authorize the disclosure of a copy of all records subpoenaed—usually the entire client chart—at the time and place commanded by the subpoena.

This is an informed-consent process because clients generally do not know the content of the information in their records, and may not remember what history was provided to a therapist during the assessment conducted at the inception of treatment. When a client is informed of the nature of the information contained in the therapist's chart and the specific history contained in notes, the client may then authorize disclosure of that information.

If an authorization signed by the client for release of treatment information accompanies written correspondence from an attorney or health care professional who has been authorized to receive the information, the generally accepted standard of practice is to comply with state law in producing the records sought. However, the best practice is to inform the client of the information contained in the chart, and ensure that the client is willing to authorize the disclosure of the records knowing their contents. After being apprised of the information contained in the chart, the client has the choice of whether to revoke the previously signed written authorization for disclosure of records.

During this informed-consent process, a client may object to any release of treatment information when notified of the subpoena served by an opposing party's attorney in litigation involving the client. If a client does not authorize the disclosure and production of treatment records or testimony by a therapist, then the client should instruct his or her attorney to oppose the subpoena and seek to have it quashed or file a motion for a protective order requesting protection of the confidential information contained in the mental health records. It should be the client's attorney who engages in legal procedures, at the client's expense, to protect the client's privacy and the confidentiality of treatment information. It is not the therapist's obligation to retain counsel at the therapist's expense to file a motion for protective order. However, if the client has no attorney, therapists can contact their professional liability insurer to determine if their insurance policy provides coverage to retain an attorney for this purpose.

If a therapist is employed by a mental health center or agency, then the therapist's supervisor should be notified immediately of the subpoena. The agency's counsel can then assist in protecting the client's privacy and the privileged information contained in records, when the client does not consent to a therapist's testimony or objects to the production of records. A form motion for protective order is contained in the Forms section of this book.

Therapists, of course, are entitled to be paid for their time for testifying in court (if called as an expert witness) and for conferring with a client's attorney, when authorized to do so, to prepare for testimony as an expert.

In situations when a therapist has received a subpoena to testify in court or to produce records, the professional cannot ignore the subpoena and must appear. If the client has not waived the therapist-client privilege and has not consented to testimony or disclosure of treatment information, the therapist should inform the court before testifying or turning over records that no client has authorized any waiver of the privilege or has consented to disclosure of treatment information.

In addition, a therapist may inform the judge that any information in the therapist's possession would be personal, private, and harmful if disclosed. This can be done without acknowledging that a professional relationship has existed in the past with any person in the courtroom. If the judge then directs that the therapist take the witness stand or produce records that have been subpoenaed, the therapist should ask, "Your Honor, are you ordering me to comply with the subpoena?" If the judge responds in the affirmative, then the therapist should comply with the court's order, trusting that the judge is properly applying and enforcing the applicable law.

The malpractice insurance policies for mental health professionals generally provide coverage for legal fees incurred in responding to a subpoena for client records. Professional liability insurers want therapists to be able to retain an attorney to assist in responding to a subpoena so that you can avoid pitfalls, and can prevent worse problems.

What issues and questions should a therapist discuss with his or her own attorney, after receiving a subpoena for testimony in court or for client records? First, was service of the subpoena proper, or can a Motion to Quash the subpoena be filed? Has the client or the client's legal representative consented in writing to disclosure of treatment information in court or to release of treatment records; or should a Motion for Protective Order be filed with the court to protect against a breach of confidentiality, which would occur if treatment information were disclosed without the client's consent? Does the subpoena comply with court rules, providing enough time to the therapist to rearrange scheduled appointments before the court appearance? Do the court rules require the therapist to travel the distance involved, especially if it is outside the county where the therapist was served? These are legal issues and questions that require legal assistance.

In what other ways can an attorney help a therapist who has received a subpoena? First and foremost, an attorney can confer with the attorneys who issued the subpoena to advise, "My client cannot help you." An attorney can also demand the expert fee that would be required, if the therapist is not released from the subpoena. And in many cases these days, an attorney can inform the attorney who issued the subpoena that the client signed a promise not to subpoena the therapist and not to request the therapist's testimony in court. In many instances, attorneys have released my clients from subpoenas, either having been confronted with a Motion to Quash or a Motion for Protective Order, or when the attorney who issued the subpoena has been confronted with the ultimate reality, "You are going to be wasting your money in this case, because you will have to pay my client an expert fee, and my client's testimony will not help you."

In terms of basic practical advice regarding subpoenas, keep in mind that a subpoena does not authorize the disclosure of confidential, privileged treatment information: It only compels you to be present at the place and time listed in the subpoena. If you receive a subpoena in the mail, which is accompanied by a card that you are asked to sign and send back, do not send the card back unless you want to appear in court and testify. The card is a waiver of service. Signing the card and returning it means that you will be required to appear in court.

So what is the first step that you should take in responding to a subpoena? Let your insurance company know that you have received a subpoena and want to hire legal counsel.

Requests for Information from Court Investigators. Judges recognize the value of recommendations by mental health professionals to assist courts in handling divorce and custody cases; in sentencing defendants in criminal cases; in imposing conditions of probation for drug or alcohol-related offenses; and in ordering treatment for juveniles who have broken the law. Family court cases involving divorce and custody litigation provide the most frequent opportunity for mental health professionals to have contact with the courts. Therapists for the husband, the wife, or the children of the parties are frequently contacted by court investigators, custody evaluators, or court-appointed special advocates (CASA advocates) seeking information for use in making recommendations to the court. These recommendations concern the award of custody, joint custody, the allocation of parental responsibilities by the court, and visitation or "parenting time."

Courts use mental health professionals as well as attorneys to conduct these investigations and to make such recommendations to the court. These investigations facilitate the judicial process, making it more efficient, so that judges do not need to spend days in court hearing the testimony of witnesses in order to rule upon disputed issues. When therapists are contacted by investigators for the court, CASA advocates, or custody evaluators, but have not received any written authorization from clients to disclose information to these individuals, they should do the following:

1. Contact the court representative without disclosing that a professional relationship has existed with anyone involved in the domestic litigation.
2. Inform the court representative that a signed, written authorization for treatment information must be received before any discussion can occur or any information can be disclosed. Usually, the custody evaluator is being paid to conduct an investigation, and can obtain the written authorization needed from the client. In these situations, courts frequently order the parties

to sign authorizations so that professionals involved with the family can provide information needed by the custody evaluator and the court. Often the court representative will have signed authorizations from the parties, which can be easily transmitted to a therapist.

3. In conferring with a court representative after having been authorized to do so, do not advocate for the client. It is the therapist's duty to provide factual information in response to questions.

When authorized to provide information to a custody evaluator, provide the least amount of information needed to satisfy the court representative's purpose. If questions are asked of the therapist concerning which parent would make the better custodian, the therapist needs to acknowledge limitations on his or her ability to respond, and acknowledge any bias or lack of objectivity that would affect the therapist's judgment in answering the questions posed. If the therapist is subsequently called as a witness to testify in a divorce or custody action, he or she should discuss the facts and not express opinions on ultimate issues that the therapist has not had an opportunity to evaluate, and not make assessments of a party whom the therapist has never met, much less assessed.

Motion for Protective Order. The Colorado Supreme Court issued a ruling that reaffirms a therapist's duty to oppose a subpoena duces tecum for treatment records in a situation where the client has not consented to the disclosure of the records. In *People v. Sisneros,* 55 P.3d 797 (Colo. 2002), the Colorado Supreme Court considered a criminal case in which charges of sexual assault on a minor had been filed and in which the defendant's attorney had issued a subpoena duces tecum to the victim's psychologist, demanding that the victim's treatment records be turned over. When the psychologist refused to turn over the records and sought a protective order from the Pueblo District Court, the judge initially ruled that he wanted to inspect the records in camera (in private) to see if any records should be turned over to the defendant. The psychologist took an immediate appeal to the Colorado Supreme Court, seeking to protect the confidential and privileged information contained in the treatment records.

The Colorado Supreme Court discussed the therapist-client privilege set forth in C.R.S. § 13-90-107. Pursuant to this privilege, a therapist may not testify in court or turn over records concerning a client's treatment without the client's consent. In its decision, the Colorado Supreme Court ruled that the trial court judge did not have the discretion to order the victim's records to be disclosed, even for the judge's in camera review. The Colorado Supreme Court also determined that the victim did not waive her privilege by testifying in court that she had received treatment from the psychologist.

This decision applies in any situation where treatment records have been subpoenaed, and the client (or clients in the case of couples or family therapy) has not consented to the disclosure of treatment information. In any criminal case in which charges of sexual assault, domestic violence, or other crimes against a person have been charged, the decision in *People v. Sisneros, supra,* should establish a precedent to be followed by the trial court. Unless the court finds that the privilege has been waived or that the client has consented to disclosure of treatment information, the court should issue a protective order, protecting against disclosure of the confidential, privileged information.

What is the duty of a therapist who receives a subpoena to testify in court or a subpoena duces tecum to turn over treatment records? To oppose the request by seeking a protective order from the court. If your client is a party to the case in which the subpoena has been issued, your client's attorney should be able to raise the issue in an appropriate manner. If it is a criminal case, then the district attorney ordinarily should be willing to raise the issue with the court in order to protect the victim's privacy. If necessary, a therapist can provide the judge hearing the case with a motion for protective order, being careful not to disclose the fact that a professional relationship exists. Keep in mind that you cannot refuse to obey a court order. If a judge orders you to testify or to disclose records in a case, the prevailing practice among therapists is to trust that the judge's ruling is legally correct and comply with it, unless an appeal is filed.

A Motion for Protective Order form is included in the Forms section of this book. This motion contains a discussion of Colorado statutes regarding confidentiality and privilege, and summarizes the legal principles regarding client confidentiality discussed in decisions issued by both the United States Supreme Court and the Colorado Supreme Court.

2.22 HIPAA Business Practices

When the Health Insurance Portability and Accountability Act (HIPAA, Pub. Law No. 104-191 (1996)) went into effect on April 14, 2003, it established procedures for compliance with standards to protect "confidential health care information" by health care professionals who transmit treatment information or billing information electronically. The primary purpose of this Act was to require insurance companies, HMOs, PPOs, and third-party payors to protect the confidentiality of the information sent to them for billing purposes. These protections are assured through identity codes, which are used instead of a client's name. In addition, diagnostic codes are used (as had been the practice in the past) along with procedure or intervention codes.

In part, the law was enacted to prevent entities that pay for health care treatment from creating data banks of information concerning consumers and our problems. Fears had existed and myths were prevalent regarding the prospect that companies were setting up data banks concerning patients who were depressed or HIV-positive, so that this information could be used to deny life insurance applications or applications for health insurance.

Confusion abounds regarding HIPAA, its applications, and its effect in relation to state law. State laws preempt HIPAA when they are more stringent than HIPAA procedures, and when the state laws provide for greater protection of confidential health information. For example, some state laws allow therapists to use their discretion in responding to a request for records and to provide a treatment summary—rather than a copy of the actual records—when therapists believe that a client might be harmed by the disclosure of the records or unable to process the data in them appropriately. Such laws and the procedures they authorize preempt HIPAA regulations and procedures.

In some jurisdictions, therapists are allowed to exercise their professional judgment and refuse a request for records. Again, such laws take precedence over HIPAA regulations. The Act recognizes that state laws that are more stringent than HIPAA standards take precedence. In practice, this means that the protections for confidential health information that existed before HIPAA went into effect still applied after HIPAA went into effect. Essentially, HIPAA did not change the procedures for protecting mental health records established by state law; it changed the amount of paperwork used by professionals.

The regulations adopted by the U.S. Department of Health and Human Services to implement HIPAA contain privacy standards, found at 45 C.F.R. §§ 164.500 to 164.534. As every consumer of health care services knows, patients (and even customers at pharmacies) were provided a HIPAA Privacy Notice, which explains the uses and disclosures of confidential health care information.

In addition, providers who are HIPAA-compliant are required to have the business associates who receive patients' confidential health care information sign a Business Associate Contract, agreeing to maintain the confidentiality of all information that the business associate may receive. For example, a contractor who conducts a billing service for mental health professionals or physicians comes into contact with extremely personal information relating to patients and their diagnoses. Pursuant to a HIPAA Business Associate Contract, the individual or billing service must agree to return or destroy all confidential information when it is no longer needed.

Other business practices required by HIPAA include providing an accounting to clients of the disclosures made by a provider, if such an accounting is requested by a patient or client. When an accounting is requested, therapists are required to provide a statement containing the following information: (1) the date of the disclosure; (2) the recipient of the information; (3) the purpose of the disclosure; (4) the nature of the information requested; and (5) a statement regarding the specific information that was disclosed.

When a request for an accounting is made by a client, providers have 60 days within which to comply with that request. In providing an accounting, professionals do not need to go back before April 14, 2003. An exception to this procedure states that health care professionals do not need to account for the disclosure of information made in billing for services or for disclosures for information made with client consent to other health care professionals.

HIPAA regulations also require that authorization forms to be signed by patients or clients when authorizing the disclosure of treatment information contain specific statements and elements in order to be HIPAA-compliant. These are discussed thoroughly in the next section. One requirement for a professional's authorization form is that it contain a statement that the authorization may be revoked, in writing, by the client at any time.

The most important new standard for mental health professionals adopted by HIPAA is the requirement that when professionals receive a request for disclosure of confidential health care information with client consent, they are to disclose the least amount of information possible to comply with the request. This new standard is important because in the past, insurers and government health care programs (such as CHAMPUS/TRICARE) at times requested a copy of the entire client chart in order to justify the reasonableness and necessity of bills for treatment as part of a utilization review. These requests were extremely invasive of clients' privacy rights. The idea that a psychologist or other mental health professional might be required to provide an entire chart with all notes to justify payment of bills was troubling because it was potentially violative of the clients' right to privacy.

The Forms section of this book contains basic HIPAA business forms for use in complying with procedures for professionals who are required to be HIPAA-compliant. The HIPAA Notice of Privacy Rights should be provided to new clients as part of the informed-consent process. It is not intended as a substitute for any client disclosure statement or informed-consent form required by state law, and does not include all of the disclosures required by the national professional associations for mental health therapists. The Forms section of this book also contains a HIPAA-compliant authorization form for disclosure of confidential, privileged treatment information.

When HIPAA was enacted by Congress, its purpose was, in part, to establish national standards for the protection of confidential health care information. As stated above, this statute and its regulations do not preempt state law to the extent that state standards for confidentiality and privilege may be more rigid and provide more protections than HIPAA standards. The basic exceptions to confidentiality contained in codes of ethics for mental health professionals, and also mandated by state law, are incorporated into the federal statute. For example, reports of child abuse or neglect, reports of imminent threats of physical violence made by clients, and procedures to hospitalize patients who are imminently dangerous to self or others were recognized under HIPAA as being exceptions to confidentiality.

One additional exception to confidentiality was created: a duty to report threats to the national security of the United States. Consistent with state laws and ethical codes, mental health professionals can comply with HIPAA by including in their disclosures to clients, in writing, a statement that the professional will report information concerning suspected threats to national security to federal officials. This disclosure would be contained in the same informed-consent form that discloses to clients the limitations on confidentiality—that treatment information is confidential, except that a mental health professional has a duty to report suspected child abuse or neglect; to warn potential victims concerning imminent threats of violence; to initiate hospitalization of clients who are imminently dangerous to self and others, and to report threats to national security to federal officials. In this way, clients give informed consent to a professional to make these reports when necessary.

Insurers, HMOs, and others who violate clients' privacy rights by improperly disclosing treatment information can have monetary sanctions imposed against them. The regulations adopted by HHS recommend that health care providers initiate commonsense practices to protect against the inadvertent disclosure of treatment information by keeping client records in locked file cabinets. Information maintained on computers must be password-protected. Other recommendations include positioning computer screens so that they are not visible to people walking by, and not leaving confidential reports, records, and files face up on a desk where they can be seen by clients entering the office.

Therapists are required to be HIPAA-compliant if they transmit treatment information electronically, either in billing for services or in transmitting information over the Internet. Be assured that if you do insurance billing, the insurer will require you to maintain compliance with all HIPAA standards and will advise you of procedures that do so. If you do not transmit billing information to third-party payors electronically, then, in all likelihood, you do not need to be HIPAA-compliant. Sending a fax containing client information or confidential health care information does not subject a therapist to HIPAA procedures.

In order to comply with the national standard of care for providing mental health treatment, therapists are required to provide treatment in accordance with the "generally accepted standards of practice." HIPAA provisions are rapidly becoming the generally accepted standards of practice for mental health professionals.

The HIPAA Privacy Rule and C.R.S. § 25-1-802. Mental health counselors are generally familiar with the HIPAA Privacy Rule, even if they cannot cite the federal regulation regarding it. The HIPAA Privacy Rule is contained in 45 C.F.R. § 164.501, and provides that "psychotherapy notes" should not be disclosed in response to a request for client records. "Psychotherapy notes" are defined as notes recorded by a mental health professional, documenting or analyzing the contents of private conversations with a client during a private counseling session.

This Privacy Rule is comparable to C.R.S. § 25-1-802, which concerns requests for client healthcare records. This Colorado law states that all healthcare providers *except* for mental health counselors must provide a complete set of records upon receipt of a signed, dated request from the client. However, when a request is made for mental health treatment records, a mental health professional may provide a treatment summary and not the psychotherapy notes and records maintained by the therapist.

The purpose of both the HIPAA Privacy Rule and this Colorado law is to protect against disclosure of information that may be extremely personal and private, and not pertinent to a request for records. Providing a treatment summary in compliance with these legal standards is consistent with another HIPAA standard. HIPAA requires that when therapists comply with requests for treatment information, they should supply the least amount of information needed to satisfy the request. This principle applies, for example, when an insurance company that is paying for client treatment asks for records to justify the need for counseling.

When a therapist receives a court order, however, requiring the disclosure of all treatment records in the therapist's possession, it means exactly that, and therapists are bound to comply with the court order, since doing so is a generally accepted standard of practice.

2.23 HIPAA Standards Concerning Authorizations to Disclose Confidential Healthcare Information

The regulations adopted by the U.S. Department of Health and Human Services contain specific requirements for the inclusion of elements and statements used in professionals' forms to be signed by clients in authorizing the disclosure of confidential treatment information. According to 45 C.F.R. § 164.508(c), authorization forms must contain the following elements (along with any additional requirements required by state law):

- A description of the information to be used or disclosed that identifies the information in a specific and meaningful fashion.
- The name or other specific identification of the person(s), or class of persons, authorized to make the requested use or disclosure.
- The name or other specific identification of the person(s), or class of persons, to whom the covered entity may make the requested use or disclosure.
- A description of each purpose of the requested use or disclosure. The statement "at the request of the individual" is a sufficient description of the purpose when an individual initiates the authorization and does not, or elects not to, provide a statement of the purpose.
- An expiration date or an expiration event that relates to the individual or the purpose of the use or disclosure. The statement "end of the research study," "none," or similar language is sufficient if the authorization is for a use or disclosure of protected health information for research, including the creation and maintenance of a research database or research repository.
- The signature of the individual and date. If the authorization is signed by a personal representative of the individual, a description of such representative's authority to act for the individual must also be provided.
- A statement adequate to place the individual on notice of the individual's right to revoke the authorization in writing, and either: (1) the exceptions to the right to revoke and a description of how the individual may revoke the authorization; or (2) to the extent that the information in (1) is included in the Notice of Privacy Practices, a reference to the covered entity's notice.
- A statement adequate to place the individual on notice of the ability or inability of the covered entity to condition treatment, payment, enrollment, or eligibility for benefits on the authorization, by stating either: (1) The covered entity may not condition treatment, payment, enrollment or eligibility for benefits on whether the individual signs the authorization when the pro-

hibition on conditioning of authorizations in the Privacy Regulation applies; or (2) The consequences to the individual of a refusal to sign the authorization when the covered entity can condition treatment, enrollment in the health plan, or eligibility for benefits on failure to obtain such authorization.

- A statement adequate to place the individual on notice of the potential for information disclosed pursuant to the authorization to be subject to re-disclosure by the recipient and no longer be protected by this rule.
- The authorization must be written in plain language.
- A copy must be given to the individual. If a covered entity seeks an authorization from an individual for a use or disclosure of protected health information, the covered entity must provide the individual with a copy of the signed authorization.
- If the authorization is for a marketing purpose that involves direct or indirect remuneration to the covered entity from a third party, the authorization must state that such remuneration is involved.

The statement that HIPAA-compliant authorizations for disclosure of treatment information "must be written in plain language" is ironic; if only the HIPAA regulations were written in plain and intelligible language!

The last element on this checklist for authorization forms is problematic. Professionals who seek testimonials from clients for marketing purposes, requiring them to obtain client authorization for this purpose, could easily be seen as exploiting the client for the benefit of the professional. A word to the wise: this is not a generally accepted practice among mental health professionals, and a licensing board might consider the use of client testimonials for marketing as a boundary violation.

2.24 Preparing a Professional Will: Protecting Clients and Their Treatment Information After a Therapist's Retirement, Disability, or Death

State licensing board rules and ethical codes for mental health professionals are beginning to require therapists to appoint an executor for their professional estate so that arrangements can be made for the proper disposition of client records or for the referral of clients in the event of a therapist's retirement, disability, or death. The American Association for Marriage and Family Therapy (AAMFT) Code of Ethics Principle 2.5 provides, "Subsequent to the therapist moving from the area, closing the practice, or upon the death of the therapist, a marriage and family therapist arranges for the storage, transfer, or disposal of client records in ways that maintain confidentiality and safeguard the welfare of clients." In Ohio, mental health counselors applying for or renewing their license must identify the professional executor who has been appointed to wind up a therapist's practice in the event of death or disability. Just as estate planning is important so that an individual's property can be disposed of through a will, which designates an executor to carry out the provisions of the will, mental health professionals are being required or encouraged to designate another therapist to be the executor of their professional estate.

Currently, a need exists for counselors in private practice to make appropriate arrangements to avoid the prospect that family members will be going through dusty old boxes of client files, found in a corner of the garage, after a therapist has died. Just as a therapist making plans for retirement should make arrangements for appropriate storage and disposition of client records, payment of bills, collection of fees, and referral of clients to ensure continuity of care, all private practitioners should also make basic contingency plans to protect clients' interests and the privacy of their treatment information in the event of a counselor's incapacity or death.

Practical Considerations. At the end of the Forms section of the book, you can find a form to use in creating a Professional Will. This form is adapted from a template created by the San Diego Psychological Association for use by mental health professionals. In reviewing the form Professional Will, you will see that a great deal of the information to be included in the document concerns logistical information, such as the location of bank accounts, account numbers for any business accounts, the location of keys for your office, and passwords for access to office computers or voicemail. The Professional Will is like a power of attorney, in that it grants authority to the professional executor to conduct business, as needed, and to close a therapist's practice. A HIPAA Business Associate Contract should be signed by the professional executor, agreeing to maintain confidentiality of all treatment information to which the professional executor will have access. The therapist's Personal Will needs to reference the fact that a Professional Will has been created, so that the personal representative of the therapist's estate can coordinate activities with the professional executor, and grant authority to the professional executor to transact business in the event of a therapist's death.

The first step is to select a colleague who would be entrusted with the responsibility for winding up your practice and either taking over your caseload or making referrals, as needed. You should determine that this colleague is willing to serve as the executor of your professional estate. In making these arrangements, you may want to reciprocate and agree to be the executor for your colleague. So that confidential treatment information may be shared with the executor in the event of an emergency, you should have the professional executor sign a HIPAA Business Associate Contract. By signing this contract, the business associate agrees to maintain clients' records and confidential treatment information appropriately within the scope of the therapist-client privilege. Then a power of attorney form should be filled out to convey to the executor the authority to take care of business matters.

The next step is to prepare a professional will, which directs the executor as to his or her duties in the event of your death or disability. The professional will need not be legalistic, nor does it require specific language. It can simply begin with the statement, "I hereby appoint my trusted professional colleague, Jane Designee, to be the executor of my professional estate." The professional will then would detail the duties to be performed and the information needed for performance of those duties.

The will should contain an appropriate checklist of matters that would require the executor's attention, such as paying any business debts, collecting fees owed by clients, providing appropriate notice to clients concerning the therapist's unavailability, and at the same time providing information to clients concerning who to contact for a referral or for continuity of care. The logistics involved in providing the executor with information and access to business records, client files, and computers requires the therapist to make the following available to the executor: (1) keys to the office and to file cabinets; (2) passwords for computers and e-mail accounts; and (3) the location of appointment calendars, billing records, client files, mailboxes, and bank accounts, along with the information specifically needed to access bank accounts, voice mail, and storage areas containing client records that have been securely stored off-site. Obviously this is a thorough planning process. We can all understand that this process is extremely important for the sake of clients to insure continuity of care, so that no client is abandoned in the event of an emergency.

What provisions does a therapist's professional will contain? It will contain all of the logistical information described above and any additional information concerning office staff or billing clerks who can help an executor perform all these duties. It would be advisable to attach to the professional will the business associate contract and the power of attorney forms discussed above. Then the will and its attachments can be given to the professional executor for safekeeping, to use in the event that it is needed. A website that provides practical information regarding the logistics involved in the contingency planning process is www.psychotherapy.net, which posts an excellent article by Ann Steiner, Ph.D., entitled, "The Empty Chair: Making Our Absence Less Traumatic for Everyone."

Ethical Considerations. The AMHCA Code of Ethics (2000 Revision) Principle 2(C) sets forth the client's basic rights, including the expectation of "complete confidentiality within the limits of the law" and the expectation "that no information will be released without the client's knowledge and written consent." Principle 3 Confidentiality affirms the duty of mental health counselors "to safeguard information about individuals obtained in the course of practice, teaching, or research." This principle recognizes the duty of therapists to protect the privacy of clients by maintaining the confidentiality of treatment information and by disposing of client files properly. A professional will is necessary, then, to insure proper handling and disposition of client files.

While the ethical codes of the professional associations for therapists require client records to be maintained, they do not prescribe specific periods of time for client records to be kept. But state laws or the rules of licensing boards do mandate the length of time that therapists must maintain records. Compliance with these ethical standards, state statutes, and board rules is only possible when therapists make arrangements for the safeguarding of client records and information in preparation for retirement or in the event of death or disability. When client records have been maintained for the requisite length of time, it would be the executor's duty to insure that the records were disposed of properly by shredding them. The executor would also be required to comply with requests for information when clients provide written authorization for disclosure of records to another professional. Under no circumstances should client records simply be mailed to clients so they can maintain their files. This would result in the same foreseeable problems that would occur if counselors failed to make proper arrangements for the safeguarding of client files and treatment information.

Principle 3(a) of the AMHCA Code of Ethics provides, "At the outset of any counseling relationship, mental health counselors make their clients aware of their rights in regard to the confidential nature of the counseling relationship. They fully disclose the limits of, or exceptions to, confidentiality and/or the existence of privileged communication, if any." One of the limitations on confidentiality that counselors must disclose at the outset of treatment is a supervisory relationship. Principle 9(f) requires, "Supervisees must make their clients aware in their informed consent statement that they are under supervision and they must provide their clients with the name and credentials of their supervisor." By the same token, any colleague designated as the executor of a mental health counselor's professional estate should also be disclosed to clients in the informed consent statement because of the possibility that the executor may need to review client files in the future in order to perform the duties required by a will.

By agreeing to serve as an executor, a mental health counselor assumes the duty to make appropriate referrals. AMHCA Code Principle 1(P) Termination and Referral provides, "Mental health counselors do not abandon or neglect their clients in counseling. Assistance is given in making appropriate arrangements for the continuation of treatment, when necessary, during interruption such as vacation and following termination." The referral process is an extremely important function and a valuable service to clients who need ongoing care when a therapist becomes incapacitated.

CHAPTER 3: TESTIFYING AS AN EXPERT

Psychotherapists are often called to testify about their knowledge or opinion of their clients. When this occurs, what can a psychotherapist expect to occur in the process of testifying? What is expert witness testimony? Is there a right to compensation for the time involved in preparing for and actually testifying? Who is responsible for paying that compensation? What happens in a deposition? What happens at trial? What rights does a witness have? The answers to these and other questions are set forth in this chapter.

3.01 Expert Witness Testimony

In general, an expert is a person who possesses special knowledge, skill, education, experience, or training in a particular field. This broad definition certainly encompasses most psychiatrists, psychologists, social workers, professional counselors, marriage and family therapists, and other mental health workers.

Rule 702 of the Colorado Rules of Evidence sets forth the admissibility of expert witness testimony as follows:

> If scientific, technical, or other specialized knowledge will assist the trier of fact to understand the evidence or to determine a fact in issue, a witness qualified as an expert by knowledge, skill, experience, training, or education, may testify thereto in the form of an opinion or otherwise.

3.02 Offered Testimony Must Be Helpful

Rule 702 requires that the court first determine whether there is a need for expert witness testimony. Thus, before a psychotherapist can testify in a trial, the court must be convinced that the testimony will help the jury or the judge to understand some factual issue in dispute.

In *People v. Beaver*, 725 P.2d 96 (Colo. App. 1986), the court excluded the testimony of a psychologist concerning certain factors that affect eyewitness testimony. A similar ruling excluding the testimony of a psychotherapist was made in *People v. Campbell,* 785 P.2d 153 (Colo. App. 1989). In these two cases, the courts determined that such testimony from a psychologist was not helpful in resolving issues, since such factors were within the realm of a juror's everyday experience.

The requirement that psychological testimony be helpful to the trier of fact was reiterated in *People v. Lomanaco,* 802 P.2d 1143 (Colo. App. 1990). In this case, the court excluded psychological testimony on the issue of irresistible impulse and heat of passion, since such issues were found to be within the experience of average laypersons.

Although the foregoing cases suggest that the testimony of psychotherapists may not be deemed helpful to the trier of fact, this is generally not the case. In practice, the courts are interested in the opinions and insights of such professionals, particularly in adoption, juvenile, child custody, mental competence, and emotional distress cases.

For example, in *People v. District Court,* 647 P.2d 1206 (Colo. 1982), the Colorado Supreme Court held that a psychiatrist could testify to the incompetence of a witness based on a review of a videotaped testimony of the witness. Also reflective of this practice are the following cases that hold that rape counselors, social workers, and others may qualify as experts, despite the fact that their testimony may be limited by application of other rules: *Farley v. People,* 746 P.2d 956 (Colo. 1987); *People v. Hampton,* 746 P.2d 947 (Colo. 1987); *People v. Snook,* 745 P.2d 647 (Colo. 1987); and *People v. Koon,* 724 P.2d 1367 (Colo. App. 1986).

In further recognition of this practice, one should note that an expert may not give an opinion on whether another witness is being truthful. *People v. Guilbeaux,* 761 P.2d 255 (Colo. App. 1988). However, according to *People v. Deninger,* 772 P.2d 674 (Colo. App. 1989), psychologists have been allowed to testify regarding the capacity of a child to fabricate sex abuse claims. *People v. Mathes,* 703 P.2d 608 (Colo. App. 1985); *People v. Koon,* 713 P.2d 410 (Colo. App. 1985); and *People v. Ashley,* 687 P.2d 473 (Colo. App. 1984).

In *People v. Gillespie,* 767 P.2d 778 (Colo. App. 1988), the Colorado Court of Appeals held that in sexual assault situations, especially where a child is very young, an opinion by a psychologist as to credibility of the witness is admissible if the testimony relates to general characteristics only.

The foregoing cases were preceded by *People v. Ortega,* 672 P.2d 215 (Colo. App. 1983), which held that the trial court erred by admitting the testimony of a clinical psychologist that a child sexual assault victim was not fabricating the incident. This case seems to conflict with those cited above. A reasonable legal prognosis is that psychotherapists will not be allowed to testify concerning the credibility of a witness or of a victim's account.

3.03 Qualifying as an Expert

Once the court has determined that expert witness testimony from a psychiatrist, psychologist, social worker, counselor, or other psychotherapist would be helpful to the trier of fact, the witness must qualify as an expert by convincing the court that he or she has the knowledge, skill, experience, training, or education to be an expert in the particular field.

This process involves the expert's recitation of his or her credentials, which should include, but not be limited to, the following:

1. Academic degrees by year, field of study, and granting institution(s);
2. Academic honors;
3. Publications by title, year of publication, and publisher;
4. Relevant professional history, stressing work related to the anticipated testimony;
5. Affiliations with relevant professional associations;
6. Licenses held, by date of issuance and body granting such licenses;
7. Professional honors;
8. Speaking appearances on topics in the field of expertise; and
9. Prior qualifications as an expert witness in other trials.

It is important that the credentials be presented in a manner that is forthright and professional. This is not the time to be humble. On the other hand, one must not become self-absorbed and egotistical. Do not forget that if a psychotherapist is testifying to a jury, it is likely that his or her qualifications and educational background will exceed those of the average juror. The psychotherapist must not alienate the jury with his or her qualifications, but must convince them that he or she is qualified and has opinions that are reasonable and consistent with all the known facts.

3.04 Types of Testimony

The testimony of a psychotherapist can be divided into three classes. First, it may relate solely to the psychotherapist's personal firsthand observations of the client, which would include events witnessed by the therapist and statements made directly to the therapist by the client. Second, it may relate solely to the psychotherapist's opinion of the mental status of the client or some other opinion, such as the therapist's assessment of the client or treatment recommendations. Third, the testimony may involve both first-hand observations and expert opinions.

Rules 702 and 704 of the Colorado Rules of Evidence specifically allow all three types of expert witness testimony from psychotherapists. However, if the case is a federal criminal matter governed by the Federal Rules of Evidence, then F.R.E. 704(b) does not allow a psychotherapist to testify with respect to whether or not the defendant had the mental state or condition constituting an element of the crime charged or a defense to it. The Colorado courts do not follow this federal restriction, and psychotherapists are allowed to render opinions on the ultimate issue in a case according to CRE 705.

3.05 Basis of Testimony

What can a psychotherapist's expert witness testimony be based upon? Rule 703 of the Colorado Rules of Evidence provides the answer as follows:

> The facts or data in the particular case upon which an expert bases an opinion or inference may be those perceived by or made known to the expert at or before the hearing. If of a type reasonably relied upon by experts in the particular field in forming opinions or inferences upon the subject, the facts or data need not be admissible in evidence . . . .

This rule allows a psychotherapist to base his or her opinion testimony on facts or data gathered from a variety of sources. Consequently, the psychotherapist is not limited to his or her own personal observations of the client.

Additionally, if the facts or data used by the psychotherapist are of a type reasonably relied upon by other experts in the field, then such facts themselves need not be admissible in evidence.

Under this rule, a psychotherapist may base his or her opinion on the following:

1. Personal observations of the client or subject;
2. Reports of other professionals who examined the client or subject;
3. Results of professional tests administered by the mental health professional or others;
4. Reports of family members, close friends, co-workers, etc., of the client or subject, provided such are customarily relied upon by other experts;
5. Sworn testimony of the client or subject or others;
6. Facts made known to him or her, at or before the hearing, which may include briefings by counsel, review of depositions, written interrogatories, and other information;
7. Opinions of other experts; and
8. Professional and academic literature, such as surveys, reports, books, learned treatises, articles, etc.

3.06 Disclosure of Underlying Facts or Data

Rule 705 of the Colorado Rules of Evidence allows an expert witness to testify in terms of opinion or inference and give the reasons therefor without prior disclosure of the underlying facts or data unless the court requires otherwise. However, Rule 705 does require disclosure of such facts and data upon cross-examination.

This rule no longer requires the expert to lay out at trial all of the facts and data that were used in developing his or her opinion. Thus, an expert may simply testify as to his or her opinion and the reasons for it.

Generally, the lawyer calling the expert witness will decide whether or not it is advisable to disclose all of the facts and data before the opinion is rendered. However, the expert witness should be prepared to reveal all of the facts and data upon which he or she relied during cross-examination. Further, the expert should offer his or her opinions to the lawyer regarding whether or not such prior disclosure aids in the effective presentation of his or her opinion at trial.

3.07 Being Retained

Psychotherapists become involved in lawsuits as experts in a variety of ways. Some have developed a reputation in a particular area and are frequently called upon by lawyers to review a case and render an opinion. For example, many psychologists and licensed therapists perform custody evaluations and are hired by a lawyer seeking such an evaluation for his or her client. Psychiatrists and psychologists are frequently involved in issues of criminal insanity and competency to stand trial and are sought out by criminal defense lawyers or prosecutors.

Psychotherapists also become involved as experts when their own clients are litigants and there is an issue as to the client's emotional or mental health. In such cases, the psychotherapist is usually contacted by the lawyer for the client and asked for his or her input regarding the specific issue. If the lawyer believes the opinion of the therapist would be helpful to the case, the lawyer will not hesitate to call the therapist at trial. This of course will result in a waiver of the therapist-client confidentiality privilege. Any authorization for disclosure of treatment information, authorizing courtroom testimony by a client's therapist, should authorize disclosure to all persons present in court, as well as all persons who may review a transcript of the testimony.

Regardless of how or why the psychotherapist becomes involved, there are certain aspects of the involvement that should immediately be clarified by the psychotherapist. These include the following:

1. The client should sign a specific release prior to any substantive discussions with any third party.
2. An understanding should be reached between the psychotherapist, client, and lawyer as to the handling of the psychotherapist's fees. For example, is the psychotherapist to look to the client for payment of his or her expert witness fees, or to the lawyer? Is an advance payment required by the psychotherapist? If so, how much? How is the fee to be determined and when is it due and payable?

3. The understanding regarding fees should be reduced to writing by the psychotherapist and signed by the client, lawyer, and psychotherapist.
4. The understanding regarding fees should include a recital of what is expected from the psychotherapist in terms of consultation, written reports, participation in depositions, and trial testimony.
5. An understanding should be reached with the lawyer as to how to handle inquiries from the opposing counsel and others involved in the litigation.

It is the responsibility of all parties to see that the foregoing items are covered. If the lawyer fails to initiate a conversation regarding these items, the psychotherapist should do so in the first conversation. For some reason, people are reluctant to discuss such matters, and assumptions are frequently made that ultimately prove to be in error. Hence, it is the better practice to confirm all business matters in writing.

Most expert witnesses are compensated at an hourly rate that is set by them. Occasionally, a witness will render his or her services for a flat fee. It is always prudent to request an advance retainer for services to be performed. Most competent and successful attorneys follow this practice, and there is no reason why a psychotherapist who has been retained as an expert should not similarly expect such treatment.

3.08 Preparing a Report

On occasion, a lawyer will request a written report from the psychotherapist regarding various aspects of his or her testimony. There is no standard format for these reports, since the contents are dictated by the needs and the particular circumstances of the case.

An attorney should make a verbal request for the report and review in detail the specific information that he or she needs to have covered in the report. This verbal request is not an attempt to dictate an opinion, but rather is simply a means of communicating what the report should cover. For example, in an evaluation of parental responsibilities and parenting time in a domestic case, there are certain statutory issues a court must consider. A good lawyer will request that the evaluation address each of the specific issues. In a case involving emotional damages, the lawyer's request will typically ask for the following kinds of information: patient background, social history, treatment history, diagnosis, prognosis, and estimated cost of future treatment.

The verbal request for a report should be confirmed in writing by the attorney. If this is not done, the psychotherapist should confirm that the lawyer has made the request for the report.

A good lawyer will want to discuss the contents of the report prior to its finalization in writing. This is typically done to assure that the expert will cover all the required areas of analysis. If this is done, it avoids the necessity of a follow-up report covering areas that were missed.

At times, an expert will feel subtle pressure from the attorney to provide a specific opinion. Lawyers are very skilled at leading witnesses and planting ideas that may not have been there in the first place. A psychotherapist should understand that this may happen and that such efforts by the lawyer should not be allowed to influence his or her ultimate opinion. A competent lawyer will respect an expert's independence, even though disappointment, anger, or frustration may be expressed over the report. But the expert's reputation in the field may be enhanced because other lawyers and judges will come to know that expert as one whose integrity is intact and whose opinion cannot be compromised.

If a psychotherapist has been appointed by the court and is not working for a particular attorney, care should be taken to avoid any appearance of impropriety or bias. The final report should be written and distributed without disclosing its contents prior to distribution. Also, it is an excellent idea to require payment for the report prior to distribution. At times, a disgruntled litigant has been known to refuse to pay for a report once it has been issued.

3.09 Deposition Practice

A deposition is a proceeding that occurs outside of the courtroom whereby one party has the right to interrogate a witness under oath in order to determine what the witness' testimony will be at trial. The attendance of the witness and the production of certain documents can be compelled through subpoena. A court reporter is present and records the entire proceeding.

If any party to a lawsuit wants to depose a psychotherapist, a written agreement should be reached regarding who will pay for the expert's time for preparing, testifying, reading, and verifying the transcribed testimony. The expert should contact his or her client's attorney and seek clarification of this issue.

Typically, it is the opposing side that is responsible for compensating the expert for his or her time in preparing, testifying, and reading the deposition. To avoid controversy regarding this matter, the psychotherapist should obtain clarification from both sides in writing.

Many medical practitioners require that their depositions be taken in their own offices. This is probably a good idea for psychotherapists, provided the office will accommodate the group.

There are several ground rules that should be followed in a deposition. Most lawyers will meet with their own expert prior to the deposition to review these practice tips and anticipated questions. The following are standard instructions given to all witnesses prior to a deposition.

1. A witness takes an oath to tell the truth. Therefore, tell the truth. Do not lie or stretch the truth.
2. Listen carefully to each question that is asked.
3. Think about the answer before responding.
4. Answer only the question that is asked.
5. Do not volunteer any information, even if you think it would be helpful.
6. If you do not understand a question, ask that it be rephrased or terms defined.
7. Never argue with the person asking the question. Simply respond and move along.
8. Ask to take a break when you become tired or need to take care of some other human need, or if you would like to consult with an attorney before responding.
9. Your answers must be verbal. Head nodding or head shaking cannot be recorded by the reporter.
10. Use your notes and refer to the client file in order to be precise in your recollection.
11. Remain calm and take your time.

After the first attorney has completed his or her questioning, the other attorney has the opportunity to ask questions to defend or rehabilitate the witness. Again, listen to the questions carefully and follow the same ground rules.

When the deposition is completed, the court reporter will ask if you would like to waive signature of the deposition. This means that it will be filed directly with the court, without the expert having read it and given the opportunity to correct mistakes. Never waive signature, even if the attorneys are agreeable to doing so. It is your right to insist that the transcription be verified, and to be paid for the time you spend in reviewing the transcript.

In a few weeks or days, you will receive the transcription of the testimony. It should be carefully reviewed and any errors noted on a correction page. You should request from the lawyer who hired you that you be given a copy for your records. If you have to testify at trial, you will definitely need to review your deposition testimony before you take the stand. Opposing counsel will have abstracted your deposition and will be eagerly waiting for you to contradict yourself at trial. Hence, it is a cardinal rule that you know what you have previously said under oath.

Frequently, at the deposition, a demand will be made for the psychotherapist to produce and allow photocopying of the client file. Generally, this is not favorably received. However, if a subpoena duces tecum has been served upon the witness and a protective order has not been obtained, there is little legal justification for withholding the file. Chapter 2 outlines the problems encountered with such disclosure. If copies are requested, the psychotherapist should make the copies. Do not simply turn the file over to someone else for this task. Keep a record of how many copies were made and to whom they were distributed. A reasonable photocopying fee may be charged for this service.

A witness who has been subpoenaed to a deposition has the right to be represented by counsel of his or her own choosing and at his or her expense. Generally, this right is not exercised where the expert is working under a retainer. However, there are cases in which a psychotherapist has been subpoenaed and questions of privilege have not been previously resolved. In such situations, it is wise to retain an attorney immediately and to have him or her present at the deposition.

3.10 Preparation for Trial

The most important aspect of testifying at a trial or hearing is adequate and thorough preparation of the testimony. This should involve (at a minimum) the following:

1. A review of the client file.
2. A review of any deposition testimony given by the expert.
3. A review of any written reports prepared by the expert.
4. Preparation of an outline of what the expected testimony will be.
5. A face-to-face meeting with the attorney at least one day prior to the trial, at which time the testimony will be finalized and rehearsed.
6. Reaching an agreement with the attorney regarding the time the expert should arrive, and the location at which the expert is to appear.
7. Reaching an understanding with the attorney as to any special dress requirements.

Each of the foregoing items is crucial to the effective presentation of trial testimony. The attorney is only as good as the expert who testifies. The first step in presenting persuasive trial testimony is to devote whatever time it takes to know the testimony inside and out. Hence, the psychotherapist's priority should be to prepare himself or herself as thoroughly as possible, in accordance with the items outlined above.

The next step is to organize the testimony in such a way that it can be presented in a clear, cogent, and convincing manner. The attorney is ultimately responsible for this task. However, most good trial lawyers appreciate input from the expert and will seek this out in the face-to-face meeting. The demands of trial work often dictate that the lawyer talk briefly with the expert on the phone or outside the courtroom just prior to trial. This is not a good practice and should be discouraged by the expert. The expert needs to have a road map of the testimony so that the attorney and the expert complement each other during trial. The only way to do this is by preparation and rehearsal.

The notion that testimony should be rehearsed may seem strange to some people. However, the practice of rehearsing simply involves the lawyer's questioning of the expert outside the courtroom, and the expert's answering of those questions as if he or she were actually in the courtroom. This provides both the attorney and the expert with a mental image of how the interrogation will go in the courtroom, as well as an opportunity to rephrase questions or answers in order to develop better timing and pacing of the testimony.

The psychotherapist should ask the lawyer for any suggestions regarding the appropriate dress at trial. This may seem odd to some professionals. However, the frequency of inappropriately dressed experts suggests that not enough attention is paid to this matter when preparing for trial.

Each lawyer and expert will have to decide for themselves the specifics of the dress requirement. However, some general rules are as follows:

1. The traditional business or professional look for both men and women is encouraged. Dark blues, tans, and beige seem to be most appropriate. Busy prints should be avoided.
2. Avoid clothing, jewelry, and makeup that tend to bring attention to the expert. The courtroom is not a place to set and establish fashion trends.

3.11 On the Witness Stand

When called as a witness, your name will be announced and at that time you should rise and walk toward the witness stand. The court clerk or judge will direct you to raise your right hand and ask you if you will swear or affirm to tell the truth. The appropriate response is, "I do." You will then be told to be seated in the witness box or stand.

If you have not been given any directions to the contrary, feel free to take your file and notes with you. You should try to testify without referring to your file; however, this is not always possible, and you should not hesitate to look at your file to refresh your memory. You may *not* read your testimony into the court record. It should be your own words, formed by you from your memory, after examining your file.

Adhere to the following rules when answering questions from attorneys:

1. Always tell the truth. Do not lie or stretch the truth.
2. Listen carefully to each question that is asked.
3. Think about the answer before responding.
4. Don't be evasive.

5. If you are presented with a yes or no question and you think it cannot be answered that way, tell the lawyer that such a question is hard to answer in that fashion and try to explain. If you are cut off and are given an ultimatum, don't argue. Your choices are to answer the questions with a yes or no, or simply restate that you cannot give a yes or no answer. If the lawyer persists, ask the judge for direction. Follow the judge's ruling.
6. Answer only the question that was asked.
7. Don't volunteer any information, even if you think it would be helpful.
8. If you do not understand a question, ask that it be rephrased or terms defined.
9. Never argue with the person asking the question. Simply respond and move along.
10. Your answers must be verbal. Head nodding or head shaking cannot be recorded by the reporter.
11. Speak slowly and deliberately.
12. Remain calm and take your time.
13. When answering a question, alternately look at the judge, jury, and the attorney doing the interrogation. Establish eye contact with each of these people.
14. Avoid technical or scientific jargon. If you must use such terminology, explain the concept in lay terms.
15. Don't hesitate to use a flip chart or blackboard to explain your testimony.
16. Remember, your goal is to persuade the judge or jury, not to impress them with how much you know. Consequently, don't adopt a superior or egotistical attitude.
17. When asked about your credentials, follow the guidelines described in section 3.03 of this book.

After your direct testimony by the lawyer who called you, the opposing side has the right to cross-examine you. This can be stressful, since the opposing counsel's job is to discredit you and your testimony. You must not take any cross-examination personally. You must suppress your feelings of pride and ego, and simply answer the questions as best you can while following the ground rules described above. Most experts get into trouble when they try to argue with an attorney, or when their emotions take over and they become defensive. Do not let this happen to you. If you understand the process, have done your homework, and follow the rules set forth earlier, you should be able to withstand any cross-examination.

Once the cross-examination has been completed, the attorney who called you as a witness has the opportunity to engage in re-direct examination. This involves questioning you about the areas brought up in the cross-examination. If the attorney has adequately prepared your testimony, he or she will ask you questions that let you explain those areas that the opposing counsel may have obscured or won in the cross-examination.

Listen to these questions very carefully. They will normally be phrased in such a manner that you will remember what you wanted to say to the opposition and were not allowed to do so. On re-direct, a good lawyer will lead you to these areas and give you the opportunity to rehabilitate yourself from any damage that the other side may have inflicted. In essence, it is your job to bolster your testimony on re-direct. The lawyer can only serve up the questions. You have to play them as winners.

3.12 Your Rights as a Witness

While serving as a witness, you have the following rights:

1. To reasonable compensation before consulting with an attorney and in advance of testimony.
2. To request cooperation from everyone regarding the scheduling of your deposition, including the date, time, and location.
3. To counsel during your deposition, at your expense.
4. To read and correct your transcribed deposition testimony.
5. To refresh your memory with the contents of your file or notes.
6. To seek a protective order from the court that declares what you must and must not do regarding confidentiality and privacy issues.
7. To be treated with respect and professionalism.
8. To absolute immunity for your testimony, as discussed in section 3.13 of this book.

3.13 Immunity

All expert witnesses under Colorado law are entitled to absolute immunity for their testimony. An expert is defined in the Colorado Rules of Evidence as a witness qualified "by knowledge, skill, experience, training, or education," whose "specialized knowledge will assist the trier of fact to understand the evidence or to determine a fact in issue." In *Merrick v. Burns,* 43 P.3d 712 (Colo. App. 2001), the Colorado Court of Appeals dismissed a lawsuit that had been filed against an attorney who had prepared a report as an expert in a malpractice case. In its decision, dated November 23, 2001, the court reaffirmed the rule in Colorado that expert witnesses are entitled to immunity for their testimony in court. In its ruling, the court stated: "[W]e agree with the trial court that [the expert's] conduct was protected by the doctrine of absolute immunity."

What does "immunity" mean as a practical matter? It means that if you are sued by anyone because of testimony that you have given as an expert witness, the suit against you must be dismissed.

In *Awai v. Kotin,* 872 P.2d 1332 (Colo. App. 1993), the Colorado Court of Appeals cited cases where therapists have been afforded immunity for their evaluations and recommendations discussed in courtroom testimony. These cases ruled that therapists are entitled to immunity for their evaluations and recommendations concerning: (1) a dependency and neglect case; (2) an evaluation regarding termination of parental rights; (3) a custody evaluation; and (4) a competency and sanity evaluation. The Colorado Mental Health Statutes extend this immunity doctrine to witnesses and consultants involved in grievances or Licensing Board matters. C.R.S. § 12-43-203 also provides that Board members are entitled to immunity for their official acts.

In *Briscoe v. LaHue,* 460 U.S. 325, 103 S. Ct. 1108, (1983), the United States Supreme Court held that "considerations of public policy support absolute immunity" for witnesses testifying in a judicial proceeding. 460 U.S. at 343, 103 S. Ct. at 1119. The Court in *Briscoe* specifically ruled that "witnesses and other persons who are integral parts of the judicial process are entitled to absolute immunity." *See Kurzawa v. Mueller,* 732 F.2d 1456, 1458 (6th Cir. 1984). The rationale for extending absolute immunity to judicial officers, witnesses, and others who serve an important function in the judicial process is to encourage these individuals to perform their duties without fear of retaliation or suit which "would hamper the duties" of such persons in fulfilling their respective roles "in judicial proceedings." *Id.*

3.14 Testifying Is Fun

Some psychotherapists are terrified of the courts and lawyers. They hate the thought of being called to testify. There are others, however, who have learned the ground rules described in this chapter, and have become accomplished expert witnesses. For them, testifying is a challenging, rewarding, and fun aspect of their profession. The same potential exists for any psychotherapist who can perceive the process of testifying in the same manner.

As the expert, you are in control whenever you are testifying in a deposition or in a courtroom setting. Have confidence in the knowledge that you know more about your client and your area of expertise than any attorney questioning you. This mindset—this confidence—should make you more comfortable as you are testifying.

CHAPTER 4: MALPRACTICE AND PROFESSIONAL LIABILITY

We live in a society that has adopted a system of justice that allows for the imposition of civil liability upon a person who, through professional negligence, has caused injury or harm to another. Psychotherapists are not exempt from this potential liability and should be intimately aware of their professional and legal obligations. This chapter outlines the major areas of potential liability for psychotherapists.

4.01 Negligence

The majority of malpractice and professional liability cases against psychotherapists involve negligence on the part of the psychotherapist.

Negligence is a breach of a duty owed to a third party that is the actual and proximate cause of injury, harm, or damage to another. Whether or not a therapist owes a specific duty to a client is an issue of law for the judge to decide.

Duty Owed. A plaintiff must establish that a psychotherapist owed a specific duty to the client. This is not difficult, since the law provides that all people owe an affirmative duty not to harm others. This is known as the "reasonable man rule."

This rule requires everyone to act as a reasonable person, and to exercise reasonable care in all activities. Hence, a psychotherapist must exercise ordinary and reasonable care in treating the client. But what is ordinary and reasonable care?

In Colorado, ordinary and reasonable care is defined as that which a reasonably prudent psychotherapist would provide, given the particular circumstances of the client. In practice, this means that expert witness testimony is necessary to establish that a psychotherapist owed a particular duty of care to a patient. If a plaintiff can locate a psychotherapist who would testify that most psychotherapists would, or would not, do a particular act in any given situation, then the plaintiff has met the burden of establishing the existence of a particular duty.

There are several sources that outline legal duties or standards of care required of psychotherapists.

The Colorado Mental Health Act, C.R.S. §§ 12-43-201, *et seq.,* states numerous statutory duties and obligations that are required of licensed and registered psychotherapists. See sections 6.07 and 6.08 of this book for more elaboration of these duties.

The Mental Health Licensing Board has promulgated numerous rules and regulations that govern the practice of psychotherapy. These rules and regulations set forth certain psychotherapeutic standards of care that also must be followed. See sections 6.04 and 6.05 of this book for an elaboration of these particular duties.

Most professional associations have promulgated practice standards, ethical codes, or guidelines that also set forth specific duties and standards. It is critical that psychotherapists know and follow these professional mandates since they, too, are legal duties psychotherapists owe to clients.

Treatment protocols, as set forth in generally accepted and well-regarded learned treatises, journals, and other professional texts also set forth specific duties that must be followed when treating clients.

Breach of Duty. Once the existence of a duty has been established, a plaintiff must then prove that the applicable standard of care owed to the patient was breached, or not followed, by the psychotherapist.

This is generally a factual question as to what was, or was not, done by the psychotherapist. In most negligence cases, an expert witness will simply testify that the care rendered by the psychotherapist fell below that standard of care required by law. The defendant will defend this claim by putting on an expert witness to rebut the testimony of the plaintiff's expert witness. The jury will determine whether or not the duty was breached, by listening to the testimony of the experts, the parties, and the other witnesses. Having a knowledgeable, respected, and persuasive expert witness is therefore critical to the outcome of the case.

Causation. The breach of duty must be the actual and proximate cause of the injury, harm, or damage suffered by the plaintiff.

Actual cause is defined as that which actually produces the injury, harm, or damage.

Proximate cause is defined as that which, in a natural and continuous sequence, unbroken by any efficient intervening cause, produces the injury and without which the result would not have occurred.

Injury, Harm, or Damage. The plaintiff must also prove that actual injury, harm, or damage has been suffered. The types of injuries, harm, or damages are numerous and include, but are not limited to, the following:

1. Pain and suffering;
2. Emotional distress;
3. Loss of enjoyment of life;
4. Lost wages;
5. Permanent impairment; and
6. Past and future treatment expenses.

Immunity. Immunity is an affirmative defense to a claim of malpractice. Under Colorado law, a therapist should be entitled to immunity in the following circumstances:

1. For reporting suspected child abuse or neglect;
2. For complying with the duty to warn and protect regarding a client's threat of imminent physical violence pursuant to C.R.S. § 13-21-117;
3. For any court-ordered evaluation or treatment recommendation;
4. For any courtroom testimony;
5. For any evaluation or treatment recommendation made to a court in seeking a short-term certification or long-term certification pursuant to C.R.S. §§ 27-65-101, *et seq.;*
6. For any court-ordered sanity or competency evaluation in a criminal case; and
7. For any court-ordered evaluation of a domestic violence perpetrator or treatment recommendation made to the court in any juvenile or criminal matter.

Based upon the decision of the United States Supreme Court in *Briscoe v. LaHue,* 460 U.S. 325, 103 S. Ct. 1108 (1983), therapists should be entitled as a matter of policy to immunity in situations where they are providing treatment pursuant to a court order in domestic litigation, where the therapists' services facilitate the judicial process of resolving conflict or domestic disputes. The interests of judicial economy are served by mental health professionals who may be appointed by the court to assist in the judicial process, thereby entitling therapists to absolute immunity for the functions which they serve. See *Briscoe v. LaHue, supra.* To the extent that therapists, mediators, or court-appointed evaluators assist the court in resolving conflict and avoiding protracted litigation that strains judicial resources, these various "agents" and "officers" of the court deserve to receive absolute immunity for serving in the judicial process without the fear of retaliation in the form of lawsuits or grievances. *Id.*

4.02 Specific Types of Negligence

The following types of mental health negligence cases appear to be the most common:

1. Failure to take steps to prevent threats of imminent suicide;
2. Failure to take steps to prevent sexual relationships with patients by staff and others;
3. Negligent placement and supervision of children;
4. Failure to warn or to protect third persons threatened by patients;
5. Failure to properly diagnose and treat a client;
6. Failure to report child abuse when mandatory;
7. Failure to obtain informed consent prior to treatment;
8. Unauthorized disclosure of confidential information;
9. Failure to develop and follow an appropriate treatment plan;
10. Failure to provide the mandatory disclosure statement required by C.R.S. § 12-43-214;
11. Failure to comply with the title use restrictions in C.R.S. § 12-43-216 (see section 6.01 of this book);
12. Engaging in the prohibited activities described in C.R.S. § 12-43-222 (see section 6.07 of this book);
13. Engaging in the unlawful acts described in C.R.S. § 12-43-226 (see section 6.08 of this book);
14. Failure to undertake steps to properly supervise those under your professional direction;

15. Failure to follow the Rules and Regulations of the State Board of Registered Psychotherapists (see section 6.05 of this book);
16. Failure to maintain appropriate professional boundaries;
17. Failure to obtain a consultation or refer a case when it is beyond or outside a psychotherapist's area of expertise;
18. Failure to provide continuity of care (abandonment); and
19. Failure to terminate therapy when continuation of treatment is not needed.

4.03 A Word of Caution

The legal definition of the term "psychotherapy" has great significance in determining the standard of care owed by a therapist to a client. C.R.S. § 12-43-201(9) defines this term as follows:

> "Psychotherapy" means the treatment, diagnosis, testing, assessment, or counseling in a professional relationship to assist individuals or groups to alleviate mental disorders, understand unconscious or conscious motivation, resolve emotional, relationship, or attitudinal conflicts, or modify behaviors that interfere with effective emotional, social, or intellectual functioning. Psychotherapy follows a planned procedure of intervention that takes place on a regular basis, over a period of time, or in the cases of testing, assessment, and brief psychotherapy, psychotherapy can be a single intervention. . . .

This definition emphasizes the fact that psychotherapy is a "planned procedure of intervention." Hence, the formulation of a treatment plan following the evaluation and diagnosis of a client is an integral aspect of the treatment process. The treatment plan should not only be formulated with care, but also reviewed on a regular basis in order to assure that the plan is appropriate and properly implemented. Documentation of treatment planning and of treatment plan reviews is of utmost importance. Failure to formulate, review, and follow a treatment plan constitutes malpractice.

When complying with the database registration requirement (see section 6.01 of this book), psychotherapists are compelled to indicate the particular psychological orientation or methodology used by them in the practice of psychotherapy. This innocent filing requirement represents a public statement of expertise in each of the areas marked by a psychotherapist on the database registration form. Consequently, it is absolutely essential that a psychotherapist be knowledgeable and informed about the underlying assumptions, principles, and techniques that comprise the orientation or methodology. A good plaintiff's lawyer will review a psychotherapist's stated orientation, become knowledgeable about that orientation, and meticulously look to determine whether the therapist's orientation, principles, and techniques were appropriately followed and applied.

Although many psychotherapists have a general knowledge of their orientation, the author has learned through depositions and general conversations with friends who are psychotherapists that many therapists are unable to readily recall or recite the following information:

1. The name and general background of the orientation's founder and chief theoretical proponent.
2. The orientation's underlying assumptions about human personality, development, and change, together with the research or theoretical basis for such beliefs.
3. The orientation's principles, treatment protocols, and techniques that are appropriate for each type of human condition.
4. The name of the major critics of the orientation and the basis for such criticism.
5. A rebuttal for each of the major criticisms of the orientation.
6. The most significant written treatises, journal articles, or publications that pertain to the orientation.

If you are unable to recite or recall the above information, a skilled trial lawyer will be able to expose this deficiency and use it as a means of persuading a jury of your incompetence. The author highly recommends that psychotherapists prepare a written outline of the above information and have it readily available in a notebook for reference.

Another observation the author has made is that many psychotherapists are not knowledgeable about recommended treatment protocols for certain conditions. I encourage psychotherapists to seek out and find state-of-the-art treatises, journal articles, and publications that outline suggested treatment protocols. You can be assured that in a malpractice action, the plaintiff's lawyer will have located such items and will question you as to why you were unaware of such protocols.

There are many psychotherapists who have adopted an eclectic orientation or methodology. The author believes that this all-encompassing orientation requires those who embrace it to be highly knowledgeable and proficient in all orientations, and be able to theoretically defend and justify the particular eclectic principles used in the practice.

There are many new therapies being advertised and used throughout the State of Colorado. These include spiritual, metaphysical, holistic, and eastern therapies. An important point to note is that these therapies often depart radically from traditional mainline therapies that are generally accepted within the psychotherapy community. It is important that practitioners of these therapies be prepared to defend the theoretical basis of these works and clearly document the appropriateness of the therapy in the client file, and that there is a treatment plan that has been reviewed with the client who has given informed consent to the therapy.

4.04 Duty to Warn and Protect

Statutory Duty. In 1986, the Colorado Legislature enacted C.R.S. § 13-21-117, which outlines the conditions under which mental health care providers have a duty to warn or protect specific persons from threats of physical violence made by a client.

The statute states that physicians, social workers, psychiatric nurses, psychologists, or other mental health care professionals, as well as mental health hospitals, community and mental health centers or clinics, or institutions and their staff, shall not be liable for damages in any civil action for failure to predict, warn, or protect any person against a mental health patient's violent behavior, *except* when the patient has communicated to the mental health care provider a serious threat of imminent physical violence against a specific person or persons.

Under this statute, a psychotherapist must apply a two-part test to determine whether or not there is a duty to warn. First, the client must make a "serious threat of imminent physical violence," although the statute does not define what constitutes that type of threat. Therefore, the psychotherapist must bring to bear all professional judgment and discretion when determining whether or not such a threat has been made by a client.

The second part of the test concerns whether a threat has been made against a "specific person or persons." Again, the statute fails to define or clarify the meaning of "specific person or persons."

Prior to the enactment of this statute, the United States District Court for the District of Colorado decided *Brady v. Hopper,* 570 F. Supp. 1333 (1983). In this case, the plaintiffs, who were all shot and seriously injured by John Hinckley in his attempt to assassinate President Reagan, brought an action against the perpetrator's psychiatrist for alleged negligence in examining, diagnosing, and treating John Hinckley. The plaintiffs also sought recovery for failure to warn others of the dangers Hinckley posed.

The psychiatrist moved to dismiss the case on the grounds that the patient had never made any threats against the President, or anyone else, and that further inquiry by the psychiatrist would have revealed only that the patient was obsessed with a certain actress and movie.

In interpreting Colorado law, and dismissing the action, the Federal District Court wrote:

> [A] therapist or others cannot be held liable for injuries inflicted upon third persons absent specific threats to a readily identifiable victim . . . . Unless a patient makes specific threats, the possibility that he may inflict injury on another is vague, speculative, and a matter of conjecture. However, once the patient verbalizes his intentions and directs his threats to identifiable victims, then the possibility of harm to third persons becomes foreseeable, and the therapist has a duty to protect those third persons from the threatened harm.

Brady v. Hopper, 570 F. Supp. at 1338. Although this case was decided prior to the enactment of the statute, it is helpful in defining and understanding the specificity requirement that there be readily identifiable victims.

The *Brady* case was appealed to the United States 10th Circuit Court of Appeals, which affirmed the trial court's dismissal of the action. In doing so, the Court of Appeals made it clear that generalized threats are insufficient to invoke the duty to warn, but that if the threats are specific and relate to specifically identifiable victims, the duty to warn arises and a psychotherapist must take action to warn or protect the intended victims.

C.R.S. § 13-21-117 specifies how the duty to warn and protect must be discharged once the duty arises. Under the statute, the mental health care provider is required to make reasonable and timely efforts to notify any person or persons specifically threatened, notify an appropriate law enforcement agency, and take other appropriate action including, but not limited to, hospitalizing the patient, as discussed in sections 2.12 and 2.13 of this book. Pursuant to this statute, a therapist who has discharged the duty to warn and protect is entitled to immunity from suit or from a grievance.

C.R.S. § 13-21-117 does *not* apply to the following cases:

1. The negligent release of a mental health patient from a mental hospital or ward; or
2. The negligent failure to initiate involuntary 72-hour treatment and evaluation after a personal patient evaluation determining that the person appears to be mentally ill and, as a result of such mental illness, appears to be an imminent danger to others.

Under these two specific circumstances, an injured victim may maintain a civil suit against a psychotherapist.

Additional Colorado Case Law. In addition to *Brady v. Hopper, supra,* there have been several other Colorado cases that have addressed the issue of a psychotherapist's duty to warn and protect others. In 1989, the Colorado Supreme Court handed down its ruling in *Perreira v. State,* 768 P.2d 1198 (Colo. 1989). In that case, the surviving spouse of a police officer who was killed by a mental patient brought a wrongful death action against the State Mental Hospital, the treating psychiatrist, and the State of Colorado. At trial, the jury rendered a verdict in favor of the spouse. The defendants appealed and the Colorado Court of Appeals reversed the trial court's decision. The Colorado Supreme Court reversed the Court of Appeals and held that the psychiatrist had a duty to exercise due care in determining whether an involuntarily committed patient had a propensity for violence and presented an unreasonable risk of bodily harm to others upon release.

The *Perreira* case arose prior to the enactment of C.R.S. § 13-21-117. Hence, the statute was not interpreted or construed specifically in the case. However, when the Colorado Supreme Court made its ruling in 1989, it cited the statute and stated that it was instructive and helpful in terms of determining the duty of the psychiatrist in treating an involuntary out-patient.

The patient had been recently released from an involuntary commitment for short-term treatment. In its holding, the Colorado Supreme Court held that a staff psychiatrist had a legal duty to exercise due care in determining whether the patient had a propensity for violence, and if released from his involuntary commitment, would represent an unreasonable risk of serious harm to others, including a police officer in the position of Officer Perreira at the time of his death. The Colorado Supreme Court further held that *if* the psychiatrist knew or should have known, in accordance with the knowledge and skill ordinarily possessed by psychiatric practitioners under similar circumstances, that the patient had a *propensity for violence,* and thus, presented an unreasonable risk of serious bodily harm to others, then the psychiatrist was obligated to take reasonable precautions to protect members of the public from the danger created by a patient's release. These precautions included giving due consideration to extending the term of the patient's commitment, and placing appropriate conditions and restrictions on the patient's release consistent with his needs and the safety of others.

In *Halverson v. Pikes Peak Family Counseling and Mental Health Ctr., Inc.,* 795 P.2d 1352 (Colo. App. 1989), the plaintiff alleged that while she was an inpatient at the defendant's crisis center, she was sexually assaulted by another patient who had a history of violent behavior. The plaintiff contended that the mental health center was negligent in failing to protect her and in failing to supervise and control the attacker after the defendants had noticed the attacker's violent propensity towards the plaintiff.

The trial judge granted the defendant's motion for dismissal for failure to state a claim. The plaintiff appealed and the Court of Appeals reversed the trial court's decision.

The defendants argued that C.R.S. § 13-21-117 provided immunity for their failure to warn or protect the plaintiff against the potential violent behavior of the defendant. The plaintiff contended that the immunity conferred by C.R.S. § 13-21-117 was inapplicable to acts of *hospitalized* patients and that the statute was intended only to provide immunity for a health care provider's failure to protect or warn others against potential violent behavior of *out-patients,* over whom the provider maintained no control. The Colorado Court of Appeals specifically rejected plaintiff's argument and held that the immunity provision of C.R.S. § 13-21-117 applied to both out-patient and in-patient mental health care providers. The case was reversed, however, on the grounds that the plaintiff had demonstrated that the violent patient had made a serious threat of imminent physical violence against the plaintiff. Thus, under the language of the statute, immunity would not apply.

Columbine and Virginia Tech: Zero Tolerance for Threats of Violence. After the Columbine tragedy in 1999, mental health professionals were reminded of their duty to warn and protect when a student makes a serious threat of imminent violence. After the Virginia Tech shootings in 2007, the entire profession is re-examining procedures and laws designed to protect the public. While we must remain tolerant of individual differences, we have learned in the past that we cannot tolerate threats of violence.

In the home, when a man threatens to kill his partner, the police are called and he goes to jail. In an airport, if you make a comment about having a bomb, you go to jail. Try to tell the police that you are just joking! Ever since Columbine, if a student makes a threat of violence, it will be taken seriously. We have zero tolerance policies in our society for threats of domestic violence, for threats in schools, for threats in airports, for threats to national security.

After Virginia Tech, school administrators and even law enforcement officials are looking to mental health professionals for an answer to the question: How do we prevent school violence from occurring? Although therapists are not mind readers and cannot know what a client is thinking, the words a client uses in making a threat of violence do indicate the individual's intent. When a person says "I am going to kill myself," those words signify an imminent risk of harm. The same is true whenever a client says "I am going to kill . . . ." Such a statement is chilling, and it justifies action to hospitalize the client due to the imminent danger that exists. Whenever a client says "I am going to kill myself" or makes a threat to kill others, it must be handled with the same attitude of zero tolerance that applies to threats of violence in the home, at airports, at schools, and in the workplace.

When a client says "I am thinking about killing myself," a thorough evaluation must be conducted, and if any question exists concerning whether hospitalization is necessary a consult with another professional is warranted. A "safety contract" is never appropriate when a person meets the criteria for hospitalization, that is, when the individual has a mental disorder and is imminently dangerous to self or others.

Keep in mind that by hospitalizing an individual, you are potentially saving lives. The conventional wisdom that you will hear everywhere is: Err on the side of safety.

4.05 Invasion of Privacy

A psychotherapist has a duty of confidentiality with respect to communications made by a client in the course of treatment. A psychotherapist could face potential civil liability if such communications are disclosed without consent and are of such a nature as to be offensive and objectionable to a reasonable person of ordinary sensibilities. Given that most communications are of a highly personal nature, a disclosure by a psychotherapist would most likely be offensive and objectionable. Accordingly, civil liability for breach of privacy could be imposed on a psychotherapist who violated this duty of confidentiality.

4.06 Outrageous Conduct

Colorado law provides that a person who engages in extreme or outrageous conduct, recklessly, or with the intent of causing emotional distress, may be found liable for the damages suffered as a result of such conduct.

Extreme and outrageous conduct is conduct that is so outrageous in character, and so extreme in degree, that a reasonable member of the community would regard the conduct as atrocious, beyond all possible bounds of decency, and utterly intolerable in a civilized community. Such outrageous conduct occurs when knowledge of all the facts by a reasonable member of the community would arouse that person's resentment against the defendant and lead that person to conclude that the conduct was extreme and outrageous.

A person intends to cause extreme emotional distress if that person engages in conduct for the purpose, in whole or in part, of causing severe emotional distress in another person, knowing that his or her conduct is substantially certain to have that result.

A person whose conduct causes severe emotional distress in another has acted recklessly if, at the time, that person knew, or because of other facts known to him or her, reasonably should have known there was a possibility that his or her conduct would cause severe emotional distress in another person.

Severe emotional distress consists of highly unpleasant mental reactions and is so extreme that no person of ordinary sensibilities could be expected to tolerate and endure it. The duration and intensity of the emotional distress are factors to be considered in determining its severity.

Under this theory of tort liability, a psychotherapist must at all times act in a manner that is forthright and professional.

Examples of outrageous conduct that readily come to mind include, but are not limited to:

1. Having sexual relations with a client; or
2. Financially defrauding a client.

4.07 Sexual Relations with a Client

C.R.S. § 18-3-405.5 provides for criminal penalties in the event of a sexual assault—that is, an intimate relationship or sexual contact with a client—by a psychotherapist with a client. The statute sets forth two types of sexual assault.

The first type is aggravated sexual assault on a client. This occurs when a psychotherapist knowingly inflicts sexual penetration or sexual intrusion on a victim who is a client of the therapist.

The second type of sexual assault is a class 1 misdemeanor and occurs when a psychotherapist knowingly subjects a client to *any* sexual contact. This statute specifically provides that consent by the client to the sexual penetration, intrusion, or contact shall *not* constitute a defense to such action.

The term "psychotherapist" is defined in C.R.S. § 18-3-405.5 to mean any person who performs or purports to perform psychotherapy, whether or not such person is licensed by the state pursuant to Title 12, C.R.S., or is certified by the state pursuant to Part 5 of Article l of Title 25, C.R.S.

Although the foregoing statute is criminal in nature, it may be used to establish the existence of a duty in a civil case for the purpose of establishing liability against a person who has violated the statute.

In *Ferguson v. People,* 824 P.2d 803 (Colo. 1992), the Colorado Supreme Court upheld the constitutionality of C.R.S. § 18-3-405.5. In that case, the defendant was charged with nine counts of aggravated sexual assault based on acts of sexual intercourse between the defendant and a client occurring between October 1988 and March 1989.

The charges against the defendant were tried to a jury, which returned guilty verdicts on four counts. Prior to sentencing, the defendant moved for a judgment of acquittal on the basis that C.R.S. § 18-3-405.5 violated his due process and equal protection rights under the Constitution. The District Court, after determining that no fundamental constitutional right was affected by the statute, concluded that it was rationally related to legitimate governmental interests of protecting psychotherapy clients. The defendant was thereafter sentenced to concurrent two-year terms on the four convictions.

It has been forcefully stated that psychotherapist-client sex is the very antithesis of effective and responsible psychotherapy. When the therapist mishandles transference and becomes sexually involved with a client, medical authorities are unanimous in considering such conduct to be malpractice. The experts would agree that there are absolutely no circumstances that permit a psychiatrist to engage in sex with his or her patient.

4.08 Failure to Report Child Abuse

As discussed in Chapter 2, C.R.S. § 19-3-304 requires certain groups of persons who have reasonable cause to know or suspect that a child has been subjected to abuse and neglect, or who have observed a child being subjected to circumstances or conditions that would reasonably result in abuse or neglect, to immediately report such fact to the County Department of Social Services or local law enforcement agency. This statute provides that any person who willfully violates this provision commits a class 3 misdemeanor criminal offense and shall be civilly liable for damages proximately caused by it.

Please refer to Chapter 2, Part II for a detailed analysis of the requirements pertaining to this statute.

4.09 Insurance Fraud

Abuse of Health Insurance. In 1985, the Colorado Legislature enacted C.R.S. § 18-13-119, which addressed the problem of abuse of health insurance by health care providers. In enacting the statute, the legislature specifically found that business practices that have the effect of eliminating the need for actual payment by the recipient of health care services of required co-payments and deductibles in health benefit plans interfered with contractual obligations entered into between the insured and insurer relating to such payments. Further, the legislature determined that such interference is not in the public interest when it is conducted as a regular business practice, because it has the effect of increasing health care costs by removing the incentive co-payments and deductibles created to make the consumer a cost-conscious consumer of health care services. The Colorado Legislature also declared that advertising such practices by health care providers might aggravate the adverse financial and other impacts on recipients of health care. Accordingly, the General Assembly declared that such business practices were illegal and that the violation thereof or the advertising of such business practices would be grounds for disciplinary actions.

The statute created a class 1 petty offense known as "abuse of health insurance." The health care provider commits abuse of health insurance if the provider knowingly:

1. Accepts from any third-party payor as payment in full for services rendered the amount the third-party payor covers; or
2. Submits a fee to a third-party payor that is higher than the fee he has agreed to accept from the insured patient with the understanding of waiving the required deductible or co-payment.

The statute created the following exceptions:

1. Reimbursements made pursuant to Articles 4 and 15 of Title 26, C.R.S.;
2. Federal Medicare laws for in-patient hospitalization; and
3. Mental health services purchased in accordance with Part 2 of Article 1 of Title 27, C.R.S.

Health care services are exempt from the provisions of C.R.S. § 18-13-119 if they are provided in accordance with a contract or agreement between the employer and an employee or employees, and the contract includes as part of any employee's salary or employment benefits terms that authorize a practice that would otherwise be prohibited by this statute.

The waiver of any required deductible or co-payment for charitable purposes is exempt if:

1. The person who provides the health care determines that the services are necessary for the immediate health and welfare of the patient;
2. The waiver is made on a case-by-case basis and the person who provides the health care determines that payment of the deductible or co-payment would create a substantial hardship for the patient; and
3. The waiver is not a regular business practice of the person who provides the health care.

The statute also states that any person who provides health care and waives the deductible or co-payment for more than one-fourth of his or her patients during any calendar year, excluding patients covered by the exemptions cited above, or who advertises through newspapers, magazines, circulars, direct mail, directories, radio, television, or otherwise that he or she will accept from any third-party payor, as payment in full for services rendered in the amount the third-party payor covers, will be presumed to be engaged in waiving the deductible or co-payment as a regular business practice.

This statute was upheld in *Parrish v. Lamm,* 758 P.2d 1356 (Colo. 1988), in which the plaintiff sought a declaration that the statute was unconstitutional, on grounds that it regulated commercial speech in violation of the First Amendment to the United States Constitution. In upholding the constitutionality of this statute, the Colorado Supreme Court held that the legislature may regulate or ban entirely commercial speech related to illegal activity, since such speech does not rise to the level of a fundamental right.

Given the foregoing restrictions, a psychotherapist should review his or her billing practices to avoid the inadvertent abuse of insurance as described in this statute.

Other Forms Of Insurance Fraud. There are other forms of insurance fraud that psychotherapists should avoid. These include, but are not limited to:

1. Billing for services that were not rendered.
2. Billing for work that was performed by another person.
3. Excessive billing or overcharging for services.
4. Miscoding of services rendered in order to qualify for insurance; e.g., coding marital counseling as treatment for anxiety.
5. Making a false representation in billing for insurance benefits.

C.R.S. § 10-1-128 addresses fraudulent insurance acts.

4.10 Billing Practices

Recently I have received numerous inquiries concerning billing standards and billing practices from therapists across the country. The following are among the frequently asked questions, with answers.

Q. If I am a clinical supervisor and I am on insurance panels, can I bill for services provided by the supervisee, if she provides treatment to clients, but is not on the insurance panels?

A. No, the only person who can bill for treatment is the actual provider. The Colorado Mental Health Boards' Supervision Rule provides that a clinical supervisor must ensure that bills accurately reflect who provided the treatment.

Q. Can I bill insurance companies for couples counseling or marital counseling, and if so, what CPT Code do I use?

A. Some health insurance plans do provide coverage for marital counseling or family therapy. The CPT Code for family therapy (conjoint) is 90847. Because marital counseling is a type of therapy, you can also use some more general CPT Codes for psychotherapy: 90804, 90806, or 90808, depending on the length of the session. If you have a question concerning whether an insurance plan provides benefits for couples counseling or will pay for marital counseling, check with the insurance representative. It may be that the clients will need to pay the old-fashioned way for treatment: out of their pockets.

Q. Can I bill insurance for telephone conferences with clients, either in emergencies where clients are in crisis or in a situation where a client cannot make it to my office due to weather conditions?

A. An excellent question. All of the CPT Codes referenced above are for "face-to-face" treatment. Therefore, if an intervention or session is done on the telephone, your bill should indicate that the place of service (POS) was the phone. Many insurance panels require that therapists be available to clients in the event of clinical emergencies. Therefore, those plans should pay for phone calls in emergencies.

Q. What are the general standards for billing?

A. Bills must be accurate, and any diagnostic code must reflect the client's presenting problem; the units of time billed must be accurate; and, of course, the provider whose name is on the bill must be the individual who provided treatment. Any misrepresentations of fact on a billing statement may be considered a "fraudulent insurance act" under Colorado law.

4.11 Responding to a Lawsuit

When a lawsuit is brought against a psychotherapist, the following procedures should be followed:

1. The date and manner in which the summons and complaint was received should be recorded.
2. Any malpractice insurance policy should be reviewed and the reporting procedures described in the policy should be followed. This will normally involve written notice to the carrier and forwarding a copy of the summons and complaint to the carrier. It is recommended that a telephone call be made to verbally report the lawsuit, and that the phone call be followed by a written confirmation of the report.
3. Correspondence with the malpractice carrier should be mailed certified mail, return receipt requested.
4. The substance of the lawsuit should not be discussed with anyone. Statements made by a party to a lawsuit are potentially admissible and may be used against that person at trial in a variety of damaging ways. Hence, the best rule is to refrain from any discussion.
5. Typically, a malpractice carrier has a duty to defend and satisfy any judgment that is entered, up to the amount of its policy

limit for liability coverage. It will fulfill its obligation by obtaining an insurance defense attorney. He or she has been hired by the insurance company to defend the psychotherapist, but simultaneously this lawyer has duties to the insurance company that may not coincide with those of the psychotherapist. Hence, the psychotherapist should obtain separate counsel for the purpose of monitoring the litigation and assuring that the defense counsel is fulfilling his or her duty to the psychotherapist.

6. If you carry no malpractice insurance, you should immediately obtain a trial attorney.

4.12 Malpractice Insurance

Professional liability insurance is highly recommended. Psychotherapists are particularly vulnerable, given the emotional and mental instability of their clientele. If the psychotherapist works for an agency or business entity, the psychotherapist should review the agency's insurance policy, determine the extent of coverage, and consider supplementing it with private insurance.

The amount of malpractice insurance should be the maximum amount that is affordable. In this day and age, a million-dollar policy is considered minimally adequate. A question arises as to the amount of the deductible. In this regard, business sense applies. The psychotherapist should realize that in the event a lawsuit is commenced, the deductible would have to be paid by the psychotherapist.

In a professional corporation, partnership, or any other association, malpractice insurance is required in order to avoid vicarious liability for the acts of the other partners. Tort law and agency law impose upon professionals who are in a partnership, or who practice in a professional corporation, joint and several liability for the acts of the other shareholders or partners. In lay terms, this means that all partners are liable, even if the tortious act is committed by only one of them. Hence, malpractice insurance is warranted.

Many insurance policies for therapists now have coverage of at least $5,000.00 for defense of a grievance. This is a feature that professionals should seek when choosing an insurance policy.

4.13 Malpractice Prevention

Psychotherapists should realize that malpractice claims can be prevented. To minimize malpractice, psychotherapists should maintain professional competence at all times. There is simply no substitute for knowledge and the proper exercise of that skill and care required of psychotherapists. Accordingly, it is recommended that psychotherapists subscribe to current professional journals and regularly attend continuing education programs. Additionally, psychotherapists should not accept a case beyond their competence level. Referring cases and jointly cooperating on cases is an excellent way to avoid getting in over your head. An important aspect of competence is knowing the law and your responsibilities. Accordingly, periodic review of the relevant mental health laws is warranted.

Often, malpractice occurs as a result of administrative oversight. Consequently, office management needs to be professional, and supervision needs to occur on a regular basis. Written policies and procedures for office management should be developed, distributed, and followed.

One area of disagreement between clients and psychotherapists is the matter of fees. Licensed professionals are required to provide each client with a disclosure statement that covers such matters as patient rights, fees, etc. All psychotherapists should consider using an engagement agreement or letter, which defines the psychotherapist-client relationship and carefully defines the expectations regarding compensation.

An important consideration in any malpractice case is the adequacy of client records, which document the services rendered and advice given. There is controversy in the field about what should and should not be documented. It is, however, highly recommended that the client's progress be adequately charted, and that all services and advice given be documented. This often is not a high priority for psychotherapists, but such oversight can have devastating results in litigation.

One major complaint levied against professionals is that they do not respond to phone calls in a timely manner. It is recommended that all phone calls be returned within 24 hours and that an adequate response system be developed. If a client feels cut off or abandoned by a professional, the first inclination is to obtain an attorney. This can be avoided by simply maintaining close contact.

All professionals, at times, have a tendency to procrastinate. In order to avoid this first step toward malpractice, psychotherapists should adopt an attitude of making a priority of doing those things they would like to avoid, rather than delaying.

From a statistical standpoint, the odds are that a psychotherapist will never be sued for malpractice. Therapists can decrease the prospect that they will be sued by adhering to some basic rules. Therapists who follow these rules will significantly decrease the chance of being sued.

1. **Know the legal standards that apply to your practice.** Therapists need to be thoroughly familiar with the laws that apply to them and to their practice. In general, these laws are contained in the Colorado Mental Health Act, which is contained in Title 12, Article 43, Sections 201, *et seq.* A copy of the Mental Health Statutes can be obtained from the Department of Regulatory Agencies, and is normally furnished to therapists along with the database application or an application for licensure. The importance of knowing and understanding these laws is surpassed only by the importance of adhering to them. Many of the specific statutes with which therapists must comply are discussed in this book. The various provisions contained in the Colorado Mental Health Statutes constitute the legal standards that apply to the practice of psychotherapy. Compliance with all of the statutes is essential, but one statute has special import: C.R.S. § 12-43-222, which is discussed in section 6.07 of this book. This law, in particular, establishes specific standards to be followed and proscribes conduct that violates the basic principles of psychotherapy.
2. **Know the ethical standards for psychotherapists and follow them.** All of the major national professional associations have adopted Codes of Ethics for their members. These Codes of Ethics establish the ethical standards that guide psychotherapists in their practice. The Codes of Ethics adopted by organizations such as the National Association of Social Workers, the American Psychological Association, American Association for Marriage & Family Therapists, and the American Counseling Association apply specifically not only to the organization's members, but also to other therapists who practice in a special discipline. For example, the AAMFT Code of Ethics establishes

the ethical standards to be followed by therapists, both licensed and unlicensed, who practice marriage and family therapy.

3. **Stay current in the field.** Membership in a national professional association or its state affiliate provides numerous benefits. These include the opportunity to attend conferences, workshops, and seminars that focus on treatment standards, professional trends, updates on the law, and current information concerning regulatory changes. In addition, professional associations provide newsletters and publications to their members that keep them informed about changes in the field. Another important benefit of membership in professional associations is professional liability insurance at group rates.

4. **Practice with informed consent.** Adhere to the basic principles of informed consent in treating your clients. These principles are discussed in section 4.13 of this book. This process will enable you to establish a better relationship with your client, and enable your client to better understand treatment goals and your treatment plan. You can elevate your practice above the "generally accepted standards" by doing the following: (1) conduct a thorough evaluation of your client, and document in your records the information on which your assessment of the client is based; (2) identify for the client the presenting problem(s) and the specific behavioral goals to be achieved in therapy (e.g., learn skills to control anger); (3) prepare a written treatment plan that identifies the probable length of treatment and method to be used to accomplish treatment goals (e.g., 36 weeks of group counseling); and (4) review the treatment plan and document in your records the process of re-evaluating the client's problems, if your client is not progressing as anticipated. The federal model for informed consent requires the client to sign off on the treatment plan, to demonstrate that the client has been informed about the process involved in treatment. Keep in mind that your disclosure statement is your informed consent form, and let it inform the client as much as possible about matters that should be disclosed.

5. **Keep good records.** Your treatment records should serve two purposes: (1) to help your client by recording basic information concerning your client's history and clinical picture at the time of your treatment, so that subsequent therapists can profit from your experience with the client; and (2) to protect you in case

questions arise years later concerning what treatment you provided and why you pursued a particular course of treatment. In addition to basic progress notes, take care to document in your records any statutory report that you are required to make, including information concerning any consultation regarding a client; a description of any treatment information disclosed, along with the authorization for disclosure of information; and documentation concerning any specific problem(s) discussed in clinical supervision. In addition, all referrals need to be documented. Refer to section 4.15 of this book for standards regarding essential record-keeping entries and for information regarding the length of time that client records must be kept.

6. **Never sue a client.** Trying to collect a fee by suing a client raises many troubling questions. How can you sue the client without breaching confidentiality? Moreover, the client will typically claim that he did not pay because the treatment was no good. A counterclaim alleging malpractice is, too frequently, the response to such a suit.
7. **Do not allow clients to tape record treatment sessions.** And if you record sessions for purposes of supervision, erase the tape after it has been used for that purpose. If a lawsuit should happen, and tapes of treatment sessions exist, your own words, taken out of context, can and will be used against you. Even if clients flatter you by saying that they want to listen to tapes of treatment sessions as homework, so that they can listen to your wise counsel and the reassuring tones of your voice, "Just say no."
8. **Maintain appropriate boundaries.** Identify ground rules for treatment that establish your role as therapist and help you to avoid problems (e.g., I cannot accept gifts from clients; our clinic policy does not allow us to hug clients). Do not engage in bartering with clients. Do not give your client legal advice—that is not your role.
9. **Refer out when a client's problems are outside of your area of expertise.** And document in writing the fact that you made a referral anytime that is done.
10. **Do not take the law into your own hands.** Anytime you are required to make a statutory report involving a 72-hour hold, child abuse, or a duty to warn, report the information that you are required to disclose. Then let the caseworker or law enforce-

ment officer whose role it is to investigate the matter conduct the investigation. As the therapist, it is your role, when necessary, to report certain information, but it is not your role to investigate cases, to interview witnesses, to confront alleged perpetrators, etc. So, do not take the law into your own hands by becoming the investigator.

11. **Maintain liability insurance.** This will enable you to aggressively defend any grievance before it becomes a lawsuit, and it will allow you, with the assistance of competent counsel, to aggressively defend any suit that may be filed. The insurance companies who write insurance policies for mental health practitioners typically hire attorneys who are excellent advocates in defending malpractice suits. In addition, a consulting expert will usually be retained to evaluate the standard-of-care issues and, hopefully, testify on your behalf. Of course, in addition to having an attorney retained by your liability insurance carrier to defend you, you can also hire personal counsel to give you a second opinion or to consult with you, if needed.

4.14 Informed Consent

Treating Adults. The Colorado Legislature has enacted a statute defining "consent" in C.R.S. § 27-10.5-102(5). This statute expresses a policy, when treating mentally ill or developmentally disabled persons, that informed consent should be given in writing, voluntarily, and should contain the following:

1. A fair explanation of the procedures to be followed, including an identification of those that are experimental;
2. A description of the attendant discomforts and risks;
3. A description of the benefits to be expected;
4. A disclosure of appropriate alternative procedures, together with an explanation of the respective benefits, discomforts, and risks; and
5. An offer to answer any inquiries concerning procedures. Wherever inherent risks in the implementation of a treatment plan exist, a psychotherapist should advise the client of those risks, and have the client sign an informed consent form, acknowledging the disclosures that have been made concerning the potential risks posed by the methods of treatment that will be employed.

Obtaining informed consent from psychotherapy clients is required by law and is an effective, proactive approach to malpractice prevention. It demonstrates that a psychotherapist is being careful in the formulation and implementation of a treatment plan and is being thoughtful of the client and the consequences that may occur as a result of treatment.

The mandatory disclosure form that must be given to clients at the initial therapy session requires that clients be informed of the right to receive information about the methods of therapy, the techniques used, the duration of therapy, and the fee structure (see section 6.02 of this book for more information on mandatory disclosures). Most psychotherapists have not undertaken the steps to develop a written summary of this information so that it can be made readily available. Surprisingly, few therapists actually provide written information of the methods and techniques of therapy. The author highly recommends that a writing be prepared that summarizes this information and that the client be given a copy. In this way, the client's choice to participate in therapy can be based upon informed consent.

Treating Juveniles. There is a controversy concerning who must give consent to the treatment of juveniles. Under common law, consent to treatment must, prior to the age of emancipation, be given by a child's parents. The age of majority in Colorado is 18. However, C.R.S. § 27-65-102(12) modifies this requirement. The statute provides:

> "Minor" means a person under eighteen years of age; except that the term does not include a person who is fifteen years of age or older who is living separately and apart from his or her parent or legal guardian and is managing his or her financial affairs, regardless of his or her source of income, or who is married and living separately and apart from his or her parent or legal guardian.

Furthermore, C.R.S. § 27-65-103 provides that a minor who is 15 years of age or older "may consent to receive mental health services to be rendered by a facility or a professional person."

As a practical matter, the author recommends avoiding treating juveniles without parental consent. The risks that a disgruntled parent will file a grievance or lawsuit are simply too great. Furthermore, payment for services, most likely, will not be readily forthcoming from a parent whose consent was not obtained.

Another problem that often occurs is the treatment of children when only one parent requests or consents to the treatment. Caution should be exercised before accepting the children as clients, since the other parent may object to the treatment. There have been several reported cases in which a parent has misrepresented his or her status as legal custodian and treatment was rendered without the legal custodian's consent. It is absolutely critical that psychotherapists obtain written verification of a parent's status as legal custodian when the other parent's consent to treatment has not been obtained. "Legal custodian" means that a parent has been allocated the primary responsibility for the residential care of a child, or the legal authority to select health care providers, in the event that a child's parents are divorced or separated.

4.15 Litigation Trends and Controversies

Repressed Memory Work. During the 1990s, the field of psychotherapy fell under organized attack by individuals and groups whose organizations sought reform of alleged abuses. For example, VOCAL (Victims of Child Abuse Laws) contends that members of law enforcement and professionals in the human services field have violated parental rights through the overly aggressive prosecution of child abuse. Members of this group contend that children have been led to make false accusations of sexual abuse through the use of leading questions or other improper, suggestive techniques.

The False Memory Syndrome Foundation (FMSF) contends that some psychotherapists created false memories of sexual abuse during therapy, thereby subjecting clients to psychological abuse. This group alleges that various types of suggestive techniques result in the implantation of false memories, including hypnosis, leading questions, and the suggestion to clients that they are exhibiting classic symptoms of repressed sexual abuse.

The False Memory Syndrome Foundation actively promotes its views, and, as a result, litigation over "false memories" has been burgeoning.

Another controversial issue that has been the focus of litigation involves Dissociative Identity Disorder (Multiple Personality Disorder). Paul R. McHugh, M.D., the Chief of Psychiatry at Johns Hopkins University

Hospital, has testified that Multiple Personality Disorder is not a natural, organic process; that it only exists in our society as a result of cultural influences such as movies and books, or as the result of suggestive techniques used by psychotherapists, who thereby create alternate personalities. Dr. McHugh contends that such a condition is "artifactual." He compares the diagnosis of Multiple Personality Disorder and the treatment of repressed memories to the wave of hysteria that resulted in the Salem witchcraft trials of the seventeenth century.

The use of hypnosis has been under attack by professionals in both the fields of psychiatry and psychology. Case law has evolved in Colorado and in other states during the past 20 years providing that memory refreshed through hypnosis is not admissible in court. In other words, most courts have ruled that memories recovered or refreshed under hypnosis are not sufficiently reliable to be presented as testimony in court.

Several professional associations are in the process of developing standards for the use of hypnosis. Because of the controversy, both medical and legal authorities recommend that informed consent be obtained from a client before using any form of hypnotherapy. It is recommended that the client be advised that hypnosis is a suggestive technique, which does not necessarily enable a person to accurately visualize or recall past events.

Psychotherapists who use hypnosis or relaxation techniques must be extremely careful, even when informed consent has been obtained. The use of leading questions should be avoided, since these may be overly suggestive under the circumstances.

Ramona v. Superior Court, 57 Cal. App. 4th 107 (1997) is a highly publicized California case in which a psychotherapist was sued for allegedly implanting memories of sexual abuse perpetrated by the client's father. Holly Ramona had sought treatment for an eating disorder. She was advised that a substantial number of people with eating disorders had been victims of sexual abuse (a statement that has not been scientifically proven and that is inaccurate, according to experts who testified in the *Ramona* case). During the process of therapy, Holly Ramona recalled previously repressed memories of sexual abuse by her father. After Holly's mother learned of those, she filed for divorce.

The father sued Holly's therapist, claiming that he had been damaged by the breakup of his marriage and by the emotional trauma that he suffered as a result of the false memories and false accusations of abuse. A jury found in his favor, and awarded him substantial damages.

These trends in litigation have demonstrated the value of one simple piece of advice, which ought to be noted: do not take the law into your own hands. If a client reports a recovered memory of previously repressed sexual abuse, you should not independently seek substantiation. Do not become embroiled in the investigation of the incident that has been recalled. If a report needs to be made of the suspected abuse, the psychotherapist should comply with any legal duty to report it. Under no circumstances should a therapist assume the role of investigator, judge, or jury. Do not tell the client that the recollection must be true. The client's feelings can be validated without any judgment being made as to whether the matter recently recalled is true or not.

Because of the controversy that surrounds "repressed memories" of abuse, a therapist who is treating a patient should be prepared to advise the client in writing that previously repressed memories, which have been recalled during therapy, may not be valid. It is recommended that informed consent from the patient be obtained before proceeding with any in-depth analysis or treatment of issues related to a recovered memory of sexual abuse. Practice in this area is highly risky and should be done only by those with a high degree of specialized training in this field.

Questions regarding the reporting of unsafe sex practices by clients who are HIV-positive occur on occasion. C.R.S. § 25-4-1402 requires that reports be made concerning HIV infections to the state or local Department of Health by physicians or by "all other persons treating a case of HIV infection in hospitals, clinics … and other private or public institutions."

Issues Regarding Informed Consent. The Board of Trustees of the American Psychiatric Association has issued a definitive statement opposing "reparative" or "conversion" therapy, which is designed to change a person's sexual orientation. The APA position statement concluded, "There is no scientific evidence that reparative or conversion therapy is effective in changing a person's sexual orientation." The statement also warned that "the potential risks of reparative therapy are great, including depression, anxiety and self-destructive behavior." The APA noted that homosexuality was removed from the DSM as a mental disorder in 1973.

The American Psychological Association adopted a resolution of its membership in 1997, opposing reparative or conversion therapy, and discussing informed consent disclosures that need to be given to a client. This resolution stopped short of decreeing that reparative therapy is unethical.

While a psychotherapist in Colorado may not be presented with the occasion to see a client who desires to change his or her sexual orientation, other situations may arise where legal, ethical, and informed consent issues exist that are similar to those which have been addressed by the APA.

Case History. A client comes to you for counseling related to relationship problems. The client is gay, and is having problems with his or her partner. You hold deeply religious beliefs based upon biblical precepts that homosexuality is sinful and morally wrong. Should you even attempt to provide counseling to this potential client under the circumstances? What are the legal and ethical issues for you to consider?

As a general matter, it is unethical for a therapist to impose his or her personal values or moral beliefs upon a client. Under the circumstances, will your professional judgment be impaired in assessing or treating the client or couple? When you can foresee that a moral conflict, no matter how subtle, may interfere in the exercise of your professional judgment, you should not attempt to treat the client, but refer the client to someone capable of providing appropriate treatment.

If you believe that homosexuality is morally wrong, and you know that your client is engaging in a lifestyle that you consider immoral, is this a matter which should be disclosed to the client before initiating treatment? The answer to this question is a resounding "yes," especially if you foresee that you may have a tendency to shame the client or to convert him or her to a straight lifestyle. A therapist who lacks the training, experience, and competence required in dealing with issues of sexual orientation has the potential to cause greater harm than good in providing treatment under the circumstances of this hypothetical case.

If you are presented with a situation where a client does request professional services in converting to a heterosexual lifestyle, you need to know that any such treatment is fraught with informed consent issues. Among the disclosures that must be made is the fact that homosexuality is not a mental disorder, that reparative therapy has not been demonstrated to be effective in changing an individual's sexual orientation, and that sexual orientation is not a conscious choice that can be voluntarily changed by an individual.

4.16 Maintaining Client Records

Each of the Mental Health Boards has a specific rule requiring maintenance of client records and specific record-keeping entries for therapists. Therapists are encouraged to keep records that document the presenting problem that requires treatment on each date that the client is seen. Using "S.O.A.P." (Subjective, Objective, Assessment, Plan) notes, a therapist can: (1) document the presenting problem for each visit; (2) evaluate the therapist's assessment of that problem and plan for treating the client; (3) refer the client to another health care provider for evaluation or treatment; or (4) consult with another professional or seek supervision on a difficult clinical issue or ethical question. Keep in mind that every disclosure of treatment information must be documented, and a therapist must also document in the client's record each statutory report that is required, e.g., a report concerning child abuse or neglect; a referral to a crisis unit of the client who requires a 72-hour hold; or a report made to law enforcement and to a potential victim, pursuant to C.R.S. § 13-21-117, when a therapist has a duty to warn and protect.

The Licensed Professional Counselor (LPC) Board Rule 19 requires that the following essential record-keeping entries be made in the client's chart, and that the entire chart be maintained by an LPC for five years after termination of treatment or the last client visit: (1) identifying data, to include the client's name, sex, telephone number, date of birth, address, and the name, address, and telephone number of the legal guardian of a child; (2) all contracts, release of information forms, and disclosure statements; (3) records of counseling including dates of service, session notes, test data, correspondence, electronic data storage, and information concerning any disclosure of information made; (4) information concerning each report made pursuant to legal duties (e.g., child abuse, duty to warn, 72-hour hold);

and (5) a final closing statement. Note that records concerning treatment of a minor child must be kept until the person is 18 years of age or for a period of 12 years, whichever comes first.

Psychology Board Rule 19 lists the essential record-keeping entries required to be prepared and maintained by a psychologist for seven years after termination of treatment or the last visit with the client.

Social Work Board Rule 18 lists the required entries and requires that records be maintained for ten years after termination of the treatment or the last client visit.

The Board of Licensed Marriage and Family Therapists Rule 19 lists the entries that an LMFT must keep, and requires that records be maintained for seven years after termination of treatment or the last client visit.

The Colorado State Board of Registered Psychotherapists Rule 12 lists the required record-keeping entries, and requires that records be maintained for seven years after termination of treatment or the last client visit with an unlicensed therapist.

Records Disposition. The Mental Health Board Rules require that records be maintained and stored in a secure manner in order to assure that only authorized persons have access to records and that confidentiality is protected. In the event of the therapist's death, disability, or the sale of a therapist's practice, the Board Rules also require that a professional executor be appointed to maintain mental health records for the period of time required.

Group Therapy Notes. Keep in mind that the standard of care for record-keeping in group therapy requires an individual note for each individual in the group. In general, the individual's session notes should not identify other members of the therapy group.

Informed Consent Issues Regarding Record Keeping. (In compliance with the NASW Code of Ethics and Social Work Board Rules)

Social workers who provide counseling to active duty military personnel, off base, are sensitive not only to the fact that treatment information is confidential and privileged, but also that it may be subject to a subpoena duces tecum seeking copies of the treatment records. Recent experience has shown that military tribunals, applying the *Uniform*

Code of Military Justice, do not recognize the same privileges that Colorado law recognizes. Therefore, active duty military clients should give informed consent in your Disclosure Statement that their treatment records may be subpoenaed and subject to disclosure pursuant to a court order enforcing the subpoena.

The NASW Code of Ethics is instructive in this situation. Section 1.07, Privacy and Confidentiality, provides in part:

> (a) Social workers should respect clients' right to privacy. Social workers should not solicit private information from clients unless it is essential to providing services or conducting social work evaluation or research. Once private information is shared, standards of confidentiality apply.
>
> . . .
>
> (d) Social workers should inform clients, to the extent possible, about the disclosure of confidential information and the potential consequences, when feasible before the disclosure is made. This applies whether social workers disclose confidential information on the basis of a legal requirement or client consent.
>
> (e) Social workers should discuss with clients and other interested parties the nature of confidentiality and limitations of clients' right to confidentiality. Social workers should review with clients circumstances where confidential information may be requested and where disclosure of confidential information may be legally required. This discussion should occur as soon as possible in the social worker-client relationship and as needed throughout the course of the relationship.
>
> . . .
>
> (j) Social workers should protect the confidentiality of clients *during legal proceedings* to the extent permitted by law. When a court of law or other legally authorized body orders social workers to disclose confidential or privileged information without a client's consent and such disclosure could cause harm to the client, social workers should request that the court withdraw the order or limit the order as narrowly as possible or maintain the records under seal, unavailable for public inspection. [emphasis added]

How might an active duty military member be harmed by disclosure of treatment information? Information concerning the use of prescription medication, mental health problems, substance abuse, domestic violence, or marital infidelity can have serious consequences, from loss of a security clearance required for a service member to do his or her job, to the filing of charges in a court martial or involuntary discharge from the military. Thus, information in a social worker's notes or records that would be relatively innocuous to a civilian may be extremely harmful to an active duty military member, if disclosed.

The information a social worker keeps in a client's file is a matter of the therapist's professional judgment. However, in the process of taking notes and keeping records, you must adhere to the basic NASW Code of Ethics and the rules and regulations of the Colorado Board of Social Work Examiners. The NASW Code of Ethics Section 3.04, Client Records, provides:

> (a) Social workers should take reasonable steps to ensure that documentation in records is accurate and reflects the services provided.
>
> . . .
>
> (c) Social workers' documentation should protect clients' privacy to the extent that is possible and appropriate and *should include only information that is directly relevant to the delivery of services.* [emphasis added.]

It is a matter of a social worker's professional judgment and discretion in taking notes to determine what information is "directly relevant to the delivery of services."

The Colorado Board of Social Work Examiners Rule 18 requires that "every social worker shall create and shall maintain records" on each of his or clients. The record entries that you must maintain include:

1. Identifying data, including the client's name;
2. Reason(s) for the professional services;
3. Dates of each contact with the client;
4. Information on each referral made and each consultation with another social worker or healthcare provider, including the date of the referral or consultation, the name of the person(s) to whom the client was referred, the name of the person with

whom consultation was sought, the outcome of the referral, and the outcome of the consultation;

5. The name of any test(s) administered;
6. Information on each mandatory report made (e.g., report of suspected child abuse); and
7. Fee information.

Therefore, although you are required to keep records, each social worker, in taking notes, determines what information is relevant to the services being provided and protects clients' privacy by keeping irrelevant information out of records.

S.O.A.P. Notes. Therapists do not necessarily learn in graduate school the best method for taking notes during treatment sessions. An excellent method is illustrated by a case that I defended in which a psychologist was sued for allegedly violating the civil rights of a client, who was an inmate in a correctional facility.

The client went to sick call one morning, telling the physician's assistant that he was waking up in the morning feeling weird, and that he was on "synthetic medication." The physician's assistant looked at his chart, saw that the individual was on psychotropic medications, and referred him to the psychologist for assessment of his problems.

When the client saw the psychologist, he told her, "I've been waking up mornings feeling weird. They've got me on synthetic medication, and I do not do well on synthetic meds." The psychologist noted these comments, reviewed the client's chart, and conducted a one-hour mental status evaluation. The chart indicated that this client had been diagnosed as Paranoid Schizophrenic and had been prescribed Prolixin, which he was taking daily, and which was also being injected every two weeks. The psychologist could also see that this client was current on his meds and had not missed his daily dose of Prolixin in over six months. During her mental status evaluation, she noted her client's demeanor, and also noted that he was responding to her questions appropriately—a significant fact since his diagnosis included delusional features.

The psychologist noted her observations of the client and her assessment of his presenting problem, the fact that he had a question concerning his medication. The psychologist then paged the doctor who was providing medication management to this client and discussed the situation with the doctor when she responded to the page. They discussed the fact that the client was showing no signs of an acute psychotic episode; that he was compensated; and that he was current on his medications and was rational, responding appropriately to questions. The doctor advised that she would meet with this client, and asked that he be scheduled to see her the following Monday so that she could ensure he was receiving the proper dosage of Prolixin.

The psychologist had been recording all of the information concerning her session with this client using the S.O.A.P. notes format. Her chart, containing the client's name and date, had the following notes:

S. "Wakes up in the mornings feeling weird; on synthetic meds."

O. Cheerful, compensated rational, current on meds.

A. Question concerning meds.

P. Contact M.D.; scheduled client to see M.D. on Monday.

That evening the client either slipped and fell from the balcony of his housing unit, or was thrown from it by another inmate. He was injured, and was airlifted to a hospital. He improved with treatment, incurred a staph infection, and died from it in the hospital. His family then initiated a lawsuit against the psychologist and the state, alleging that the client's civil rights had been violated. A consulting expert provided a report to the plaintiff's attorney, expressing the opinion that this client had been suicidal and should have been placed in administrative segregation to protect him from harming himself. (The expert's opinion was absurd, in view of the psychologist's session note!) The lawsuit was summarily dismissed, based upon the S.O.A.P. notes concerning this session.

In 50 words or less, this session note enabled the psychologist to paint an accurate clinical picture of her client's presentation at the time of this session. He was cheerful, not depressed; compensated, not decompensated; and rational, not delusional. This was not an acute psychotic episode by an individual who was noncompliant with his medications. The note enabled all of the essential information concerning the treatment session to be recorded. The client's **S**ubjective data, his presenting problem, is recorded, along with the psychologist's **O**bjective information concerning her observations of the client's demeanor and his mental state. The psychologist's **A**ssessment of the client was also recorded, as well as her **P**lan for followup care.

The S.O.A.P. note format, therefore, enables therapists to record information concerning their client's presenting problem on a particular day, thereby documenting the reason for the services provided. This is important in this era of managed healthcare, when insurance carriers and federal healthcare programs conduct utilization reviews to determine whether treatment on specific dates was reasonable and necessary. Such questions can be answered easily when S.O.A.P. notes have been taken.

This format answers the frequently asked question, "How extensive should my session notes be?" While note taking is a matter of a therapist's style to some degree, with some therapists being minimalists and others being more obsessive, this format enables therapists to maintain the essential data that should be recorded regarding a session.

4.17 Pastoral Counseling/Spiritual Counseling

The statute that defines the authority of the Colorado Department of Regulatory Agencies to license, regulate, and discipline mental health professionals limits the Board's jurisdiction. C.R.S. § 12-43-215(1) provides that:

> Any person engaged in the practice of religious ministry shall not be required to comply with the provisions of this article; except that such person shall not hold himself or herself out to the public by any title incorporating the terms "psychologist", "social worker", "licensed social worker", "LSW", "licensed clinical social worker", "clinical social worker", "LCSW", "licensed marriage and family therapist", "LMFT", "licensed professional counselor", or "LPC" unless that person has been licensed pursuant to this article.

The right to religious freedom, guaranteed by the First Amendment to the United States Constitution, prohibits states from regulating the practice of a religion or from inhibiting religious freedom.

The Mental Health Boards have all adopted rules that distinguish psychotherapy from spiritual counseling based on the practice of a religious ministry. The Colorado State Board of Registered Psychotherapists Rule 1 lists the following factors to be used by the Board in determining whether a person is engaged in the "practice of religious ministry" or in the practice of psychotherapy under the Board's jurisdiction:

1. Whether the client or guardian had received notice or reasonably understood that the therapy in question was part of a religious practice/ministry.
2. Whether the client or guardian was seeking therapy from a religious entity to which the complainant belonged at any time.
3. Whether a written agreement or statement exists indicating the therapy in question was part of a religious practice/ministry.
4. Whether the therapy sessions were conducted in a house of worship or on property belonging to or controlled by a religious entity.
5. Whether the person conducting the therapy normally represented himself or herself as a religious official who was counseling as part of a religious ministry.
6. Whether therapy services were part of an ongoing relationship, formed because the provider is a spiritual counselor to the client.
7. Whether the provider of therapy holds a position of trust within a religious entity.
8. Whether the provider advertises therapy to the general public for a fee.
9. Whether the provider collects fees or expects/requires donations, offerings, tithes, or other compensation for therapy.
10. Whether the therapy provided is based on any religious orientation or viewpoint.
11. Whether the provider engaged in the practice of therapy is accountable or subject to any religious entity or person for misdeeds or acts of misconduct.
12. Whether the provider of therapy is a member of a religious entity holding tax-exempt status (e.g., does the entity hold 501(c)(3) tax-exempt status?).
13. Whether the provider is trained in theology or any other field, area, or specialty related to the study of the religious or spiritual orientation.
14. Whether the provider has a declaration of religious mission or a statement identifying the religious views or belief of the entity or person.
15. Whether the provider of therapy services is recognized by consumers as a religious minister or spiritual healer.

Other factors in individual cases will also be considered by a Board in determining whether it has jurisdiction over a minister, pastoral counselor, or other spiritual counselor.

C.R.S. § 13-90-107(1)(c) provides that a clergy member, minister, priest, or rabbi-client privilege exists, and that a clergy member, minister, priest, or rabbi "shall not be examined without both his or her consent and also the consent of the person making the confidential communication as to any confidential communication made to him or her in his or her professional capacity in the course of discipline expected by the religious body to which he or she belongs." A "priest-penitent" privilege has long existed, which protects communications made by a penitent who confesses sins to a priest or other clergy member. If a church member admits wrongdoing or confesses sins to a minister, expecting absolution and expecting complete confidentiality for any admissions made, then a privilege exists which is inviolate.

C.R.S. § 19-3-304(2)(aa)(I) requires that a clergy member must report child abuse or neglect, but states that this requirement shall *not* apply to a person "who acquires reasonable cause to know or suspect that a child has been subjected to abuse or neglect during a communication about which the person may not be examined as a witness pursuant to Section 13-90-107(1)(c), C.R.S., unless the person also acquires such reasonable cause from a source other than such a communication." This language is obviously confusing. What C.R.S. § 19-3-304 essentially provides is that if a church member confides or confesses that he or she has committed an act of child abuse in confidence to a clergy member, then a legal privilege exists protecting the confidentiality of these statements. If a clergy member has knowledge concerning suspected child abuse or neglect from his or her own observations or from statements made to the clergy member from a victim, then a duty exists to report the suspected child abuse or neglect.

Best Practice for a Pastoral Counselor. When ministers, priests, rabbis, or other clergy members engage in pastoral counseling as part of their religious ministry, it would be prudent for the clergy member to provide a statement to the person being counseled which acknowledges that the counseling is being conducted as part of a religious ministry, and that the clergy member is not providing psychotherapy or mental health counseling. Such a statement should be signed by the individual who is to receive counseling in order to avoid any confusion regarding the nature of the counseling being provided and to protect the clergy member, in the event that the Department of Regulatory Agencies attempts to exercise jurisdiction over him or her. If a minister or pastoral counselor is licensed by one of the Mental Health Boards, it is essential that the pastoral counselor not use his or her licensure status or honorific title such as "LPC," "LMFT," "LCSW," etc. on any written forms provided to the client or on any signs or office markings in the office where counseling occurs, unless the counselor is willing to submit to the jurisdiction of the Mental Health Boards and to comply with all of the laws, regulations, and ethical standards applicable to psychotherapists.

4.18 Legal Standards for Forensic Evaluations

Models for Forensic Evaluations. These include Social Security examinations, competency and sanity evaluations in criminal cases, independent medical evaluations or psychological evaluations for lawsuits, court-ordered psychological testing in domestic relations cases, and parental responsibility and parenting time evaluations in domestic cases.

Confidentiality and Privilege. The laws regarding confidentiality and privilege, which apply where healthcare providers have professional relationships with patients, do not apply to forensic evaluations. For example, C.R.S. § 12-43-218 contains an exception for competency and sanity evaluations, which are not deemed to be confidential, since they will be shared with the court and with attorneys in the case. Similarly, the subjects being evaluated by a forensic examiner are not required to give "informed consent" for the examination, since there is no treatment being provided. C.R.S. § 12-43-214, which mandates that informed consent for treatment be obtained by mental health professionals providing treatment to a client, contains an exception for court-ordered evaluations. Nevertheless, disclosures are appropriate for an individual being evaluated by a forensic examiner so that (1) the forensic examiner's role is clearly defined, and (2) it is understood that the forensic examiner will not be providing treatment to the person being evaluated.

Ethical Standards. American Psychological Association Ethical Principles regarding the conduct of forensic evaluations include the following:

APA Ethics Code 2002

Ethical Principle 9.01 Bases for Assessments

(a) Psychologists base the opinions contained in their recommendations, reports, and diagnostic or evaluative statements, including forensic testimony, on information and techniques sufficient to substantiate their findings.

(b) Except as noted in 9.01c, psychologists provide opinions of the psychological characteristics of individuals only after they have conducted an examination of the individuals adequate to support their statements or conclusions. When, despite reasonable efforts, such an examination is not practical, psychologists document the efforts they made and the result of those efforts, clarify the probable impact of their limited information on the reliability and the validity of their opinions, and appropriately limit the nature and extent of their conclusions or recommendations.

(c) When psychologists conduct a record review or provide consultation or supervision and an individual examination is not warranted or necessary for the opinion, psychologists explain this and the sources of information on which they based their conclusions and recommendations.

Ethical Principle 9.02 Use of Assessments

(a) Psychologists administer, adapt, score, interpret, or use assessment techniques, interviews, tests, or instruments in a manner and for purposes that are appropriate in light of the research on or evidence of usefulness and proper application of the techniques.

(b) Psychologists use assessment instruments whose validity and reliability have been established for use with members of the population tested. When such validity or reliability has not been established, psychologists describe the strengths and limitations of test results and interpretation.

(c) Psychologists use assessment methods that are appropriate to an individual's language preference and competence, unless the use of an alternative language is relevant to the assessment issues.

> *Ethical Principle 9.03 Informed Consent in Assessments*
>
> (a) Psychologists obtain informed consent for assessments, evaluations, or diagnostic services, as described in Standard 3.10, Informed Consent, except when (1) testing is mandated by law or governmental regulations; (2) informed consent is implied because testing is conducted as a routine educational, institutional, or organizational activity (e.g., when participants voluntarily agree to assessment when applying for a job); or (3) one purpose of the testing is to evaluate decisional capacity. Informed consent includes an explanation of the nature and purpose of the assessment, fees, involvement of third parties, and limits of confidentiality and sufficient opportunity for the client/patient to ask questions and receive answers.
>
> (b) Psychologists inform persons with questionable capacity to consent or for whom testing is mandated by law or government regulations about the nature and purpose of the proposed assessment services, using language that is reasonably understandable to the person being assessed.

Disclosures signed by the person to be evaluated concerning the forensic examiner's role and the use of the information being shared with the forensic examiner, as well as the report being prepared, are important in order to comply with these APA Ethical Principles.

Legal Standards. Pursuant to C.R.S. § 12-43-201(9), psychologists and other mental health professionals under Colorado law are engaging in the practice of psychotherapy when they are attempting to accomplish a psychotherapeutic objective *in a professional relationship with the client.* C.R.S. § 12-43-201(9) defines "psychotherapy" as:

> "Psychotherapy" means the treatment, diagnosis, testing, assessment, or counseling *in a professional relationship* to assist individuals or groups to alleviate mental disorders, understand unconscious or conscious motivation, resolve emotional, relationship, or attitudinal conflicts, or modify behaviors which interfere with effective, emotional, social, or intellectual functioning. Psychotherapy follows a planned procedure of intervention which takes place on a regular basis, over a period of time, or in the cases of testing, assessment, and brief psychotherapy, it can be a single intervention. [emphasis added]

Risk Management Principles. When an independent medical evaluation of a client is performed, the medical examiner does not have a duty to provide treatment to the person being examined. When there is no psychologist-patient relationship, there is no duty to (1) provide treatment to the person being examined, (2) make appropriate referrals for that individual, (3) make appropriate treatment recommendations concerning the individual, or (4) provide needed treatment to the individual. Where no professional relationship exists and no duty of care exists, the person being examined cannot sue for malpractice. Colorado courts have recognized a duty on the part of an independent examining physician not to harm the person being examined.

The forensic examiner has a duty to report any previously unreported child abuse or neglect, pursuant to C.R.S. § 13-90-107. That legal requirement should be disclosed to the person to be evaluated. Other disclosures that should be made to the individual being examined, in order to protect the forensic examiner from any kind of claim, include the forensic examiner's role and the fact that he or she is not providing treatment or establishing a relationship with the person being evaluated. The boundaries between the forensic examiner and the subject of the examination need to be clearly defined in appropriate disclosures.

An important consideration regarding the relationship of a forensic examiner to people being tested or evaluated concerns confidentiality and privilege. If a professional relationship exists between a treatment provider and the patient, then the medical records and treatment information are confidential and privileged, and cannot be disclosed without the consent of the patient pursuant to C.R.S. §§ 12-43-218 and 13-90-107(1)(g).

From a risk management perspective, establishing correct boundaries between the forensic examiner and the examinee assist the professional in defending any potential liability claim that may be made for alleged "breach of confidentiality" or "violation of privilege." In a forensic evaluation where no professional relationship exists, there is no duty of confidentiality or legal privilege preventing disclosure of the examiner's report to the court or agency that requested it.

Record Keeping. Any records maintained by a forensic examiner should be kept locked, with access available only to authorized individuals on a need-to-know basis. The person evaluated is not necessarily entitled to a copy of any report or to the forensic examiner's file.

Social Security Administration Regulations mandate that the forensic examiner share information only with the Social Security Administration.

a. Request for Records: The subject of the evaluation and report, not being a client, does not have any right to receive copies of reports or other records, and should be informed of that fact in the Disclosures provided. If the court or other authority allows disclosure of the forensic examiner's report or other data, then such disclosure is permissible. Records should not be disclosed to anyone who does not have a "need to know."

Model Disclosures. In the Forms section of this book is a form for making disclosures to persons being evaluated. This form clearly establishes that no duty of confidentiality exists, explains how the examiner's report will be used, and makes it clear that no professional relationship or duty to provide care has been established.

The disclosures should divulge the fact that a forensic examiner will report any threat of imminent harm against a specific person and will also notify law enforcement of such a threat.

Reports. All reports should identify the basis for any opinions or conclusions stated and should disclose any limitations on the forensic examiner's ability to state conclusions or opinions. The examiner must, of course, remain objective in the entire process of a forensic evaluation. The report should state with specificity that the examiner has not assumed a duty to provide treatment, and is neither making treatment recommendations nor conducting an evaluation for purposes of treatment. The scope of the forensic examiner's role and the fact that no professional relationship has been established may be stated in the report. In formulating any conclusions or opinions, a professional must state any conclusions or opinions "to a reasonable degree of probability" in the professional's discipline or field.

4.19 College and University Counseling Programs: Best Practices

History is a great teacher. Experience has taught that foreseeable problems arise in certain situations brought by students to university counseling programs. For example, if a student reports that she has been sexually harassed by a professor or other university official, a therapist will inevitably be conflicted in attempting to treat the student in this situation. If a student presents to a campus counselor, needing treatment for trauma after being raped by a football player being recruited by the university, foreseeable problems will arise. If a student has been disciplined by a university for engaging in violent conduct, cheating, making threats of violence, or for stalking a student, and the student wants to seek counseling from a university counselor for the anxiety or depression caused by the discipline, inevitable conflicts for a counselor within the university will occur.

What are the foreseeable problems and conflicts associated with these scenarios? In these litigious times, students who feel wronged by a university employee, official, or program may find an attorney to sue the university. If a therapist at the university's counseling program has been providing services to the claimant, then that therapist will be the star witness for the client in the suit against the university. What a conflict will then ensue! The therapist will be torn between his or her therapeutic alliance with the client and loyalty to his or her employer, the university. Imagine being a therapist in a university counseling program and finding yourself cross-examined by the university's legal counsel, who is attempting to impeach your credibility, undermine your opinions, demonstrate that you are incompetent, and embarrass your client in any way possible. Enormous pressure is placed upon therapists in such situations, who may feel compromised regardless of what they do.

The practical solution for such problems is to avoid the situation. A student who has emotional problems allegedly caused by a university professor, employee, or program should be referred off campus. This prevents the therapist's ethical judgment from being questioned, impaired, or compromised. History has shown that attempting to handle such situations "in house" at campus counseling centers is ill-advised.

4.20 Testifying in Divorce Litigation: Prevention of Foreseeable Risks

In Colorado and across the nation, the most frequent type of board complaint involving therapists arises from testimony in divorce and custody cases. Clients or the parents of children receiving treatment from a therapist, who are involved in bitterly contested custody battles, often consider the treating professional as an ally in the custody battle. These clients and their attorneys have unreasonable expectations concerning the role of a therapist who is providing treatment.

They expect the therapist to make favorable recommendations to the court concerning parental responsibilities and parenting plans. However, that is not the proper role of a treatment professional. Such recommendations should only be made by custody evaluators, child and family investigators, guardians ad litem or child representatives appointed by the court to conduct investigations and evaluations of parenting issues. Their recommendations can then be made to the court regarding the allocation of parental responsibilities and the implementation of parenting plans.

Therapists must comply with AAMFT Code of Ethics Principle 3.14 which states: "To avoid a conflict of interest, marriage and family therapists who treat minors or adults involved in custody or visitation actions may not also perform forensic evaluations for custody, residence, or visitation of the minor. The marriage and family therapist who treats the minor may provide the court or mental health professional performing the evaluation with information about the minor from the marriage and family therapist's perspective . . . ." For example, if a therapist is subpoenaed to court and is then asked by a client's attorney for recommendations concerning who should have custody of the parties' children or concerning whether it is appropriate for a parent to have parenting time with a child, the only appropriate response should be, "I have not conducted the evaluation necessary to provide an opinion on this issue, so I cannot answer the question."

However, problems arise when a client has unreasonable expectations concerning a therapist's role, and the client feels betrayed when the therapist does not support the client's position in the litigation. For example, if a child's mother does not want her estranged spouse to have any contact with their children, she may be outraged if the therapist expresses an opinion that fathers should have relationships with their children, and then pull the children out of treatment with the therapist. This is an all too frequent experience for therapists nationwide who have testified in court: their clinical relationship with clients is either damaged or destroyed as a result of testimony in court in a domestic case.

How can therapists avoid these risks? First, therapists should not agree to testify in court. Second, therapists should disclose to clients who are involved in custody battles at the outset of treatment that it is not the therapist's role to make recommendations to the court for purposes of domestic litigation, and that any courtroom testimony may damage the clinical relationship. The mandatory Disclosure Statement is a vehicle by which an appropriate disclosure can be made. In it you can disclose:

> If you are involved in a divorce or custody litigation, you need to understand that my role as a therapist is not to make recommendations for the court concerning custody or parenting issues or to testify in court concerning opinions on issues involved in the litigation. By signing this disclosure statement, you agree not to call me as a witness in any such litigation. Experience has shown that testimony by therapists in domestic cases causes damage to the clinical relationship between a therapist and client. Only court-appointed experts, investigators, or evaluators can make recommendations to the court on disputed issues concerning parental responsibilities and parenting plans.

Such an agreement by a client is not enforceable if the client's attorney issues a subpoena to a therapist; however, these disclosures may correct any unrealistic expectations that clients might have.

To avoid the foreseeable risks that result from testimony in domestic litigation, therefore, therapists should not agree to testify in court and, if subpoenaed, should acknowledge their limitations as treating professionals, who have not evaluated and ethically cannot evaluate issues to be decided by the court or make recommendations concerning them. And, of course, compliance with the AAMFT Code of Ethics is the best way to prevent such risks.

CHAPTER 5: RESTRICTION OF CLIENT LIBERTIES

There are several legal proceedings that are intended to protect clients but result in the deprivation of their civil liberties. This chapter describes these proceedings so psychotherapists can be better equipped to serve the client who is involved in such proceedings.

5.01 Guardianship

Colorado law on guardianship is found in C.R.S. §§ 15-14-101 to 15-14-318. A distinction is made with respect to the appointment of guardians for minors and the appointment of guardians for incapacitated persons. The following definitions are helpful with respect to understanding the distinctions that are drawn by the law with respect to these two types of guardianship:

1. A **guardianship** is generally thought of as a trust relationship in which one person, called a "Guardian," acts for another called the "Ward" or "Incapacitated Person" or "Protected Person," who the law regards as incapable of managing his or her own affairs.
2. A **guardian** is lawfully invested with the power and charged with the duty of taking care of and managing the rights of another person who, for some peculiarity of status or defect of age, understanding, or self-control, is considered incapable of ministering his or her own affairs. A guardian is generally empowered to facilitate a protected person's education and social or other activities, and to authorize medical or other professional care, treatment, or advice for the benefit of the protected person. The guardian may also consent to the marriage or adoption of his or her ward. In general, the guardian is thought of as the person who is responsible for assisting the incapacitated person with respect to making life decisions. In cases where the incapacitated person is unable to make a life decision, the guardian is empowered to make that decision for the incapacitated person.
3. A guardian must be distinguished from a guardian ad litem and a conservator. A **guardian ad litem** is an attorney appointed by

the court to represent the interests of the minor, ward, incapacitated person, or person to be protected in a legal proceeding.

4. A **conservator** is appointed by the court to manage the financial affairs of the minor, ward, incapacitated person, or person to be protected. Thus, in most cases, a guardian ad litem protects the incapacitated person with respect to a specific legal proceeding, while a conservator manages the financial affairs of such a person.
5. A **minor** means any person who is under the age of 18 years.
6. An **incapacitated person** means a person who is impaired by reason of mental illness, mental deficiency, physical illness or disability, advanced age, chronic use of drugs, chronic intoxication, or other cause (except minority), to the extent that he or she lacks sufficient understanding or capacity to make or communicate responsible decisions concerning his or her person.
7. A **protected person** is a minor or other person for whom a conservator has been appointed or some other protective order has been made.
8. A **ward** is a person for whom a guardian has been appointed.

Guardians of Minors. A person becomes a guardian of a minor by accepting a testamentary appointment, by a written instrument appointing the guardian, or upon appointment by the court.

A testamentary appointment of a guardian occurs when a parent of a minor appoints a guardian in the parent's last will. The testamentary appointment becomes effective upon the guardian's filing of a written acceptance in the court in which the will is probated.

The appointment of a guardian by a written instrument occurs when such a document is filed in the court having probate jurisdiction over the last parent of the ward to die, and when such guardian files with the court an acceptance of the guardianship.

C.R.S. § 15-14-203 allows a minor of 12 years of age or older to prevent an appointment of his or her guardian from becoming effective by filing a written objection to the appointment before it is accepted or within 30 days after notice of its acceptance. In such a case, the court will, in a proper proceeding, appoint a guardian over the written objection by the minor.

C.R.S. § 15-14-206 provides that the court may appoint as a guardian any person whose appointment would be in the best interests of the minor. Unless the court finds the prospective appointment contrary to the best interests of the minor, qualified persons have priority for appointment in the following order:

1. A person nominated by the minor, if the minor is 12 years of age or older;
2. A person appointed by a will or by a written instrument of a parent of the minor; and
3. Any other interested person.

C.R.S. § 15-14-205 outlines the procedure that is to be followed for the court appointment of a guardian for a minor. Upon receipt of a petition for the appointment of a guardian, the court may, if requested, appoint a temporary guardian. The appointment shall not last longer than nine months. Notwithstanding this temporary appointment, the court will set the matter for a hearing. The person filing the petition for appointment must provide notice of the time and place of the hearing to: (1) the minor if he or she is 14 years of age or older; (2) to the person who has had the principal care and custody of the minor during the 60 days preceding the date of the petition; and (3) to any living parent of the minor. If at any time during the proceeding the court determines that the interests of the minor are or may be inadequately represented, it may appoint an attorney to represent the minor, giving consideration to the preference of the minor if the minor is 12 years of age or older.

C.R.S. §§ 15-14-207 and 15-14-208 set forth the powers and duties of a guardian of a minor. Under the statute, a guardian of a minor has the responsibilities of a parent who has not been deprived of custody of his or her minor unemancipated child, except that a guardian is not legally obligated to provide from his or her own funds for the ward and, except as specifically provided by law, is not liable to third persons by reason of the parental relationship for acts of the ward. The statute specifically requires a guardian to take reasonable care of the ward's personal effects and commence a conservatorship, if necessary to protect other property of the ward. A guardian may receive money payable for the support of the ward otherwise made payable to the ward's parent, guardian, or custodian under the terms of any statutory benefit, insurance system, or private contract, devise, trust, conservatorship, or custodianship. Any sum so received must be applied to the ward's current needs for support, care, and education. The guardian must exercise due care to conserve any excess for the ward's future needs, unless a conservator has been appointed for the estate of the ward, in which case the excess shall be paid over at least annually to the conservator. Sums so received by the guardian are not to be used as compensation for his or her services, except as approved by order of the court or as determined by a duly appointed conservator other than the guardian.

A guardian is empowered to facilitate the ward's education and to consent to authorized medical or professional care. A guardian is not liable by reason of his or her consent for injury to the ward resulting from the negligence or acts of third persons, unless it would have been illegal for a parent to consent. A guardian may consent to the marriage or adoption of his or her ward. Additionally, a guardian must report on the condition of his or her ward and the ward's estate that has been subject to his or her possession or control as ordered by the court.

C.R.S. § 15-14-210 provides that a guardian's authority and responsibility for a minor terminates upon the death, resignation, or removal of the guardian, or upon the minor's death, adoption, marriage, or attainment of majority at age 18.

Guardians of Incapacitated Persons. The appointment process for a guardian of an incapacitated person is somewhat different from that for a minor. C.R.S. § 15-14-310 provides that the parent of an unmarried incapacitated person may appoint a guardian for that person, by will or other writing signed by the parent and attested to by at least two witnesses. Such parental appointment becomes effective when, after having given seven days' prior written notice of his or her intention to do so to both the incapacitated person and the person having the care of the incapacitated person or his or her nearest adult relative, the guardian files an acceptance of appointment in the court in which the parent's will is probated. In the case of a non-testamentary nominating instrument, the acceptance of appointment may be filed in the court where the incapacitated person resides or is present.

C.R.S. § 15-14-310 also provides that the spouse of a married incapacitated person may appoint, by will or other writing signed by the spouse and attested to by at least two witnesses, a guardian of the incapacitated person. The appointment becomes effective when, after having given seven days' prior written notice of his or her intention to do so to both the incapacitated person and the person having the care of the incapacitated person or his or her nearest adult relative, the guardian files an acceptance of appointment in the court in which the will is probated. In the case of a non-testamentary nominating instrument, acceptance may be filed in the court at the place where the incapacitated person resides or is present.

C.R.S. § 15-14-304 provides that an incapacitated person ("respondent") or any person interested in his or her welfare may petition the court for a finding of incapacity, the appointment of a guardian, or other protective orders. In such case, the court shall set a date for a hearing on the issues of incapacity and, unless the incapacitated person has counsel of his or her own choice, it shall appoint a visitor who shall have the following duties:

1. To meet, interview, and consult with the allegedly incapacitated person regarding the proceeding, and to explain, in a manner such person can reasonably be expected to understand, the substance of the petition; the nature, purpose, and effect of the proceedings; and the general powers and duties of a guardian.
2. To ascertain such person's views with regard to the proposed guardian and his or her powers and duties, the proposed guardianship, and the scope and duration thereof.
3. To inform such person of his or her right to obtain and consult with an attorney at his or her own expense, but that, if he or she cannot afford to pay an attorney, one will be provided by the court without costs; and to advise such person of each of his or her rights.
4. To inform such person that all costs and expenses of the proceeding, including his or her attorney fees, will be paid from his or her estate, unless the court directs otherwise.
5. To interview the petitioner.
6. To interview the person seeking appointment as guardian.
7. To visit or otherwise obtain information regarding the present place of abode of the person alleged to be incapacitated and the place where it is proposed that he or she will be detained or reside if the requested appointment is made.

8. To interview any physician or other person who is known to have evaluated or rendered care, counsel, treatment, or service to the person in the recent past.
9. To make any other investigation the court directs.
10. To provide the court with a written report.

The written report of the visitor must include the following:

1. A recommendation, if any, as to whether or not an attorney or a guardian ad litem should be appointed to represent the respondent;
2. A summary of daily functions the respondent can manage without assistance, could manage with assistance of supportive services or benefits (including use of appropriate technological assistance) and cannot manage;
3. A recommendation regarding the appropriateness of guardianship, including whether less restrictive means of intervention are available, the type of guardianship, and if a limited guardianship, the powers to be granted to the limited guardian;
4. An evaluation of the qualifications of the guardian whose appointment is sought, any recommendation to limit any of the guardian's powers, and the reasons for any such recommendation;
5. Any expression of approval or disapproval made by the respondent concerning the proposed guardian or his or her powers and duties, the proposed guardianship, or the scope thereof;
6. A statement as to whether the proposed dwelling meets the respondent's individual needs;
7. Any other information bearing upon the proposed guardian or guardianship that should be brought to the attention of the court; and
8. A recommendation as to whether or when the guardianship should be reviewed by the court.

The investigation and the report of the visitor is to occur within ten days after the visitor's appointment, unless an extension of time is granted by the court for good cause shown. The visitor is to forward a copy of his or her report to the court, with copies to the respondent, the person seeking appointment as guardian, and his or her attorney.

The court may appoint a physician to examine the allegedly incapacitated person, and the physician shall submit a report to the court. The report must include: (1) a description of the nature, type, and degree of any current incapacity or disability, including the medical history if reasonably available; (2) a medical prognosis specifying the estimated severity and duration of any current incapacity or disability; (3) a statement as to how or in what manner the person's ability to make or communicate responsible decisions concerning his or her person has been affected by the underlying condition of his or her physical or mental health; (4) a statement as to whether any current medication affects the demeanor of the person or his or her ability to participate fully in any court proceeding; and (5) any other matter required by the court or by court rule.

The person alleged to be incapacitated is entitled to be present at any court proceeding in person and to see and hear all evidence bearing upon his or her condition. He or she is entitled to be present by counsel, to present evidence, to cross-examine witnesses (including the court-appointed visitor and any court-appointed physician) and to trial by jury upon written demand and without payment of a jury demand fee. The proceeding may be determined at a closed hearing if the person alleged to be incapacitated so requests. If at any time in any court proceeding the allegedly incapacitated person requests that an attorney be appointed to represent him or her or expresses a desire to contest the petition or object to the appointment of the proposed guardian or his or her powers or duties, or objects to the creation of the proposed guardianship or its scope or duration, the court will appoint an attorney to represent such person in the proceeding when such person does not have an attorney. The court also has the power to appoint an attorney if, in the opinion of the court, the rights and interests of the allegedly incapacitated person cannot otherwise be adequately protected or represented.

C.R.S. § 15-14-311 requires that in all cases where a person is found to be incapacitated, the court shall determine the nature and extent of the care, assistance, protection, or supervision that is necessary or desirable under all of the circumstances. The court must consider less restrictive alternative means of providing the necessary protective services for such person and may enter any appropriate order to provide for such person's care, assistance, protection, or supervision. The court may appoint a special guardian to assist in the accomplishment of any such protective order, and this guardian will have the authority conferred after making such report as the court requires.

In appointing a guardian, the court must be satisfied that the person for whom care is sought is incapacitated and that the appointment is necessary or desirable as a means of providing continuing care and supervision of the incapacitated person. Prior to the entry of any protective order or the appointment of a guardian, the court must consider the wishes of the incapacitated person concerning his or her care, counsel, treatment, service, and supervision, as well as the incapacitated person's views concerning the selection of the guardian, the duties of the guardian, the scope and duration of the guardianship, and any limitations or restrictions that should be imposed on the powers of the guardian.

C.R.S. § 15-14-318 provides that the authority and responsibility of a guardian for any incapacitated person terminates upon the death of the guardian or ward or the removal or resignation of the guardian.

C.R.S. § 15-14-312 provides that if an incapacitated person has no guardian and an emergency exists, the court may exercise the power of a guardian or may appoint a temporary guardian pending notice and hearing. Such temporary guardian is entitled to the care and custody of the ward.

C.R.S. § 15-14-102(4) provides that any qualified person 21 years of age or older may be appointed guardian of any incapacitated person. C.R.S. § 15-14-310 states that persons seeking appointment as guardian of an incapacitated person have priority for the appointment in the following order:

1. A guardian, other than a temporary or emergency guardian, currently acting for the respondent in this state or elsewhere.
2. A person nominated as guardian by the respondent, including the respondent's specific nomination of a guardian made in a durable power of attorney or in a designated beneficiary agreement.
3. An agent appointed by the respondent under a medical durable power of attorney pursuant to C.R.S. § 15-14-506.
4. An agent appointed by the respondent under a general durable power of attorney.
5. The spouse of the respondent or a person nominated by will or other signed writing of a deceased spouse.

6. An adult child of the respondent.
7. A parent of the respondent or an individual nominated by will or other signed writing of a deceased parent.
8. An adult with whom the respondent has resided for more than six months immediately before the filing of the petition.

C.R.S. § 15-14-314 sets forth the general duties of a guardian. This statute provides that a guardian of an incapacitated person has the same powers, rights, and duties respecting his or her ward that a parent has respecting an unemancipated minor child. However, according to C.R.S. § 15-14-316, a guardian is not required to provide from his or her own funds for the incapacitated person, and, except as specifically provided by law, a guardian is not liable to third persons for acts of the ward solely by reason of the parental relationship. Unless limited or restricted by the court, the guardian of an incapacitated person determines the ward's place of abode, within or outside of the state. C.R.S. § 15-14-316 also provides that to obtain hospital or institutional care for the mental illness of a ward, a guardian must proceed as provided under C.R.S. §§ 27-65-101, *et seq.*, and if a guardian seeks care and treatment for a ward with developmental disabilities, he or she is required to proceed under C.R.S. §§ 27-10.5-101, *et seq.* Further, to obtain care and treatment for alcoholism, a guardian must proceed under C.R.S. §§ 27-81-101, *et seq.* No guardian has the authority to consent to any such care or treatment against the will of the ward.

If a guardian is entitled to custody of the ward, the guardian must make provision for the ward's care, comfort, and maintenance, and whenever appropriate, arrange for his or her training and education. Without regard to custodial rights of the ward's person, the guardian must take reasonable care of his or her ward's clothing, furniture, vehicles, and other personal effects and commence a conservatorship action if other property of his or her ward is in need of protection.

The court is required to determine the extent to which a guardian will be permitted to give any consent or approval that may be necessary to enable the ward to receive medical or other professional care, counsel, treatment, or service, taking into account the ward's wishes, if any, and the prevention of unnecessary or excessive treatment. If the court at any time determines that there is any category of care, counsel, treatment, or service that might not be in the best interest of the ward, the court shall require the guardian to obtain prior court approval for any such care, counsel, treatment, or service.

C.R.S. § 15-14-315 also provides that if no conservator for the estate of the ward has been appointed, the guardian may institute proceedings to compel any person under a duty to support the ward, or to pay sums for the welfare of the ward, to perform that duty. In such cases, the guardian may receive money and tangible property deliverable to the ward and apply the money and property for the support, care, and education of the ward. However, the guardian may not use funds from the ward's estate for room and board that the guardian has furnished for the ward, unless the charge for the service is approved by order of the court and made upon notice to at least one of the next of kin of the ward. If a conservator has been appointed, all of the ward's estate received by the guardian in excess of those funds expended to meet current expenses for support, care, and education of the ward must be paid to the conservator for management and the guardian must account to the conservator for funds expended.

Any guardian of a person for whom a conservator has also been appointed shall control the custody and care of the ward, and is entitled to receive reasonable sums for his or her services and for room and board furnished to the ward as agreed upon between him or her and the conservator.

The role of a psychotherapist in a guardianship generally involves testifying as to a person's capacity to handle his or her own personal affairs. The person for whom the guardianship is sought may be a client of the psychotherapist. Therefore, the psychotherapist must be keenly aware of his or her duty of non-disclosure with respect to confidential and privileged matters. When confronted with a request for information from one who seeks to impose a guardianship on a psychotherapist's client, the psychotherapist should generally decline to release any information unless required to do so by court order.

5.02 Conservatorship

A conservatorship is a court proceeding whereby the court appoints an interested person to manage or protect the business affairs of a minor or an incapacitated person.

The court may appoint a conservator for a minor if the court determines that a minor has money, property, or business affairs requiring management or protection; or the minor needs funds for his or her support and education, and protection is necessary or desirable to obtain or provide the funds.

The court may appoint a conservator for any other person if the court determines that the person is unable to manage his or her property and affairs effectively for reasons such as mental illness, mental deficiency, physical illness or disability, advanced age, chronic use of drugs, chronic intoxication, etc., and that the person has property which will be wasted or dissipated unless proper management is provided, or that funds are needed for the support, care, and welfare of the person or those entitled to be supported by him.

A conservatorship is commenced by the filing of a petition for appointment as conservator with the District Court. The respondent is served with a copy of the petition, as well as a notice of the date on which the hearing for the conservatorship will be held by the court.

The court may order that the person to be protected be examined by a physician and the court may send a visitor, who may be a guardian ad litem or an officer or employee of the court, to interview the person to be protected.

Unlike a guardian, a conservator's powers are limited to financial affairs and, as such, a conservator has no right to decide non-financial or non-business-related matters for the person in need of protection.

As in a guardianship, a psychotherapist's role generally involves testimony concerning whether the respondent is capable of managing his or her own financial or business affairs. If the respondent is a client of the psychotherapist, the psychotherapist must be keenly aware of his or her duty of non-disclosure with respect to confidential and privileged matters. When confronted with a request for information from one who seeks to impose a conservatorship on a psychotherapist's client, the psychotherapist should generally decline to release any information unless required to do so by court order.

5.03 Restraining Orders

A restraining order is a court order issued by the court for the purpose of preventing domestic violence. There are various types of restraining orders:

1. A restraining order to prevent domestic abuse under C.R.S. § 13-14-102;
2. The automatic temporary injunction, which occurs upon the filing of a petition for dissolution of marriage or separation under C.R.S. § 14-10-107(4); and
3. A restraining order to prevent emotional abuse of the elderly pursuant to C.R.S. § 13-14-102.

Violation of a restraining order is a crime pursuant to C.R.S. § 18-6-803.5.

Prevention of Domestic Violence. "Domestic violence" is defined by C.R.S. § 18-6-800.3 as "an act or threatened act of violence upon a person with whom the actor is or has been involved in an intimate relationship" and it includes "any other crime against a person, or against property, including an animal . . . when used as a method of coercion, control, punishment, intimidation, or revenge directed against a person with whom the actor is or has been involved in an intimate relationship." Controlling a victim's finances, documents, or property in a way that makes the victim "more likely to return to an abuser due to fear of retaliation or inability to meet basic needs" is also a form of domestic violence. C.R.S. § 13-14-102.

Under C.R.S. § 13-14-102, a municipal court, county court, and district court may issue temporary and permanent restraining orders to prevent domestic abuse. Such temporary or permanent orders may include a provision:

1. Restraining a party from threatening, molesting, or injuring any other party of the minor children of either of the parties;
2. Restraining a party from contacting any other party or the minor child of either of the parties;
3. Excluding a party from the family home or from the home of the other party upon a showing that physical or emotional harm would otherwise result;
4. Awarding temporary care and control of any minor children of either party involved for a period of not more than 120 days;
5. Determining visitation rights for the other party;
6. Restraining a party (for up to 120 days) from ceasing to make payments for mortgage or rent, insurance, utilities or related

services, transportation, medical care, or child care when the defendant has a prior existing duty or legal obligation; or

7. Restraining a party (for up to 120 days) from transferring, encumbering, concealing, or in any way disposing of personal effects or real property, except in the usual course of business or for the necessities of life.

In order to obtain a temporary restraining order to prevent domestic abuse, a party must file a verified complaint alleging that the other party has committed acts constituting domestic abuse. The court, after hearing evidence and being fully satisfied that sufficient cause exists, may issue a temporary restraining order to prevent domestic abuse and issue a citation directed to the other party demanding that the defendant appear before the court at a specific time and date to show cause, if any, why such temporary restraining order should not be made permanent. Such temporary restraining order may be issued only if the issuing judge finds that an imminent danger exists to the life or health of one or more persons.

A copy of the complaint, together with a copy of the temporary restraining order and a copy of the citation, must be served upon the defendant. The citation must inform the defendant that if the defendant fails to appear in court in accordance with the terms of the citation, a bench warrant may be issued for the arrest of the defendant.

Any person against whom a restraining order is issued pursuant to C.R.S. § 13-14-102, which excludes such person from a shared residence, may return to such shared residence one time to obtain sufficient undisputed personal effects as are necessary for such person to maintain a normal standard of living during any period prior to a hearing concerning such order. Such person is permitted to return to such shared residence *only if* such person is accompanied at all times by a peace officer.

On the date of the hearing, the judge will examine the record and the evidence and, if he or she believes that the defendant has committed acts constituting domestic abuse to the plaintiff or a minor child and if not restrained and enjoined will continue to commit such acts constituting domestic abuse, the judge may order that the temporary restraining order by made permanent or order a permanent restraining order with different provisions than the temporary restraining order. The judge will inform the defendant that the violation of the restraining order will constitute contempt of court and subject the defendant to such punishment as may be provided by law.

The foregoing procedure requires affirmative action by the party seeking the restraining order. In particular, the party seeking the order must obtain the appropriate paperwork, file it with the county court, and take the appropriate steps to have the paperwork properly served upon the defendant.

Frequently, psychotherapists will find themselves in a situation where they must provide emotional support for their client who is a victim of such abuse. In such cases, referral to a competent attorney should be considered as a means of relieving the anxiety and burden on the victim. If finances are a consideration, the procedure can be accomplished by a person of average abilities and competence without the assistance of an attorney.

Emergency Protection Orders. Colorado law recognizes that there are circumstances that make it impossible to follow the restraining order procedure described in C.R.S. § 13-14-102. For example, there are times when the courts are closed for judicial business and an emergency order is needed. In such circumstances, a peace officer who has reasonable grounds to believe that an adult is in immediate and present danger of domestic abuse, based upon an allegation of a recent incident of actual domestic abuse or threat of domestic abuse, may telephone the on-call judge and request the issuance of a written or verbal emergency protection order. These emergency protection orders may include a provision:

1. Restraining a party from threatening, molesting, or injuring any other party or minor children of either of the parties;
2. Excluding a party from the family home or from the home of another party upon a showing that physical or emotional harm would otherwise result; and
3. Awarding temporary care and control of any minor children of a party involved.

The emergency protective order will expire not later than the close of judicial business on the next day of judicial business following the day of issue, unless otherwise continued by the court. The court may continue any emergency protection order only if the plaintiff has filed a complaint or restraining order to prevent domestic abuse pursuant to

C.R.S. § 13-14-102, and the judge is unable to set a hearing on a plaintiff's request for a temporary restraining order on the day the complaint is filed.

A verbal emergency protection order may be issued only if the issuing judge finds that an imminent danger exists to the life or health of one or more persons. Such an order must be reduced to writing and signed by the peace officer and must include a statement of the grounds for the order asserted by the officer.

The role of the psychotherapist with respect to an emergency protection order is much more limited than in those instances where a restraining order to prevent domestic abuse is sought. Since the emergency protection order is initiated by a peace officer, the opportunity for a psychotherapist to become involved is limited. However, when a psychotherapist believes that a client may be the victim of domestic abuse, the psychotherapist should explain the availability of a restraining order under C.R.S. § 13-14-102. In many cases, knowledge of the availability of this procedure may be comforting to a client.

Divorce Injunction. Upon filing a petition for dissolution of marriage or legal separation by a party, and upon personal service of the petition and summons on the other party, an automatic temporary injunction is in effect against both parties, which:

1. Restrains both parties from transferring, encumbering, concealing, or in any way disposing of, without the consent of the other party or an order of the court, any marital property, except in the usual course of business or for the necessities of life, and requires each party to notify the other party of any proposed extraordinary expenditures and to account to the court for all extraordinary expenditures made after the injunction is in effect;
2. Enjoins both parties from molesting or disturbing the peace of the other party; and
3. Restrains both parties from moving the minor child or children of the parties, if any, from the state without the consent of the other party or an order of the court.

This automatic temporary injunction can be modified or supplemented if either party petitions the court for a more definite or specific temporary order based upon the belief that irreparable injury would result to the moving party if no order were issued. The party may request that the court:

1. Restrain any party from transferring, encumbering, concealing, or in any way disposing of any property, except in the usual course of business or for the necessities of life, and, if so restrained, require him or her to notify the moving party of any proposed extraordinary expenditures made after the order is issued;
2. Enjoin a party from molesting or disturbing the peace of the other party or of any child; and
3. Exclude a party from the family home or from the home of the other party upon a showing that physical or emotional harm would otherwise result.

Such a temporary injunction may be obtained without notice to the other party. However, the party to whom the temporary injunction is directed may appear before the court and move for dissolution or modification of the temporary injunction.

C.R.S. § 18-6-803.5 provides that whenever a police officer is shown a certified copy of a restraining order that restrains and enjoins any person from threatening, beating, striking, or assaulting any other person, or requires the person to remove himself or herself from certain premises and to refrain from loitering, entering, or remaining near the premises thereafter, or requires the doing or refraining from doing of any other act stated therein, it is the duty of the police officer to remove the violator from the premises or arrest said violator and take him or her immediately before the court that issued the restraining order. If that court is not in session, the violator is to be taken to the nearest jail to await further action of the court until the convening of the court's next session.

When a client consents, a psychotherapist may be asked to testify at the temporary orders hearing and to render opinions as to the effects of any emotional abuse inflicted upon a victim.

Summary. Psychotherapists should recognize that the temporary restraining orders described above are effective only to the extent that the party to whom they are directed complies with them. Although the court will undertake appropriate steps to punish a violation of its restraining order, the nature of domestic violence limits the overall effectiveness of such orders. Accordingly, a psychotherapist should counsel that such orders do not stop bullets, nor do they, in all cases, stop the violence. Hence, temporary residence at a safe-house or shelter should be considered. One should not rely solely upon restraining orders for safety.

5.04 Involuntary Mental Health Commitments

C.R.S. §§ 27-65-101, *et seq.*, provide limitations and standards for the care and treatment of the mentally ill. The statutes were enacted by the General Assembly in order to:

1. Secure for each person who may be mentally ill such care and treatment as will be suited to the needs of the person and ensure that such care and treatment are skillfully and humanely administered with full respect for the person's dignity and personal integrity.
2. Deprive a person of his or her liberty for purposes of treatment or care only when less restrictive alternatives are unavailable and only when his or her safety or the safety of others is endangered.
3. Provide the fullest possible measure of privacy, dignity, and other rights to persons undergoing care and treatment for mental illness.
4. Encourage the use of voluntary rather than coercive measures to secure treatment and care for mental illness.
5. Provide appropriate information to family members concerning the location and fact of admission of mentally ill persons to inpatient or residential care and treatment.
6. Encourage the appropriate participation of family members in the care and treatment of a mentally ill person and, when appropriate, provide information to family members in order to facilitate such participation.

Emergency 72-Hour Hold. C.R.S. § 27-65-105 sets forth two emergency procedures by which a person appearing to be mentally ill may be taken into custody and confined for a 72-hour evaluation and treatment. Under C.R.S. § 27-65-105, a person may be held for a 72-hour evaluation when he or she appears to be mentally ill (and as a result, an imminent danger to self or others) or gravely disabled. Mental retardation, however, is insufficient to either justify or exclude a finding of mental illness within the provisions of this article.

C.R.S. § 27-65-105(1)(a) provides that a peace officer, a medical doctor or psychologist, a registered professional nurse, a licensed marriage and family therapist, a licensed professional counselor, or a licensed clinical social worker may temporarily commit a mentally ill person into custody, or cause such person to be taken into custody and placed in a facility of the Department of Human Services for a 72-hour treatment and evaluation. In order for an intervening professional to initiate a 72-hour hold, the following conditions must be present:

1. The person must appear to be mentally ill, meaning that he or she suffers a substantial disorder of cognitive, volitional, or emotional processes that grossly impairs judgment or capacity to recognize reality and control behavior.
2. As a result of such mental illness, the person appears to be an imminent danger to others, or to himself or herself, or appears to be gravely disabled.
3. The intervening professional must have *probable cause* to believe that there is in fact an appearance of mental illness or that the person is an imminent danger to self or others or is gravely disabled.

A Form M-1 is included in the Forms section of this book. A Form M-1 may be signed by a licensed mental health professional or by a peace officer when probable cause exists to detain a client for a 72-hour hold.

A 72-hour hold may also be ordered by the court when an affidavit sworn to or affirmed before a judge contains sufficient facts to establish that the person appears to be mentally ill and, as a result of such mental illness, appears to be an imminent danger to others or to himself or herself, or appears to be gravely disabled. The court may then order the person described in the affidavit to be taken into custody and placed on hold for a 72-hour evaluation at a designated facility.

Any person taken into custody for a 72-hour hold must not be detained in a jail, lockup, or other place used for the confinement of persons charged with or convicted of penal offenses. Such place may be used, however, if no other suitable place of confinement for treatment and evaluation is readily available. In such cases, the person must be detained separately from those persons charged with or convicted of penal offenses and must be held for a period not to exceed

24 hours, excluding Saturdays, Sundays, and holidays, after which time he or she shall be transferred to an appropriate facility.

Each person taken into custody and confinement under 72-hour detention must be examined at least every 12 hours by a peace officer, nurse, or physician, or by an appropriate staff professional of the nearest designated or approved mental health treatment facility to determine if the person is receiving appropriate care consistent with his or her mental condition.

Any person admitted to a 72-hour treatment and evaluation facility must receive an evaluation as soon after admittance as possible and must receive such treatment and care as his or her condition requires for the full period he or she is held. Such person must be released before 72 hours have elapsed if, in the opinion of the professional in charge of the evaluation, the person no longer requires evaluation or treatment. Persons who have been detained for 72-hour evaluation and treatment must be released, referred for further care and treatment on a voluntary basis, or certified for short-term treatment by a court.

Court-Ordered Evaluations. C.R.S. § 27-65-106 provides that any person alleged to be mentally ill, who, as a result of mental illness, is a danger to others or to himself or herself, or is gravely disabled, may be ordered to submit to an evaluation of his or her condition. Such an order may be issued when any individual petitions the court in the county where the mentally ill person resides or is physically present and alleges that the person appears to be mentally ill and, as a result of such mental illness, appears to be a danger to others or to himself or herself, or appears to be gravely disabled, and requests that an evaluation of the person's condition be made.

The petition for a court-ordered evaluation must contain the following:

1. The name and address of the petitioner and his or her interest in the case.
2. The name of the person for whom the evaluation is sought (who will be designated as the respondent) and, if known to the petitioner, the address, age, sex, marital status, and occupation of the respondent.
3. Allegations of fact indicating that the respondent may have a mental illness and, as a result of the mental illness, may be a

danger to others or to himself or herself, or gravely disabled and showing reasonable grounds to warrant an evaluation.

4. The name and address of every person known or believed by the petitioner to be legally responsible for the care, support, and maintenance of the respondent, if available.
5. The name, address, and telephone number of the attorney, if any, who has most recently represented the respondent. If there is no attorney, there will be a statement as to whether, to the best knowledge of the petitioner, the respondent meets the criteria established by the legal aid agency operating in the county or city and county to represent a client.

Upon receipt of a petition containing the above requirements, the court must designate a facility, approved by the Executive Director of the Department of Human Services or a professional person, to provide screening of the respondent to determine whether there is probable cause to believe the allegations.

Following the screening, the facility or professional person must file a report with the court. This report must make a recommendation as to whether there is probable cause to believe that the respondent is mentally ill and, as a result of mental illness, is a danger to others or to himself or herself, or is gravely disabled, as well as a report on whether the respondent will voluntarily receive evaluation or treatment. A copy of the report must be furnished to the respondent or his or her attorney or personal representative.

Whenever, by petition and the foregoing screening, it appears to the satisfaction of the court that probable cause exists to believe that the respondent is mentally ill and, as a result of such mental illness, is a danger to others or to himself or herself, or is gravely disabled, and that efforts have been made to secure the cooperation of the respondent who has refused or failed to accept evaluation voluntarily, the court will issue an order for evaluation authorizing a peace officer to take the respondent into custody and place him or her in a facility designated by the Executive Director of the Department of Human Services for 72-hour treatment and evaluation. At the time of taking the respondent into custody, a copy of the petition and the order for evaluation must be given to the respondent and promptly given thereafter to any one person designated by such respondent and to the person in charge of the 72-hour treatment and evaluation facility.

The respondent must be evaluated as promptly as possible and shall in no event be detained longer than 72 hours under the court order, excluding Saturdays, Sundays, and holidays if treatment and evaluation services are not available on those days. Within that time, the respondent must be released, referred for further care and treatment on a voluntary basis, or certified for short-term treatment.

At the time the respondent is taken into custody for evaluation, or within a reasonable time thereafter, unless a responsible relative is in possession of the respondent's personal property, the peace officer taking the respondent into custody must take reasonable precautions to preserve and safeguard the personal property in the possession of or on the premises occupied by the respondent.

When a person is involuntarily admitted to a 72-hour treatment and evaluation facility, such person or his or her duly appointed representative must be advised by the facility director that such person is going to be examined with regard to his or her mental condition. The person must also be advised of his or her right to obtain and consult with any attorney at any time, and if he or she cannot afford to pay an attorney, upon proof of indigence, one will be appointed by the court without cost.

M-1 Process/Certification for Short-Term Treatment. C.R.S. § 27-65-107 provides that if a person has been detained for 72 hours under C.R.S. § 27-65-105 or a respondent has been detained under court order for evaluation pursuant to C.R.S. § 27-65-106, and has received an evaluation, he or she may be certified for not more than three months of short-term treatment under the following conditions:

1. The 72-hour treatment and evaluation staff have found the person has a mental illness and, as a result of the mental illness, is a danger to others or to himself or herself, or is gravely disabled.
2. The person has been advised of the availability of, but has not accepted, voluntary treatment. If reasonable grounds exist to believe that the person will not remain in a voluntary treatment program, his or her acceptance of voluntary treatment shall not preclude certification.

The facility must file a certification of such facts with the court in the county in which the respondent resided or was physically present immediately prior to being taken into custody. Thereafter and within

24 hours, copies of the certification must be personally delivered to the respondent, and a copy kept by the evaluation facility as part of the respondent's record. The respondent must also be asked to designate one other person whom he or she wishes informed regarding certification. If he or she is incapable of making such a designation at the time the certification is delivered, he or she must be asked to designate such person as soon as he or she is capable. The respondent must also be given a written notice that a hearing on his or her certification for short-term treatment may be had before the court or a jury upon written request directed to the court.

Whenever a certificate is filed with the court, the court will appoint an attorney for the respondent. If the respondent cannot afford any attorney, the court will appoint counsel from the legal services program or private counsel to represent the respondent. The attorney will be provided with a copy of the certification immediately upon his or her appointment. Any waiver of the right to counsel must be knowingly and intelligently made in writing and filed with the court by the respondent.

The respondent may at any time file a written request that the certification for short-term treatment be reviewed by the court or that the treatment be on an out-patient basis. If requested, the court must hear the matter within ten days of the request and give notice to the respondent, his or her attorney, and the certifying and treating professional of the time and place of the hearing. At the conclusion of the hearing, the court may enter or confirm the certification for short-term treatment, discharge the respondent, or enter any other appropriate order, subject to available appropriations.

C.R.S. § 27-65-108 provides that if the professional person in charge of the evaluation and treatment of the respondent believes that a period longer than three months is necessary for treatment, he or she must file an extended certification with the court. No extended certification for treatment can be for a period of more than three months. The respondent is entitled to a hearing on the extended certification under the same conditions of the original certification.

Long-Term Care and Treatment. C.R.S. § 27-65-109 provides that whenever a respondent has received short-term treatment for five consecutive months, the professional person in charge of the evaluation and treatment may file a petition with the court for long-term care and treatment under the following conditions:

1. The professional staff member providing short-term treatment has analyzed the respondent's condition and has found that the respondent has a mental illness and, as a result of the mental illness, is a danger to others or to himself or herself, or is gravely disabled.
2. The respondent has been advised of the availability of, but has not accepted, voluntary treatment. If reasonable grounds exist to believe that the respondent will not remain in a voluntary treatment program, his or her acceptance of voluntary treatment shall not preclude an order pursuant to C.R.S. § 27-65-109.
3. The facility that will provide long-term care and treatment has been designated or approved by the Executive Director of the Department of Human Services to provide such care and treatment.

Every petition for long-term care and treatment must include a request for a hearing before the court prior to the expiration of six months from the date of original certification. A copy of the petition must be delivered personally to the respondent and mailed to his or her attorney of record. Within ten days after receipt of the petition, the respondent or his or her attorney may request a jury trial.

The court or jury will determine whether the foregoing conditions have been met and whether the respondent is mentally ill and, as a result, is a danger to others or to himself or herself, or is gravely disabled. The court will thereupon issue an order of long-term care and treatment not to exceed six months, or discharge the respondent for whom the long-term care and treatment was sought, or enter any other appropriate order, subject to available appropriations.

Any order for long-term care and treatment must grant custody of the respondent to the Department of Human Services for placement with an agency or facility. When a petition contains a request that a specific legal disability be imposed or that a specific legal right be deprived, the court may order the disability imposed or the right deprived if it or a jury has determined that the respondent is mentally ill or gravely disabled and that, by reason thereof, the person is unable to competently exercise the right or perform the function for which the disability is sought to be imposed.

An original order of long-term care and treatment expires upon the date it specifies, unless further extended. If an extension is sought, the professional in charge of the evaluation and treatment must certify to the court at least 30 days prior to the expiration date of the order that an extension of such order is necessary for the care and treatment of the respondent. A copy of the certification must be delivered to the respondent and mailed to his or her attorney of record. At least 20 days before the expiration of the order, the court must give written notice to the respondent and his or her attorney that a hearing on the extension may be had before the court or a jury upon written request to the court within ten days after receipt of the notice. If no hearing is requested within such time, the court may proceed. However, if a hearing is timely requested, it must be held before the expiration date of the order in force. If the court or jury finds that the mental illness continues and, as a result, the respondent is a danger to others or to himself or herself, or is gravely disabled, the court must issue an extension of the order. Any extension must be for a period of not more than six months, but there may be as many extensions as the court orders.

Termination and Escape. Certifications for short-term treatment, extended certification, or an order for long-term care and treatment, or any extensions thereof, must terminate as soon as, in the opinion of the professional person in charge of treatment of the respondent, the respondent has received sufficient benefit from such treatment for him or her to leave. Whenever this occurs, the professional person in charge of providing treatment must notify the court in writing within five days of the termination. The professional person may also prescribe day care, night care, or any other similar mode of treatment prior to termination.

Before termination, an escaped respondent may be returned to the facility by order of the court without a hearing, or by the superintendent or director of such facility without order of court.

Right to Treatment. C.R.S. § 27-65-116 provides that any person receiving evaluation or treatment is entitled to medical and psychiatric care and treatment that is suited to meet his or her individual needs, delivered in such a way as to keep him or her in the least restrictive environment and to include the opportunity for participation of family members in his or her program or care and treatment when appropriate.

Patient's Rights. C.R.S. § 27-65-117 sets forth the following rights for persons receiving evaluation, care, or mental health treatment:

1. To receive and send sealed correspondence, without such correspondence being opened, delayed, held, or censored.
2. To have access to letter-writing materials, including postage, and to have staff members of the facility assist him or her if he or she is unable to write, prepare, and mail correspondence.
3. To have ready access to telephones, both to make and to receive calls in privacy.
4. To have frequent and convenient opportunities to meet with visitors and to see his or her attorney, clergy, or physician at any time.
5. To wear his or her own clothes, keep and use his or her personal possessions, and keep and be allowed to spend reasonable sums of his or her own money.
6. To receive a written copy of all of his or her rights.

The person's rights may be denied for good cause only by the professional person providing treatment. Denial of any right, however, shall in all cases be entered into the person's treatment record and made available, upon request, to the person or his or her attorney. No person admitted to a facility shall be fingerprinted unless required by other provisions of law. A person may be photographed upon admission for identification and administrative purposes of the facility. However, such photographs shall be confidential and shall not be released by the facility, except pursuant to a court order.

In addition to the foregoing, C.R.S. § 27-65-120 provides that any person receiving evaluation, care, or treatment shall be given the opportunity to exercise his or her right to register and to vote in primary and general elections. The agency or facility providing evaluation, care, or treatment shall assist such persons, upon their request, in obtaining voter registration forms and applications for absentee ballots.

Federal Law Concerning Patients' Rights. The federal statute that guarantees rights to patients in a federal mental health program or facility is 42 U.S.C. § 9501. This statute ensures for mental health patients the following rights:

1. The right to appropriate treatment and services in a setting that is supportive of the person's personal liberty, under conditions that restrict liberty only to the extent necessary, considering the individual's treatment needs.
2. The right to an individualized written treatment plan, which is to be developed promptly. A patient has the right to treatment based on this plan, the right to periodic review of treatment, and the right to appropriate revision of the plan, including a description of mental health services that may be needed after the individual is discharged from the mental health program or facility.
3. The right to ongoing participation, in a manner appropriate to the individual's capabilities, *in the planning of the mental health services* that will be provided. In this regard, a patient has the right to be provided with a reasonable explanation, in terms appropriate to the individual's condition, of the following:
    a. The person's general mental condition;
    b. The objectives of treatment;
    c. The nature of the treatment, and any significant adverse effects of it;
    d. The reasons why a particular treatment is considered appropriate;
    e. The reasons why access to certain visitors may not be appropriate; and
    f. Any appropriate alternative treatments, services, and mental health providers that are available.
4. The right *not* to receive a course of treatment pursuant to the treatment plan unless the person has given voluntary, informed consent in writing. This does not apply to emergency treatment or to a situation where a person has been committed by a court to a treatment program or a facility.
5. The right not to participate in experimentation in the absence of voluntary informed consent in writing, and the right to appropriate protection in connection with such participation, including the right to a reasonable explanation of the procedure to be followed, the benefits to be expected, the relative advantages of alternative treatments, and the potential discomfort and risks, as well as the right and opportunity to revoke such consent.
6. The right to freedom from restraint or seclusion, other than as a course of treatment or during an emergency, if such restraint or

seclusion is ordered and documented in writing by a mental health professional.

7. The right to a humane treatment environment that affords reasonable protection from harm and appropriate privacy with regard to personal needs.
8. The right to confidentiality.
9. The right to access, upon request, to such person's mental health records, except a patient may be refused access to information that was provided by a third party under assurances that it would remain confidential. In addition, a patient may be refused access to information if a mental health professional determines, in writing, that access would be detrimental to the patient's health.
10. The right, in a residential or in-patient setting, to converse with others privately, to have convenient and reasonable access to the telephone and mail, and to see visitors during regularly scheduled hours, except that a patient may be refused access to visitors if a mental health professional determines that it may be detrimental to the patient.
11. The right to be informed of these rights at the time of admission and periodically thereafter in terms appropriate to the individual's condition.
12. The right to assert grievances with respect to infringement of these rights, including the right to have grievances considered in a fair, timely, and impartial grievance procedure established by the program or facility.
13. The right to a qualified advocate, as well as the right of access to any available rights protection services within the program or facility and within the state mental health system, for the purpose of receiving assistance in understanding, exercising, and protecting these rights.
14. The right to exercise these rights without reprisal in any form.
15. The right to an appropriate referral to other providers of mental health services upon discharge from in-patient treatment.

Confidentiality of Records. C.R.S. § 27-65-121 and C.R.S. § 27-65-122 set forth detailed procedures for the maintenance of records and the release of information to third parties. See section 2.16 of this book for a discussion of such requirements.

Imposition of Legal Disability and Deprivation of Legal Rights. C.R.S. § 27-65-127 sets forth the procedures that must be followed by any interested person desiring to obtain a determination as to the imposition of a legal disability or the deprivation of a legal right for any person who has a mental illness and is a danger to himself or herself or others, or is gravely disabled or insane. Such interested person may petition the court for a specific finding as to such disability or deprivation of a legal right. The petition must set forth the disability to be imposed or the legal right to be deprived and the reasons therefor. The court may impose disability or may deprive a person of a legal right only upon finding that the respondent has a mental illness and is a danger to himself or herself or others, or is gravely disabled or insane, and that the requested disability or deprivation is both necessary and desirable.

No legal disability may be imposed, nor a legal right be deprived, for a period of more than six months without a review hearing by the court at the end of six months, at which time the findings previously entered by the court may be reaffirmed to justify continuance of the disability or deprivation.

Whenever any proceedings are instituted for the imposition of a legal disability or deprivation of a legal right, the court must appoint (1) an attorney to represent the respondent, and (2) other professional persons to assist the respondent in the preparation of his or her case. Upon demand, the respondent shall have the right to a trial on all issues by a jury of six. The burden of proof is upon the person seeking imposition of disability or deprivation of a legal right, and such must be proven by clear and convincing evidence.

5.05 Care and Treatment of a Minor

The provision of mental health services to a minor (one who is under the age of 18) raises various legal issues. These include: (1) whether the minor may consent to treatment, or whether parental consent is required for treatment; (2) whether the minor, or his or her parents, must be provided with the disclosure statement and must sign it; (3) whether, in treating a minor, the duty of confidentiality prevents a psychotherapist from disclosing confidential communications with the client's parents; (4) whether a minor may consent to in-patient mental health treatment; (5) whether the minor, or his or her parents, will be obligated to pay for treatment expenses; and (6) whether the due process rights of a minor who is subject to a 72-hour hold or who is receiving treatment under a court-ordered certification vary in any way from the due process rights of an adult.

C.R.S. § 27-65-103 provides that a minor who is 15 years of age or older "may consent to receive mental health services to be rendered by a facility or a professional person." A "facility" means a public hospital, a licensed private hospital, a community mental health center, a clinic, or a residential childcare facility that provides treatment for mentally ill persons. A "professional person," from whom a 15-year-old may consent to receive mental health services, is "a person licensed to practice medicine in this state or a psychologist certified to practice in this state."

Regarding the issue of confidentiality, C.R.S. § 27-65-103(2) provides: "The professional person rendering mental health services to a minor may, with or without the consent of the minor, advise the parent or legal guardian of the minor of the services given or needed."

Note that C.R.S. § 27-65-103(2) only authorizes disclosure by the therapist of the fact that services are needed or are being given.

With regard to the due process rights of a minor who is the subject of a voluntary commitment, C.R.S. § 27-65-103(5) provides that the need for continuing hospitalization of all minors who are voluntary patients shall be formally reviewed at least every two months. This review shall be conducted by an independent professional person, who is not a member of the minor's treatment team. The independent professional person shall determine whether the minor continues to meet the criteria for hospitalization.

In circumstances where a minor does *not* consent to mental health treatment, consent for treatment must be obtained from the minor's parent, guardian, or other legal representative authorized to provide such consent. In general, if a minor has voluntarily consented to mental health treatment, the minor should give consent to the release of any records or information concerning treatment. On the other hand, if parental consent was necessary in order to provide mental health services to the minor, then authorization from the parent or guardian must be obtained for release of confidential information.

In Colorado, a parent or legal guardian is obligated to provide support for minor children up to the age of their majority (age 18) or up to the time when they become emancipated. Accordingly, it is the parent's obligation to pay for any mental health services provided to a minor.

The Child Mental Health Treatment Act. In 1999, the Colorado Legislature enacted the Child Mental Health Treatment Act. The public policy supporting this enactment states that "it is desirable to assist children with mental health needs and such children's families ... [and] to make mental health services more available to these families desiring such treatment for their children." The legislative declaration contained in C.R.S. § 27-67-102 provides that in many situations, an action in dependency or neglect under the Children's Code is neither appropriate nor warranted in circumstances where "the parents are loving, caring parents who have become increasingly frustrated in their attempts to navigate the various governmental systems including child welfare, mental health, law enforcement, juvenile justice, education, and youth corrections in an attempt to find help for their children."

C.R.S. § 27-67-104 provides that a parent or guardian may apply to a mental health agency on behalf of a minor child for mental health treatment services in a situation where the parent believes that his or her child is "at risk of out-of-home placement." The term "mental health agency" means the community mental health center serving children in a particular area or the mental health assessment and services agency serving children in a particular area who are receiving Medicaid.

At the time of the assessment of a child by the mental health agency, the agency shall evaluate the child and clinically assess the child's need for mental health services and, when warranted, provide treatment services as may be necessary and in the best interests of the child and the child's family. Subject to available state appropriations, the mental health agency "shall be responsible for providing the treatment services, including any in-home family mental health treatment, other family preservation services, residential treatment, or any post-residential follow-up services that may be appropriate for the child's or family's needs." At the time of the assessment by the mental health agency, if residential services are denied, the mental health agency shall advise the family in writing of the appeal process available.

This statute further provides for its repeal, unless it is re-enacted by the Colorado Legislature.

5.06 Treatment of Alcoholics

Emergency Commitment. C.R.S. § 27-81-111 provides that when any person is intoxicated or incapacitated by alcohol and clearly dangerous to the health and safety of himself or herself or others, such person shall be taken into protective custody by law enforcement authorities or an emergency service patrol, acting with probable cause, and placed in an approved treatment facility. If no such facilities are available, such person may be detained in an emergency medical facility or jail, but only for so long as necessary to prevent injury to himself or herself or others or to prevent a breach of the peace. A taking into protective custody under this statute is not an arrest, and no entry or other record is made to indicate that the person has been arrested or charged with a crime.

Under C.R.S. § 27-81-111, a law enforcement officer, emergency service patrolman, physician, spouse, guardian, relative of the person to be committed, or any other responsible person may make a written application for emergency commitment to the administrator of an approved alcohol treatment facility. The application must state the circumstances requiring the emergency commitment, including the applicant's personal observations and the specific statements of others, if any, upon which he or she relies in making the application. A copy of the application must be furnished to the person to be committed.

If the approved treatment facility administrator or his or her authorized designee approves the application, the person shall be committed, evaluated, and treated for a period not to exceed five days. The person will be brought to the facility by a peace officer, the emergency service patrol, or any interested person. If necessary, the court may be contacted to issue an order to the police or sheriff's department to transport the person to the facility.

If the approved treatment facility administrator or his or her authorized designee determines that the application fails to sustain the grounds for emergency commitment, the commitment request will be refused and the person detained will be immediately released, and the person shall be encouraged to seek voluntary treatment if appropriate.

When the administrator determines that the grounds for commitment no longer exist, he or she must discharge the person committed. No person committed under this statute may be detained in any treatment facility for more than five days, except that a person may be detained for longer than five days at the approved treatment facility if, in that period of time, a petition for involuntary commitment has been filed pursuant to C.R.S. § 27-81-112. A person may not be detained longer than ten days after the date of filing of the petition for involuntary commitment.

Whenever a person is involuntarily detained pursuant to C.R.S. § 27-81-111, he or she must immediately be advised by the facility administrator or his or her authorized designee, both orally and in writing, of his or her right to challenge such detention by application to the courts for a writ of *habeas corpus,* to be represented by counsel at every stage of any proceedings relating to his or her commitment and recommitment, and to have counsel appointed by the court or provided by the court if he or she wants the assistance of counsel and is unable to obtain counsel.

Involuntary Commitment of Alcoholics. C.R.S. § 27-81-112 provides that a person may be committed to the custody of the Division of Alcohol and Drug Abuse upon the petition of a spouse, guardian, relative, physician, an advanced practice nurse, the administrator in charge of any approved treatment facility, or any other responsible person. The petition must allege that the person is an alcoholic and that he or she has threatened, attempted to inflict, or inflicted physical harm on himself or herself or on another, and that unless committed, he or she is likely to inflict physical harm on himself or herself or on another, or that he or she is incapacitated by alcohol. A refusal to undergo treatment does not constitute evidence of lack of judgment as to the need for treatment. The petition must be accompanied by a certificate of a licensed physician who has examined the person within two days before submission of the petition, unless that person whose commitment is sought has refused to submit to a medical examination, in which case the fact of refusal must be alleged in the petition. The certificate must set forth the physician's findings in support of the allegations of the petition.

The petition for commitment will not be accepted unless there is documentation of the refusal by the person to be committed to accessible and affordable voluntary treatment. Such documentation may include, but shall not be limited to, physician's statements, advanced practice nurse's statements, notations in the person's medical or law enforcement records, or witnesses' statements.

Upon the filing of the petition, the court will fix a date for a hearing no later than ten days after the date the petition was filed. A copy of the petition and of the notice of the hearing will be personally served on the petitioner, the person whose commitment is sought, and one of his or her parents or legal guardian if he or she is a minor. Additionally, a copy of the petition and notice of hearing must be mailed: (1) to the Division of Alcohol and Drug Abuse; (2) to counsel for the person whose commitment is sought; (3) to the administrator in charge of the approved treatment facility to which the person may have been committed for emergency treatment; and (4) to any other person the court believes advisable.

At the hearing, the court will hear all relevant testimony, including, if possible, the testimony of at least one licensed physician who has examined the person whose commitment is sought. The person must be present unless the court believes that his or her presence is likely to be injurious to him or her. In this event, the court will appoint a guardian ad litem to represent him or her throughout the proceeding. If the person has refused to be examined by a licensed physician, he or she will be given an opportunity to be examined by a court-appointed licensed physician. If he or she refuses and there is sufficient evidence to believe that the allegations of the petition are true or if the court believes that more medical evidence is necessary, the court may commit the person to a licensed hospital for a period of not more than five days for a diagnostic examination. In such event, the court will schedule a further hearing for final determination of commitment, in no event later than five days after the first hearing.

If, after hearing all relevant evidence, the court finds that grounds for involuntary commitment have been established by clear and convincing proof, it must make an order of commitment to the division. The division has the right to delegate physical custody of the person to an appropriate approved treatment facility. It may not order commitment of a person unless it determines that the division is able to provide adequate and appropriate treatment.

Upon commitment of a person to the Division of Alcohol and Drug Abuse by the court, the court may issue an order to the sheriff to transport the person committed to the facility designated by the division.

A person committed as provided in C.R.S. § 27-81-112 will remain in the custody of the division for treatment for a period of 30 days unless sooner discharged. At the end of the 30-day period, he or she must be discharged automatically unless the division, before expiration of the period, obtains a court order for his or her recommitment for a further period of 90 days unless sooner discharged.

A person recommitted who has not been discharged by the division before the end of the 90-day period must be discharged at the expiration of that period unless the division, before expiration of the period, obtains another court order. Only two recommitment orders are permitted.

Upon the filing of a petition for recommitment, the court will fix a date for hearing no later than ten days after the date the petition was filed, and the court will proceed with a hearing.

A person committed to the custody of the Division of Alcohol and Drug Abuse must be discharged at any time before the end of the period for which he or she has been committed if either of the following conditions is met:

1. In case of an alcoholic committed on the grounds that he or she is likely to inflict physical harm upon another, that he or she no longer has an alcoholic condition that requires treatment or the likelihood no longer exists; or
2. In case of an alcoholic committed on the grounds of the need for treatment and/or incapacity, that the incapacity no longer exists, further treatment will not be likely to bring about significant improvement in the person's condition, or that treatment is no longer appropriate.

The court must inform the person whose commitment or recommitment is sought of his or her right to contest the application, to be represented by counsel at every level of any proceedings relating to his or her commitment and recommitment, and to have counsel appointed by the court or provided by the court if he or she wants the assistance of counsel and is unable to obtain counsel. If the court believes that the person needs the assistance of counsel, the court must appoint counsel for him or her regardless of his or her wishes. The person whose commitment or recommitment is sought must be informed of his or her right to be examined by a licensed physician of his or her choice. If the person is unable to obtain a licensed physician and requests examination by a physician, the court will employ a licensed physician.

Patients in any approved alcohol treatment facility must be granted opportunities for continuing visitation and communication with their families and friends consistent with an effective treatment program. Patients shall be permitted to consult with counsel at any time. Neither mail nor other communication to or from a patient in any approved treatment facility may be intercepted, read, or censored.

5.07 Care and Treatment of the Developmentally Disabled

C.R.S. §§ 27-10.5-101, *et seq.,* set forth in general terms provisions for the care and treatment of the developmentally disabled. Developmental disability means a disability that is manifested before the person reaches 22 years of age. It constitutes a substantial handicap of the affected individual and is attributable to mental retardation or related conditions that include cerebral palsy, epilepsy, autism, or other neurological conditions when such conditions result in impairment of general intellectual functioning or adaptive behavior similar to that of mentally retarded persons.

In C.R.S. § 27-10.5-101, the rights of the developmentally disabled are identified in a compassionate legislative declaration, which promotes community support for developmentally disabled persons to "ensure the fullest measure of privacy, dignity, rights, and privileges" for developmentally disabled persons.

Limitation on Liability of Developmental Disability Service Providers

In 2003, the Colorado Legislature enacted C.R.S. § 13-21-117.5, which limits the liability of developmental disability service providers. The law provides that neither developmentally disabled individuals nor their family members may file a lawsuit against a service provider, unless the claimant has pursued "dispute resolution or other applicable intervention … within one year after the date of the discovery of the injury or grievance …."

A claimant's submission of proof that a dispute resolution request has been filed and no action was taken by the department within 90 days "shall be a jurisdictional prerequisite to any action" brought by the claimant. Therefore, whenever a developmental disability service provider receives a letter from an attorney threatening a suit or forwarding a complaint, that provider should immediately respond by agreeing that the matter be submitted for dispute resolution pursuant to C.R.S. § 13-21-117.5.

Another provision of the same statute states that a provider of services "shall not be liable for damages in any civil action for failure to warn or protect any person against the violent, assaultive, disorderly, or harassing behavior of a person with a developmental disability, nor shall any such provider be held civilly liable for failure to predict or prevent such behavior," except where a "serious and credible threat of imminent physical violence and serious bodily injury against a specific person or persons" has been made by a person with a developmental disability.

If there is a duty to warn of such a threat, that duty shall be discharged "by the provider making reasonable and timely efforts to notify any person or persons specifically threatened." If the person threatened with imminent physical violence is a person with a developmental disability under a provider's care, "the provider shall take reasonable action to protect such person from serious bodily injury until the threat can reasonably be deemed to have abated."

Imposition of Legal Disability. C.R.S. § 27-10.5-110 sets forth the conditions under which a legal disability may be imposed or a legal right removed from a person with developmental disabilities. Under C.R.S. § 27-10.5-110, any interested person may petition the court to impose a legal disability or to remove a legal right that affects the rights of the disabled person to contract, determine a place of abode or provisions of care and treatment, to operate a motor vehicle, or other similar rights.

Prior to granting the petition, the court must find that the person subject to the petition has been determined to be a person with developmental disabilities and that the requested disability or removal is both necessary and desirable in order to implement the individual habilitation plan developed for the person with developmental disabilities under the supervision of a developmental disabilities professional.

If a petition seeks to impose a disability or remove a legal right related to the selection of a place of abode, the court must also find that, based on the recent overt actions or omissions of the person subject to the petition, and because of his or her developmental disability, without the removal of said right, such person poses a probable threat of serious physical harm to himself or herself or others, or is unable to care for his or her own needs to the extent that his or her own life or safety is seriously threatened, and that the place of abode requested in the petition is the least restrictive habilitation setting appropriate for the individual needs of the person with developmental disabilities.

Within six months after legal disability has been imposed or a legal right has been removed, the court shall hold a hearing to review its order and either reaffirm the findings and continue the legal disability or removal, or remove the legal disability or restore the legal rights to the person subject to the petition.

When a petition is filed, the court shall appoint an attorney to represent the person subject to the petition. Such person may retain his or her own counsel at any time. Additionally, the court, at the request of an indigent respondent, shall appoint one or more developmental disabilities professionals of the respondent's choice to assist the respondent in the preparation of his or her case. The fees for both the attorney and the developmental disabilities professionals shall be paid for by the court for all indigent respondents.

The burden of proof is upon the party seeking imposition of a disability or removal of a legal right, and the standard of proof is by clear and convincing evidence.

Rights of the Developmentally Disabled. Pursuant to C.R.S. § 27-10.5-112, developmentally disabled persons have the same legal rights and responsibilities guaranteed to all other individuals under the federal and state constitutions and laws. Other statutes confer the following rights on developmentally disabled persons:

1. The right to have an individualized plan developed jointly by professional persons, the person receiving the services, and such person's parent or guardian (C.R.S. § 27-10.5-113);
2. The right to receive appropriate dental and medical care and treatment for any physical ailments and for the prevention of any illness or disability (C.R.S. § 27-10.5-114);
3. The right to be free from unnecessary or excessive medication (C.R.S. § 27-10.5-114(4));
4. The right to humane care and treatment (C.R.S. § 27-10.5-115);

5. The right to be free from physical restraint except when absolutely necessary to protect the person receiving services from injury to himself or herself or to prevent injury to others, and only if alternative techniques have failed and such restraint imposes the least possible restriction consistent with its purposes (C.R.S. § 27-10.5-115(8));
6. The right to fair employment practices (C.R.S. § 27-10.5-118);
7. The right to religious belief, practices, and worship (C.R.S. § 27-10.5-116);
8. The right to communicate freely and privately with persons of his or her own choosing (C.R.S. § 27-10.5-117(1));
9. The right to receive and send sealed, unopened packages and correspondence without incoming or outgoing packages or correspondence being opened, delayed, held, or censored by any person (C.R.S. § 27-10.5-117(2) and (3));
10. The right to reasonable access to telephones, both to make and receive calls in privacy (C.R.S. § 27-10.5-117(5));
11. The right to reasonable and frequent opportunities to meet with visitors (C.R.S. § 27-10.5-117(5));
12. The right to suitable opportunities for the resident's interaction with persons of their choice (C.R.S. § 27-10.5-117(6));
13. Sterilization rights (C.R.S. § 27-10.5-128);
14. The right to vote in all primary and general elections and to assistance in registering to vote, obtaining applications for absentee ballots, and obtaining absentee ballots (C.R.S. § 27-10.5-119);
15. The right to possession and use of his or her own clothing and personal effects, including the right to receive reasonable amounts of his or her own money or funds held in trust (C.R.S. § 27-10.5-121);
16. The right to establish committees to hear the views and represent the interests of all persons served by an agency serving developmentally disabled persons and to attempt to influence the policies of the agency to the extent that they influence provision of services (C.R.S. § 27-10.5-122);

17. The right to read or have explained any rules or regulations adopted by an approved service agency pertaining to such person's activities (C.R.S. § 27-10.5-123); and
18. The right to be free from discrimination (C.R.S. § 27-10.5-124).

Limitations on Sterilization. C.R.S. § 27-10.5-128 provides that any person with developmental disabilities who is over the age of 18 years and who has given informed consent may be sterilized if all the following conditions are met:

1. The lawful parent or legal guardian of the person with developmental disabilities has consented to the procedure.
2. A psychiatrist or psychologist, who consults with and interviews the person with developmental disabilities, consents to the procedure.
3. A person who works in the field of developmental disabilities who is knowledgeable in it, and who consults with and interviews the person with developmental disabilities, consents to the procedure.

In no event shall a person with developmental disabilities who has not given consent be sterilized.

Any person with developmental disabilities, or the parent, legal guardian, or custodian of said person may, pursuant to C.R.S. § 27-10.5-129, file a petition with the court for sterilization. The only issue before the court will be the capacity to give consent for voluntary sterilization. The court will set a hearing to determine the person's competency to give such consent. The person with developmental disabilities must be physically present at the entire proceeding, represented by counsel, and provided with the opportunity to present testimony and cross-examine witnesses.

5.08 Criminal Insanity

Colorado's criminal statutes recognize the defense of not guilty by reason of insanity. The current test of insanity is set forth in C.R.S. § 16-8-101.5(1) as follows:

> (a) A person who is so diseased or defective in mind at the time of the commission of the act as to be incapable of distinguishing right from wrong with respect to that act is not accountable; except that care should be taken not to confuse such

> mental disease or defect with moral obliquity, mental depravity, or passion growing out of anger, revenge, hatred, or other motives and kindred evil conditions, for, when the act is induced by any of these causes, the person is accountable to the law; or
>
> (b) A person who suffered from a condition of mind caused by mental disease or defect that prevented the person from forming a culpable mental state that is an essential element of the crime charged. . . .

In March 1992, the Colorado Supreme Court decided the case of *People v. Serravo,* 823 P.2d 128 (Colo. 1992). In this case, the jury found the defendant not guilty by reason of insanity in connection with the stabbing of his wife. The defendant contended that God directed him to establish a sports complex in Denver and that this godly mission required him to sever his relationship with his wife, who opposed his efforts. The defendant terminated his relationship with his wife by stabbing her in the back.

The prosecution appealed the acquittal of the defendant and asked the appellate courts to clarify the meaning of the phrase "right from wrong" and to decide from whose viewpoint "right" and "wrong" should be considered, i.e., that of the individual, society generally, or society as expressed by positive law. The defendant contended that right and wrong should be defined by his own personal reference and understanding of right and wrong, while the prosecution argued that right and wrong should be defined by reference to legal right and wrong.

The Colorado Supreme Court rejected both approaches and held that right and wrong refers to a cognitive inability to distinguish right from wrong under existing societal standards of morality rather than under a purely subjective and personal standard of morality.

In deciding the case, the court noted that the use of the prosecution's proposed definition (i.e., knowledge that an act was illegal rather than knowledge that it was immoral) would result in the acquittal of a person who knew that his or her actions were profoundly immoral but did not know that they were prohibited by law. The court determined that such a person should be considered sane, and therefore held accountable for his or her criminal act. Conversely, the court noted that the prosecution's proposed definition would result in the conviction of a person who knew that his or her actions were prohibited by law but did not have any comprehension of the immoral nature of the acts. In the court's opinion, such a person should not be held criminally accountable. Accordingly, it held that right and wrong should always be measured by a societal standard of morality.

Temporary Insanity. Unique legal issues have arisen when defendants have contended that they were temporarily insane for reasons beyond their control. For example, in *People v Low,* 732 P.2d 622 (Colo. 1987), a defendant offered evidence that he had ingested a large quantity of cold medication, which rendered him temporarily incapable of distinguishing right from wrong. The trial court allowed the evidence and found the defendant temporarily insane.

On appeal, the Colorado Court of Appeals ruled that the trial court erred, because temporary insanity is not a mental state recognized under Colorado law. The court held that the defendant should have been required to plead and prove that his insanity was caused by an ongoing mental disease or defect.

Procedural Matters. When a defense of not guilty by reason of insanity is entered, the defendant seeks to avoid legal responsibility on the grounds of his or her insanity. Once the plea has been entered, the trial court orders a sanity examination pursuant to C.R.S. § 16-8-105(1) or C.R.S. § 16-8-105.5. Upon receipt by the court of the sanity examination report, the matter is set for trial on the issue of whether the defendant was sane at the time the offense was committed. There is a presumption of sanity and the defendant carries the burden of introducing evidence of insanity. Once the evidence is introduced, the prosecution then bears the burden to prove that the defendant was sane beyond a reasonable doubt. In such hearings, expert opinions from psychiatrists and psychologists are inevitable. However, evidence of the defendant's sanity or insanity is not limited to experts, since C.R.S. § 16-8-109 allows a lay person to render an opinion as to a defendant's insanity, provided the lay witness had sufficient opportunity to observe the person whose sanity is at issue.

If the defendant is found sane, the case proceeds to trial on the merits. If, on the other hand, the defendant is found not guilty by reason of insanity, the defendant is committed to the custody of the Executive Director of the Department of Human Services until he or she is deemed eligible for release. This commitment is for the purpose of treatment and not punishment.

C.R.S. § 16-8-120(3) sets forth the current test for releasing a defendant who has been found not guilty by reason of insanity and committed. The statute provides that the defendant may be released if the defendant has no abnormal mental condition that would be likely to cause him or her to be dangerous either to himself or herself or to the community in the reasonably foreseeable future, and if he or she is capable of distinguishing right from wrong and has substantial capacity to conform his or her conduct to the requirements of the law.

This issue is determined at a hearing, which may be brought by the court, the prosecutor, or the defendant. The burden of proof is on the defendant to show his or her sanity by a preponderance of the evidence. If the jury or court finds the defendant eligible for release, the trial court has the power to place certain conditions on the release. If such conditions are imposed by the court, the Department of Human Services retains jurisdiction to monitor compliance with the conditions imposed by the court, and to report periodically to the District Attorney concerning the defendant's status. The trial court is also required by C.R.S. § 16-8-115(3) to review the status of the conditionally released defendant every 12 months.

A conditional release may be revoked. This generally occurs when someone has reason to believe that the defendant has violated a condition of the release and reports it to the appropriate authority. When the state has probable cause to believe that a conditional release should be revoked, the prosecutor may apply for a warrant to take the defendant into custody or proceed by way of a summons. Once the defendant is in custody, a petition for revocation of the conditional release must be filed within 72 hours. Thereafter, the defendant is entitled to a preliminary hearing. If no probable cause for revocation is found at this temporary hearing, the defendant will be released. However, the finding that probable cause does exist will result in a temporary revocation and commitment of the defendant, pending a final hearing, which must be held within 30 days.

At the final hearing, the prosecution has the burden to prove by a preponderance of the evidence that the defendant has become ineligible to remain on conditional release. This does not mean that the court has to find that the defendant is dangerous, but only that there has been a violation of the terms or conditions of the conditional release. If the defendant is found ineligible to remain on conditional release, the court will recommit the defendant. If the prosecution fails to fulfill its burden of proof, the defendant is released on the same or modified conditions.

5.09 The Role of the Psychotherapist

Psychotherapists who get involved in any of the foregoing proceedings often become frustrated with the process and results. One explanation for this frustration is that the trial courts are given discretion over such issues, but are required to exercise that discretion consistent with the express public policy of the law. This may not coincide with the psychotherapist's own set of standards and beliefs. The best advice for a psychotherapist involved in such proceedings is to have a clear understanding of the specific nature of the proceedings, as well as those concepts outlined in Chapter 3 concerning how best to testify as an expert.

If a psychologist is appointed by the court to conduct a sanity or competency evaluation, the psychologist should provide the disclosures discussed in Section 4.18 to the defendant who is being evaluated. A form for providing these disclosures is included in the Forms section of this book.

CHAPTER 6: LICENSING CONSIDERATIONS

6.01 Licensed Professionals

The Colorado Legislature has declared that in order to safeguard the public health and safety of the people, and in order to protect the people of this state against the unauthorized, unqualified, and improper application of psychotherapy, psychology, clinical social work, marriage and family therapy, professional counseling, and school psychology, it is necessary that certain regulatory agencies be established. To fulfill this declaration of public policy, Title 12, Article 43, of the Colorado Revised Statutes was enacted in 1988 and has been amended in subsequent years.

The Colorado Legislature has created a new category for those who are seeking licensure as Psychologists, Licensed Marriage and Family Therapists, or as Licensed Professional Counselors, and who have begun the process of completing the required supervised hours of therapy for licensure. The new categories are Psychologist Candidate, Marriage and Family Therapist Candidate, and Licensed Professional Counselor Candidate. To qualify as a candidate, an individual should apply to DORA for this status, after a clinical supervisor has been obtained. Note that in the form Disclosure Statement in the Forms Section of this book, those who are candidates for licensure can disclose this fact to potential clients.

Definitions. Title 12, Article 43, governs the following persons:

1. A "psychologist" is defined as a person who practices psychotherapy and who is a licensed psychologist pursuant to the provisions of Article 43.
2. "Psychology" is defined as the observation, description, evaluation, interpretation, treatment, or modification of behavior, cognitions, or emotions by the application of psychological, behavioral, and physical principles, methods, or procedures, for the purpose of preventing or eliminating symptomatic, maladaptive, or undesired behavior, cognitions, or emotions and of enhanc-

ing interpersonal relationships, work and life adjustment, personal effectiveness, behavioral health, and mental health.

3. "Licensed social worker, licensed independent social worker, or licensed clinical social worker" means a social work practitioner, licensed by the state pursuant to the Mental Health Act.
4. "Social work practice" means the professional application of social work theory and methods by a graduate with a master's degree in social work, a doctoral degree in social work, or a bachelor's degree in social work from an accredited social work program, for the purpose of prevention, assessment, diagnosis, and intervention with individual, family, group, organizational, and societal problems, including alcohol and substance abuse and domestic violence, based on the promotion of biopsychosocial developmental processes, person in environment transactions, and empowerment of the client system. Social work theory and methods are based on known accepted principles that are taught in professional schools of social work in colleges or universities accredited by the Council on Social Work Education.
5. A "marriage and family therapist" is defined as a person who practices psychotherapy and who is a marriage and family therapist licensed pursuant to Article 43.
6. "Marriage and family therapy" means the rendering of professional marriage and family therapy services to individuals, couples, and families, singly or in groups, whether such services are offered directly to the general public or through organizations, either public or private, for a monetary fee. Marriage and family therapy utilizes established principles that recognize the interrelated nature of individual problems and dysfunctions to assess, understand, diagnose, and treat emotional and mental problems, alcohol and substance abuse, and domestic violence, and to modify intrapersonal and interpersonal dysfunctions.
7. A "licensed professional counselor" is defined as a person who practices psychotherapy and who is a professional counselor licensed pursuant to the provisions of Article 43.
8. "Professional counseling" means those activities that assist the person receiving counseling in developing and understanding personal, emotional, social, educational, and vocational development, alcohol and substance abuse, and domestic violence, and in planning and effecting actions to increase functioning or

gain control of his or her behavior in such areas. Such activities include, but are not limited to, skill-building in communications, decision making, problem solving, clarifying values, promoting adaptation to loss and other life changes, developing social skills, restructuring cognitive patterns, defining educational and career goals, and facilitating adjustment to personal crises and conflicts. It includes testing and assessment, and individual and group counseling. Professional counseling follows a planned procedure of intervention that takes place on a regular basis, over a period of time; or, in the cases of testing, assessment, and brief professional counseling, it can be a single intervention.

9. "Registered psychotherapist" means any person whose primary practice is psychotherapy or who holds himself or herself out to the public as being able to practice psychotherapy for compensation and who is not licensed under this Article to practice psychotherapy. "Registered psychotherapist" also means a person who is a certified or licensed school psychologist, licensed pursuant to C.R.S. § 22-60.5-210, who is practicing outside of a school setting.
10. "Psychotherapy" is defined in C.R.S. § 12-43-201(9) as:

    > The treatment, diagnosis, testing, assessment, or counseling in a professional relationship to assist individuals or groups to alleviate mental disorders, understand unconscious or conscious motivations, resolve emotional, relationship, or attitudinal conflicts, or modify behaviors that interfere with effective emotional, social, or intellectual functioning. Psychotherapy follows a planned procedure of intervention that takes place on a regular basis, over a period of time, or in the cases of testing, assessment, and brief psychotherapy, it can be a single intervention.

11. An "Addiction Counselor" is defined as follows. A "Licensed Addiction Counselor" is a person licensed by the Board to provide professional behavioral health disorder treatment, according to C.R.S. § 12-43-801; a "Certified Addiction Counselor" means an individual who has a certificate issued by the Board authorizing the individual to practice addiction counseling commensurate with his or her certification level and scope of practice.

Title Use Restrictions. A person who is licensed pursuant to Title 12, Article 43, is subject to certain defined duties and enjoys certain privileges.

Pursuant to C.R.S. § 12-43-216, the following titles are limited to those who have been licensed or registered: "Licensed clinical social worker," "clinical social worker," "LCSW," "licensed social worker," "LSW," "marriage and family therapist," "LMFT," "professional counselor," "LPC," "psychologist," "psychologist candidate," "psychology," or "psychological." No other persons shall hold themselves out to the public by any title or description of services using those terms, unless authorized to do so by virtue of their licensure or their having registered as a social worker.

A person who is not licensed under Title 12, Article 43, but whose primary practice is psychotherapy or who holds himself or herself out to the public as being able to practice psychotherapy for compensation, is considered to be an registered psychotherapist. These individuals are subject to the provisions of Title 12, Article 43 and therefore must abide by the requirements set forth therein.

Database Registration Requirement. C.R.S. § 12-43-702.5 requires the Board of Registered Psychotherapists to maintain a database of all unlicensed persons practicing psychotherapy in Colorado. Each registered psychotherapist is required to report to the State Board of Registered Psychotherapists such therapist's name, current address, educational qualifications, disclosure statements, therapeutic orientation or methodology, and years of experience in each specialty area for inclusion in the database. At the time of recording of the above information, the psychotherapist must indicate whether or not he or she has been convicted of or entered a plea of guilty or a plea of nolo contendere to any felony or misdemeanor. Each psychotherapist is required to update the above information.

Effective July 1, 1998, no unlicensed person may practice psychotherapy if such person is not included in the database required to be maintained by the State Board of Registered Psychotherapists. Any person who violates this provision commits a class 2 misdemeanor. A subsequent violation is a class 6 felony. Notwithstanding the reporting requirements, no registered psychotherapist may use the term "regulated," "certified," "clinical," "state registered," "state-approved," or any other term, abbreviation, or symbol that would falsely give the impression that the psychotherapist or the service which is being provided is recommended or approved by the state, based solely on inclusion in the database.

Pursuant to C.R.S. § 12-43-215(8), an employee of a community mental health center is not required to comply with the database registration provision unless, as an registered psychotherapist, such a person is practicing psychotherapy outside the scope of his or her employment as an employee of a community mental health center.

Scope of the Mental Health Act. Pursuant to C.R.S. § 12-43-215, the State of Colorado Mental Health Boards do not regulate the following persons:

1. Any person engaged in the practice of religious ministry;
2. Any person who is engaged in the practice of employment or rehabilitation counseling performed in the private and public sectors; except that Title 12, Article 43 does apply to employment or rehabilitation counselors practicing psychotherapy in the field of mental health;
3. Employees of the Department of Social Services, employees of county departments of social services, or personnel under the direct supervision and control of the Department of Social Services or any county department of social services for work undertaken as part of their employment;
4. Certified school psychologists licensed pursuant to C.R.S. § 22-60.5-210, and persons who are not licensed under Article 43 for work undertaken as part of their employment with public schools;
5. Mediators resolving judicial disputes under Part 3 of Title 13, Article 22; and
6. A professional coach, including a life coach, executive coach, personal coach, or business coach, who has had coach-specific training and who serves clients exclusively as a coach, so long as the professional coach does not engage in the practice of psychotherapy or addiction counseling.

6.02 Mandatory Disclosure of Information

C.R.S. § 12-43-214 states that every registered psychotherapist, licensee, or registrant must provide a written disclosure statement containing the following information to each client during the initial client contact:

1. The name, business address, and business phone number of the registered psychotherapist, licensee, or registrant.
2. An explanation of the levels of regulation applicable to mental health professionals under this article and the differences between licensure, registration, and certification, including the educational, experience, and training requirements applicable to the particular level of regulation.
3. A listing of any degrees, credentials, certifications, registrations, and licenses held or obtained by the licensee, registrant, or certificate holder, including the education, experience, and training the licensee, registrant, or certificate holder was required to satisfy in order to obtain the degree, credentials, certifications, registrations, or licenses.
4. A statement indicating that the practice of both licensed or registered persons in the field of psychotherapy is regulated by the division, and an address and telephone number for the board that regulates the licensee, registrant, or certificate holder.
5. A statement indicating that:
    a. In a professional relationship, sexual intimacy is never appropriate and should be reported to the board that licenses, registers, or certifies the licensee, registrant, or certificate holder;
    b. The client is entitled to receive information about the methods of therapy, the techniques used, the duration of therapy, if known, and the fee structure;
    c. The client may seek a second opinion from another therapist or may terminate therapy at any time;
    d. The information provided by the client during therapy sessions is legally confidential, except as provided in C.R.S. § 12-43-218, and except for certain legal exceptions that will be identified by the licensee, registrant, or certificate holder should any such situation arise during therapy; and
    e. If the mental health professional is a registered psychotherapist, a statement indicating that a registered psychotherapist is a psychotherapist listed in the State's database and is authorized by law to practice psy-

chotherapy in Colorado but is not licensed by the State and is not required to satisfy any standardized educational or testing requirements to obtain a registration from the State.

Unless the client, parent, or guardian is unable to write, or refuses or objects, the client, parent, or guardian shall sign the disclosure form *not later than the second visit* with the psychotherapist. You must then give the client a copy of the disclosure statement. If a client or the client's legal representative refuses to sign the disclosure statement, thereby refusing to consent to treatment, the therapist must honor the client's exercise of the right to refuse treatment.

The statute provides that if the client is an adolescent over the age of 15 who is consenting to mental health services pursuant to C.R.S. § 27-65-103, disclosure shall be made to the adolescent. If the client is a child whose parent or legal guardian is consenting to mental health services, disclosure shall be made to the parent or legal guardian.

In residential, institutional, or other settings where psychotherapy may be provided by multiple providers, disclosure shall be made by the primary therapist. The institution shall also provide a statement to the patient concerning the regulation of psychotherapy and the client's right to see information on methods of therapy, the right to seek a second opinion, the inappropriateness of sexual intimacy, and the legal confidentiality of communications.

The statute does not require any disclosure of information in the following circumstances:

1. In an emergency;
2. Pursuant to a court order or involuntary procedures pursuant to C.R.S. §§ 27-65-105 to 27-65-109;
3. Where the sole purpose of the professional relationship is for forensic evaluation;
4. When the client is in the physical custody of either the Department of Corrections or the Department of Institutions and such department has developed an alternative program to provide similar information to such client and such program has been established through rule or regulation; or

5. When the client is incapable of understanding such disclosure and has no guardian to whom disclosure can be made.
6. By a person licensed or certified pursuant to this article or by a registered psychotherapist practicing in a hospital that is licensed or certified under C.R.S. § 25-1.5-103(1)(a).

If the client has no written language or is unable to read, the statute requires that an oral explanation shall accompany the written copy.

Colorado State Board of Registered Psychotherapists Rule 8(f) reiterates that if a psychotherapist practicing outside the school setting fails to make mandatory disclosure in accordance with C.R.S. § 12-43-214 and Rule 12, he or she is subject to disciplinary action, criminal prosecution, and civil damages.

As a matter of good practice, all psychotherapists should prepare a disclosure statement fulfilling the requirements of C.R.S. § 12-43-214 and Rule 12, have such reviewed by competent legal counsel, give a copy of it to the client, and get a signed copy of it from the client, acknowledging receipt of the disclosure statement at the time of the initial client contact.

According to C.R.S. § 12-43-226, it is unlawful for any person to violate C.R.S. § 12-43-214 by failing to provide to the client the required disclosure statement and to obtain the client's signature acknowledging receipt. A violation of C.R.S. § 12-43-226 is a class 2 misdemeanor. Committing "a second or any subsequent offense" is a class 6 felony. In addition, C.R.S. § 12-43-226(5) provides that the civil penalties for a violation of C.R.S. § 12-43-214 include recovery of the amount of any fees paid for services by the psychotherapist, and also "damages for injury or death occurring as a result of the services may be recovered ... without any showing of negligence." *Id.*

Psychotherapists who are supervised by a licensed professional must include in their disclosure statement the name and address of the supervisor and an explanation that the client's case will be discussed with the supervisor. Whenever there is a change in the supervisory relationship, a disclosure statement must be given including the new supervisor's information.

Because of the confusion surrounding the exceptions to confidentiality, it is highly recommended that disclosure statements specifically list the possible instances where confidentiality may not apply. The use of an informed consent document that contains the client's waiver of confidentiality in those specific instances (addressed in Chapter 2, Part II) is highly recommended. A form disclosure statement is contained in the Forms section of this book. This form may be modified for specific areas of practice, adding appropriate disclosures as needed.

6.03 Non-Disclosure of Confidential Communications

C.R.S. § 12-43-218 provides that a psychotherapist shall not disclose, without the consent of the client, any confidential communications made by the client to the psychotherapist, or the advice given thereon, in the course of professional employment; nor shall a psychotherapist's employee or associate, whether clerical or professional, disclose any knowledge of said communications acquired in such capacity; nor shall any person who has participated in any therapy conducted under the supervision of a licensee or registered psycholotherapist, including, but not limited to, group therapy sessions, disclose any knowledge gained during the course of such therapy without the consent of the person to whom the knowledge relates.

This duty of non-disclosure of confidential communications does not apply when:

1. A client or the heirs, executors, or administrators of a client file suit or a complaint against a psychotherapist on any cause of action arising out of the care or treatment of such client.
2. A mental health practitioner was in consultation with a physician, registered professional nurse, licensee, registrant, or registered psychotherapist against whom a complaint was filed, based on the case out of which the suit or complaint arises.
3. A review of services of a psychotherapist is conducted by one of the following groups:
    a. A board or a person or group authorized by such board to make an investigation;
    b. The governing board of a hospital where the psychotherapist practices or the medical staff of such hospital if the medical staff operates pursuant to written bylaws; or
    c. A professional review committee established pursuant to C.R.S. § 12-43-203(11) if said person has signed a release authorizing such review.

4. C.R.S. § 12-43-218 does not apply to any delinquency or criminal proceeding, except as provided in C.R.S. § 13-90-107.
5. This statute does not prohibit any other disclosures required by law.
6. This statute does not apply to covered entities, their business associates, or health oversight agencies pursuant to HIPAA, the Health Insurance Portability and Accountability Act of 1996.

C.R.S. § 12-43-218(4) provides that the duty of nondisclosure and confidentiality does not apply to any delinquency or criminal proceeding, except as provided in C.R.S. § 13-90-107, the statute pertaining to privilege.

For a more detailed discussion of confidentiality, see Chapter 2.

6.04 Grievance Procedures

If a licensee, registrant, or registered psychotherapist has violated any of the provisions of C.R.S. § 12-43-222, the board that licenses, registers, or regulates such psychotherapist may (1) deny, revoke, or suspend any license, registration, or listing of any registered psychotherapist; (2) issue a letter of admonition; (3) issue a confidential letter of concern; (4) place a psychotherapist on probation; or (5) apply for an injunction pursuant to C.R.S. § 12-43-227 to enjoin a therapist from practicing psychotherapy.

Typical types of grievances that are submitted by clients against psychotherapists concern the same types of complaints which lead to litigation. These include:

1. Failure to conform to generally accepted treatment practices;
2. Treating outside a therapist's area of expertise;
3. Failure to refer a client to a specialist or to another therapist when a client is not making progress in therapy;
4. Failure to comply with C.R.S. § 12-43-214, which requires that each client receive a disclosure statement at the time of the initial visit;
5. Boundary violations; and
6. Breach of confidentiality.

When a complaint is submitted by a client or other person to a mental health regulatory board, the psychotherapist named in the complaint is required to respond to it; disciplinary action can be taken against a therapist for failing to respond to the complaint. Then, in most cases, the Board investigates the complaint. If probable cause exists to believe that a violation of state laws or regulations pertaining to the practice of psychotherapy has occurred, then the case is referred to the Attorney General's office for prosecution. Those cases involving violations that are less serious in nature may be resolved by the issuance of a letter of admonition.

Where a violation occurs, which does not disqualify a psychotherapist from maintaining a license, the Board generally issues a letter of admonition or places the licensee on probation for a period of two to three years with the imposition of various conditions. The conditions include (1) having the psychotherapist submit to a mental health evaluation; (2) requiring practice monitoring, which usually means a weekly monitoring of cases by a practice monitor; and (3) requiring additional training or education in specific areas of ethics or practice.

In the grievance process, the Assistant Attorney General handling a complaint will generally make an offer of discipline, which is designed to resolve the grievance proceeding if the therapist agrees to accept the discipline imposed. If no such agreement is made, then the case proceeds to a hearing before an administrative law judge (ALJ), who issues findings of fact and a determination concerning whether a disciplinary violation has occurred. Regardless of the decision entered by the ALJ, the Board itself has the right to reject the ALJ's determination and substitute its own decision in the case.

6.05 Rules of the Mental Health Boards

The mental health regulatory boards have adopted rules for the regulation of the psychotherapists or addiction counselors under their jurisdiction. Every psychotherapist should, as a matter of good practice, obtain a copy of the most current rules and know their requirements. A number of the rules pertain to procedural matters regarding the handling of a grievance against a licensed or unlicensed professional. There are several rules, however, that require greater familiarity. These rules are discussed below.

Rule 6—Declaratory Orders (C.R.S. § 24-4-105(11)). Rule 6 of the Board of Registered Psychotherapists provides that anyone may petition the Board for a ruling (declaratory order) "to terminate a controversy or to remove uncertainty as to the applicability *to the petitioner* of any statutory provision or of any Board rule or order." This means, in practical terms, that a therapist could request a ruling from the Board concerning any duty to report suspected child abuse, for example, where the professional's duty is unclear under the attendant facts and circumstances. This Rule contains specific procedures that must be followed in requesting a ruling.

Rule 7—Mandatory Disclosure. Rule 7 of the Board of Registered Psychotherapists clarifies the requirements of the mandatory disclosure of information required under C.R.S. § 12-43-214. Section 6.02 of this book sets forth the important aspects of Rule 7.

Rule 8—Mandatory Reporting. Rule 8 provides that therapists are required to report to the Board of Registered Psychotherapists violations of C.R.S. 12-43-222, if a therapist has direct knowledge that a psychotherapist has violated a provision of C.R.S. § 12-43-222 and if the report would not violate the prohibition of disclosure of confidential information without client consent.

The rule defines direct knowledge to mean:

1. Having seen, heard, or participated in the alleged violation; or
2. Having been informed by the client/victim and having obtained an informed consent to release information as to the event or the client's name; or
3. Having been informed of a violation by the violator; or
4. Having been informed by a guardian of a minor or adult and having obtained informed consent from the guardian to release information.

A duty to report a violation exists if a licensee has a reasonable belief that a psychotherapist has engaged in a prohibited activity under C.R.S. § 12-43-222. Section 6.07 of this book sets forth those prohibited activities and should be consulted as a means of determining the extent of a psychotherapist's duty to report violations.

Rule 8 sets forth a specific procedure that must be followed once direct knowledge has been established. The rule states that the therapist must report the alleged violation as soon as practicable, and within 60 days. A special procedure must be followed when direct knowledge of a violation is obtained from a client. In such cases, Rule 8 requires that the psychotherapist:

1. Inform the client a violation may have occurred;
2. Encourage the client to report the violation;
3. Provide the client with a packet entitled "Your Options as a Psychotherapy Client;" and
4. Obtain the client's informed consent before reporting the alleged violation.

Rule 8 also requires that the report be in writing and include the specifics of the violation, to the degree known, as well as all relevant information and supporting documentation.

Rule 9—Standards for Supervision. The Board of Registered Psychotherapists has promulgated Rule 9, which was intended to establish a legal minimum standard that protects the public (i.e., client, supervisor, supervisee) from harm, educates the public as to the minimum standards for supervision, promotes the professional growth of both supervisor and supervisee, and gives the professional a documented standard against which he or she will be measured for disciplinary action.

Definitions. Rule 9(b) sets forth the following definitions:

1. "**Clinical supervision**" occurs when there is close, ongoing review and direction of a supervisee's clinical practice.
2. "**Consultation**" describes a voluntary relationship between professionals of relative equal expertise or status, wherein the consultant offers his or her best advice or information on an individual case or problem for use by the consultee as he or she deems appropriate in his or her professional judgment.
3. "**Administrative supervisor**" is the person who bears responsibility for the non-clinical functioning of an employee, such as performance appraisals, personnel decisions, etc. The administrative supervisor may be held accountable for misconduct by a psychotherapist when he or she knew or should have known of a violation of generally accepted standards of practice or any prohibited activity, and when he or she had responsibility for corrective administrative action and failed to act.

4. "**Modes of supervision**" include but are not limited to individual, group, telephone, audio-visual, process recording, direct observation, telecommunication (teleconferencing, fax, videotapes), and hospital round supervision. The appropriate modality of supervision shall be determined by the training, education, and experience of the supervisee and the treatment setting (i.e., urban/rural or the availability of resources, at all times based on community standards and client needs). The level of supervision provided, including whether every case is directly supervised and whether the supervisor meets with the client, is determined by the education, training, and experience of the supervisee, the specific needs of the clients being served, and the professional judgment of the supervisor. Nothing in this rule should be assumed to abridge the rights of the client to be a reasonable standard of care.

Rule 9(b)(5) sets forth a definition of "conflictual dual relationship." This is deemed to include, but not be limited to, blood relatives, spousal relationships or significant others (either current or former), current or former therapist and/or client and any other relationship that might command therapist/client, supervisor/supervisee, and supervisor/client akin to the term fiduciary relationship, whether or not money changed hands. The rule goes on to provide that any administrative supervisor shall not be prohibited from a conflictual dual relationship so long as he or she conforms to the specific personnel policies and procedures of the agency and is not engaged in clinical supervision involving the conflicted relationship.

The rule also provides that any supervisor or psychotherapist claiming an exception to a conflictual dual relationship due to practice in a rural location or accredited training institution of formal learning, or due to special needs of the clinical population being served, shall have the burden to show by a preponderance of the evidence that:

1. The client was fully informed of the dual relationship and the possibilities for conflicts of interest.
2. The client's access to quality care has not been compromised.
3. The supervisor and psychotherapist have not benefited from the relationship over and above a reasonable fee for service (i.e., that the power in the therapeutic relationship has not been used to influence the therapeutic relationship for personal gain).

4. The therapeutic and supervisory relationships have not been compromised and the best interests of the client are served by the relationship.

The definition of conflictual dual relationships is significant, since one of the duties of a supervisor is to assure that no conflictual dual relationship exists between a client and therapist, supervisor and supervisee, or supervisor and client.

Specific Duties. Rule 9(c) imposes upon supervisors a number of detailed responsibilities. Specifically, the rule requires that all supervisors:

1. Monitor the supervisee's clinical activities to assure he or she is providing psychotherapy that meets minimal standards.
2. Have experience, training, and competence adequate to perform and direct the services provided by the supervisee, as well as appropriate knowledge, skills, and expertise in supervision.
3. Assure that it is the practice of any supervisee to provide the mandatory disclosure form at the initial client contact and ensure that the form contains at least the minimum information required under the statutory requirements, and a statement that this supervisor is providing supervision in this case with the supervisor's address and telephone number, or a statement that this supervisor is not providing supervision on this case, and information regarding the broadened limits of confidentiality inherent in supervision.
4. Assure that clients are informed as to any changes in the supervisory relationship, and that an adequate process of termination of supervision with both the supervisee and his or her clients is undertaken.
5. Keep records documenting that the supervision has met the generally accepted standards of practice.
6. Provide documentation of the supervisory relationship, spelling out terms and conditions and financial agreements, unless already covered by formal personnel policies and procedures. This agreement shall not abridge the rights of the client to appropriate care.
7. Assist the supervisee in becoming aware of and adhering to all legal, ethical, and professional responsibilities.

8. Assure that all insurance forms and other official documents are filled out accurately and express who provided the service and who provided the supervision.
9. Have sufficient knowledge of legal, ethical, and professional standards relevant to the client being served.
10. Assure that no conflictual dual relationships exist between the client and therapist, supervisor and supervisee, or supervisor and client.

As a practice guide, those psychotherapists who may have assumed positions of supervision should develop and incorporate a checklist of the foregoing duties in order to assure that their duties as supervisor have been fulfilled. A supervisor should note that the failure to reasonably perform any of the foregoing supervisory responsibilities could subject such person to a malpractice claim.

6.06 Standards for Clinical Supervision

Clinical supervision in Colorado is conducted pursuant to Licensing Board Rules. For example, Psychology Board Rule 9 defines clinical supervision and sets forth the supervisor's duties. This rule states that it is the supervisor's duty to "[assist] the supervisee in becoming aware of and adhering to all legal, ethical, and professional responsibilities," and, in general, to direct the supervisee's clinical practice to assure that the therapist "is providing services that meet minimal standards." This is an awesome undertaking on the part of supervisors, and provides an enormous contribution to the profession through the training that is given and the experience imparted to the supervisee.

A supervisor's failure to comply with the duties set forth in the Board's supervision rules could impose liability on the supervisor, if he or she knew or should have known of the fact that treatment was being provided that did not comply with clinical or ethical standards. I have often advised clinical supervisors to include a provision in a written contract with supervisees that the supervisee will comply with the applicable ethical code (e.g., the NASW or AAMFT Code of Ethics). In addition, the clinical supervision contract should provide that the supervisee will (1) maintain a policy of liability insurance, with a minimum of $1,000,000 in coverage, and (2) provide the supervisor with a Certificate of Insurance. See the Clinical Supervision Contract in the Forms section, page 295.

When the professional relationship between a clinical supervisor and the supervisee has ended, that fact should be confirmed in writing, so that no claim can be made that the supervisor remains responsible for monitoring and directing the supervisee's practice.

The situation that most often leads to a malpractice suit is a critical incident where a client commits suicide or kills another person. Therefore, supervisors should be most vigilant in consulting with a supervisee in cases where a client may be dangerous to self or others. In addition, supervisors should keep thorough notes concerning all individual and group clinical supervision sessions, and should especially keep thorough records concerning consultations regarding whether a client is suicidal or dangerous to others.

Keep in mind that supervisors must maintain accurate records concerning the number of hours of clinical supervision when the supervisee is seeking licensure, since the supervisor will be required to certify to the appropriate licensing board the number of hours of clinical supervision with the supervisee.

Requirements for Clinical Supervisors. Clinical supervisors must ensure that their supervisees provide disclosure statements to clients identifying the clinical supervisor and his or her role. The purpose for this practice is twofold: (1) to disclose the fact that treatment information will be shared with the supervisor in clinical supervision; and (2) to identify any conflictual dual relationship that may exist between the client and the clinical supervisor.

For example, when the therapist is going through the disclosure statement with the client during the first treatment session and mentions the clinical supervisor's name, the client may say, "Oh, I know her; she is my psychology professor." Or, a client might inform the therapist that the clinical supervisor is a close friend, a relative, or is otherwise engaged in a relationship with the client that creates a conflictual dual relationship between the supervisor and the client. Any prior relationship that would impair the supervisor's judgment in directing the treatment process creates a prohibited dual relationship.

Clinical supervisors must keep records of the supervision. C.R.S. § 12-43-222(1)(n) prohibits the failure "to render adequate professional supervision of persons practicing pursuant to this article under such person's supervision." Record-keeping practices vary widely among supervisors. Experience has demonstrated, however, that the licensing boards expect clinical supervisors to maintain their own notes concerning each case discussed in supervision, notes concerning each issue on which the supervisor was consulted, and detailed records concerning the amount of face-to-face supervision or group supervision conducted by the supervisor.

Each supervisor must use his or her professional judgment to determine whether to maintain a copy of each client file for purposes of clinical supervision. At a minimum, supervisors should maintain thorough notes concerning directions they give to supervisees concerning specific clients' cases, as well as notes concerning each consultation with supervisees on difficult issues encountered in treatment. For risk-management purposes, supervisors should maintain copies of any records or notes from the client file concerning mandatory reports made by the supervisee of suspected child abuse or neglect, a duty to warn and protect, or situations concerning threats of suicide or harm to others.

Each clinical supervisor should have a list of resources and reference materials that supervisees are required to have and to consult. Such resources include:

- *The Legal Guide for Practicing Psychotherapy in Colorado;*
- A copy of the Colorado mental health statutes;
- The Board Rules for the Licensing Board to which the supervisee is applying for licensure;
- A copy of the Code of Ethics for the professional association that is most applicable to the supervisee's practice; and
- A copy of the supervision contract. A contract for clinical supervision is contained in the Forms section of this book as Form 7.

Each supervisor must have a contract for clinical supervision, which discusses the fees and policies for the supervision. The contract should set forth specifically all ground rules and expectations for the supervision process. As stated in the previous section, the supervision contract should require the supervisee to maintain professional liability insurance at all times and to provide a copy of the current Certificate of Insurance to the supervisor.

In the rare instances when a supervisor learns of a client's dissatisfaction with the therapist, indicated by the filing of a grievance or the submission of correspondence threatening a lawsuit, the clinical supervisor should direct the therapist to put his or her malpractice insurer on notice of the potential claim. The supervisor should do the same, providing notice to the therapist's insurance carrier of the potential liability claim. If a client commits suicide, it would also be prudent at that time to put insurers on notice of the situation in the event that a lawsuit is filed.

The Board Supervision Rules, e.g., State Board of Registered Psychotherapists Rule 10 and Psychology Board Rule 9, impose upon the supervisor the duty to ensure that billing records are accurate. It is *never* appropriate for a clinical supervisor to submit a bill for a treatment session that was actually conducted by the therapist and not by the supervisor; to do so constitutes billing fraud.

The duties of a clinical supervisor encompass all aspects of treatment, requiring the supervisor to ensure that:

- Assessments are done thoroughly and accurately;
- Disclosure statements are signed by every client;
- Record-keeping practices adhere to legal and ethical standards;
- Adequate session notes are being kept;
- Appropriate treatment plans are formulated to meet the clients' goals of treatment;
- The therapist is aware of all ethical standards;
- The therapist is charting any disclosure of treatment information; and
- Appropriate billing records are being maintained.

Clinical supervisors should meet with the therapists whom they are supervising so that each therapist receives (at a minimum) one hour of supervision for every 20 hours of treatment. If audio recordings or videotapes of treatment sessions are made so that the supervisor can see or hear treatment sessions, the supervisor must ensure that the tapes are erased or recorded over when they are no longer needed for supervisory purposes.

Clinical Supervision and Consultations: Confidentiality. Recently, in preparation for an ethics seminar on clinical supervision, my co-presenter and I researched state laws and ethics codes regarding the confidentiality of information obtained in clinical supervision by a supervisor. The generally accepted standard, established by ethical codes and practices nationwide, is that clinical supervision is a confidential process, the same as the counseling done by a supervisee with a client. Some states have exceptions to this rule, established by their state licensing board rules, but in general the supervision process is as confidential as mental health treatment itself. The Colorado Mental Health Boards' Supervision Rule, does not contain in it any special exceptions to the confidentiality of this treatment process.

The AAMFT Code of Ethics Principle 4.7 provides that clinical supervision is confidential and confidences may not be disclosed except by written waiver.

Imagine informing your clinical supervisor of action you had taken to save a client's life by calling the police for a welfare check, and having the supervisor inform you: "What you did constitutes a breach of confidentiality. You did not have consent to call the police. I am required to file a complaint against you." The supervision process is intended to be confidential, just as treatment is required to be confidential, in order to encourage disclosures and discussion. Clinical supervision is part of the treatment process. The same exceptions to confidentiality that apply in a counseling relationship also apply in clinical supervision: reporting of child abuse and neglect, compliance with the *Tarasoff* duty, initiation of a 72-hour hold, etc. Colorado law, C.R.S. § 12-43-224(9), prohibits a Board complaint containing confidential treatment information from being submitted, unless the client consents.

Consider another hypothetical. A therapist comes to you for peer consultation, and advises you of a situation where a client is experiencing suicidal ideation, but does not have a plan. The client had phoned the therapist to cancel a treatment session, and spoke with slurred speech. The client is on painkillers for chronic pain problems. The therapist informs you that she contacted the police for a welfare check on the client, who was not at home when the police arrived. In this situation would it be proper for you, as consultant, to say, "You breached confidentiality when you called the police and sent them to the client's home, so I must file a grievance against you"? Because consultations are a form of supervision according to the Licensing Boards' Supervision Rule, they, too, are confidential.

If clinical supervision were not a confidential process, supervisees would not be encouraged to ask questions about difficult situations involved in their practice or to discuss problems that arise in counseling. Confidentiality in the clinical supervision process serves an important purpose, just as it does in a counseling relationship.

6.07 Prohibited Activities

Pursuant to C.R.S. § 12-43-222, a person practicing psychotherapy under Title 12, Article 43, is in violation of the law if he or she:

1. Has been convicted of a felony or has pled guilty or *nolo contendere* to a felony; or has received a deferred sentence to a felony charge.
2. Has violated or attempted to violate, directly or indirectly, or assisted or abetted the violation of, or conspired to violate any provision or term of the article, rule, or regulation promulgated pursuant to the article or any order of a Board established pursuant to the article.
3. Has used advertising that is misleading, deceptive, or false.
4. Has committed abuse of health insurance pursuant to C.R.S. §18-13-119.
5. Has advertised through newspapers, magazines, circulars, direct mail directories, radio, television, or otherwise that he or she will perform any act prohibited by C.R.S. § 18-13-119.
6. Habitually or excessively uses or abuses alcohol, a habit-forming drug, or a controlled substance, as defined in C.R.S. § 12-22-303.
7. Fails to notify the Board that regulates his or her profession of a physical or mental illness or condition that affects the person's ability to treat clients with reasonable skill and safety, or that may endanger the health or safety of persons under his or her care; fails to act within the limitations created by physical or mental illness or a condition that renders the person unable to treat clients with reasonable skill and safety or that may endanger the health or safety of persons under his or her care; or fails to comply with the limitations agreed to under a confidential agreement pursuant to C.R.S. § 12-43-221.5.
8. Has acted or failed to act in a manner that does not meet the generally accepted standards of the professional discipline under which the person practices. Generally accepted standards may

include, at the Board's discretion, the standards of practice generally recognized by state and national associations of practitioners in the field of the person's professional discipline.

9. Has performed services outside of his or her area of training, experience, or competence.
10. Has maintained relationships with clients that are likely to impair his or her professional judgment or increase the risk of client exploitation, such as treating employees, supervisees, close colleagues, or relatives.
11. Has exercised undue influence on a client, including the promotion or the sale of services, goods, property, or drugs in such a manner as to exploit the client for the financial gain of the practitioner or third party.
12. Has failed to terminate a relationship with a client when it was reasonably clear that the client was not benefiting from the relationship and was not likely to gain such benefit in the future.
13. Has failed to obtain a consultation or perform a referral when such failure is not consistent with generally accepted standards of care.
14. Has failed to render adequate professional supervision for persons practicing psychotherapy under his or her supervision, according to the generally accepted standards of care.
15. Has accepted commissions or rebates or other forms of remuneration for referring clients to other professional persons.
16. Has failed to comply with any of the requirements pertaining to mandatory disclosure of information.
17. Has offered or given commissions, rebates, or other forms of remuneration for the referral of clients (although a licensee, certified school psychologist, or registered psychotherapist may pay an independent advertising or marketing agent compensation for advertising or marketing services rendered on his or her behalf by such agent, including compensation that is paid for the results of performance of such services on a per-patient basis).
18. Has engaged in sexual contact, sexual intrusion, or sexual penetration with a client during the period of time in which a therapeutic relationship exists or for up to two years after the period in which such a relationship exists.

19. Has resorted to fraud, misrepresentation, or deception in applying for or in securing licensure or taking any examination provided for in this article.
20. Has engaged in any of the following activities and practices: Repeated ordering or performing of demonstrably unnecessary laboratory tests or studies without clinical justification for the tests or studies; ordering or performing any service or treatment that is contrary to the generally accepted standards of the person's practice and is without clinical justification.
21. Has falsified or repeatedly made incorrect essential entries or repeatedly failed to make essential entries on patient records.
22. Has used or recommended rebirthing or any therapy technique that may be considered similar to rebirthing as a therapeutic technique. "Rebirthing" means the re-enactment of the birthing process through therapy techniques that involve any restraint that creates a situation in which a patient may suffer physical injury or death.
23. Has committed a fraudulent insurance act in violation of C.R.S. § 10-1-128.
24. Has sold or fraudulently obtained or furnished a license, certification, or registration to practice as a social worker, marriage and family therapist, professional counselor, psychologist, or addiction counselor or has aided and abetted such conduct.
25. Has failed to respond in the manner required by the Board to a complaint filed with or by the Board against the licensee, registrant, or certificate holder.

6.08 Unauthorized Practice

C.R.S. § 12-43-226 states that it is unlawful for any person to practice or offer or attempt to practice "as a social worker, marriage and family therapist, professional counselor, addiction counselor, or psychologist without an active license, certification, or registration issued under [Article 43]."

Any person who violates this provision commits a class 2 misdemeanor. Any person who subsequently violates this provision commits a class 6 felony.

The statute also provides that when a client has been the recipient of services that are prohibited by this article, his or her personal representative is entitled to recover the amount of any fee paid for the services. Damages for any injury or death occurring as a result of the services may be recovered without any showing of negligence.

6.09 Professional Service Corporations

C.R.S. § 12-43-211 provides that licensees, registrants, or certificate holders may form professional service corporations for the practice of psychology, social work, marriage and family therapy, professional counseling, psychotherapy, or addiction counseling under the "Colorado Business Corporation Act," if the corporations meet the following requirements:

1. The name of the corporation must contain the words "professional company," "professional corporation," or the abbreviations.
2. The corporation may be organized with any other person, and any other person may own shares, if the professional practice is performed under the supervision of a licensee and the licensee remains individually responsible for its professional acts and conduct.
3. Lay directors and officers must not exercise any authority whatsoever over professional matters.
4. The articles of incorporation provide, and all shareholders of the corporation agree, that either all shareholders of the corporation shall be jointly and severally liable for all acts, errors, and omissions of the employees of the corporation or that all shareholders of the corporation shall be jointly and severally liable for all acts, errors, and omissions of the employees of the corporation, except during periods of time when the corporation shall maintain, in good standing, professional liability insurance that meets the following standards: (a) the insurance insures the corporation against liability imposed upon the corporation by law for damages resulting from any claim made against the corporation arising out of the performance of professional services for others by those officers and employees who are licensed to practice or who are certified school psychologists or by those who provide professional services under supervision; (b) the insurance policy insures the corporation against liability imposed upon it by law for damages arising out of the acts, errors, and omissions of

all nonprofessional employees; (c) the insurance is in an amount for each claim of at least $100,000, multiplied by the number of persons licensed, registered, or certified to practice who are employed by the corporation. The policy may provide for an aggregate maximum limit of liability per year for all claims of $300,000, also multiplied by the number of licensees, registrants, or certificate holders employed by the corporation, but no corporation is required to carry insurance in excess of $300,000 for each claim with an aggregate maximum limit of liability for all claims during the year of $900,000.

6.10 Psychiatrists

A psychiatrist is not subject to the provisions of C.R.S. §§ 12-43-101, *et seq.* However, the provisions of the Colorado Medical Practice Act, as embodied in C.R.S. §§ 12-36-101, *et seq.*, govern the conduct of psychiatrists. Additionally, the Colorado State Board of Medical Examiners promulgates specific rules that apply to all physicians.

C.R.S. § 12-36-117 defines unprofessional conduct for physicians as follows:

1. Resorting to fraud, misrepresentation, or deception in applying for or securing a license, or in taking the examination.
2. Procuring, or aiding and abetting in procuring, criminal abortion.
3. Conviction of an offense involving moral turpitude or a felony.
4. Administering, dispensing, or prescribing any habit-forming drug or any controlled substance other than in the course of legitimate professional practice.
5. Any conviction of violation of any federal or state law regulating the possession, distribution, or use of any controlled substance.
6. Habitual intemperance or excessive use of any habit-forming drug or any controlled substance.
7. The aiding or abetting, in the practice of medicine, of any person not licensed to practice medicine as defined under this article or of any person whose license to practice medicine is suspended.
8. Practicing medicine as the partner, agent, or employee of, or in joint venture with, any person who does not hold a license to

practice medicine within this state, or practicing medicine as an employee of, or in joint venture with, any corporation other than a professional service corporation for the practice of medicine. Any licensee holding a license to practice medicine in this state may accept employment from any person to examine and treat the employees of such person.

9. Violating, or attempting to violate, directly or indirectly, or assisting in or abetting the violation of or conspiring to violate, any provision or term of C.R.S. §§ 12-36-101, *et seq.*
10. Exhibiting such physical or mental disability as to render the licensee unable to perform medical services with reasonable skill and with safety to the patient.
11. Advertising in a way that is misleading, deceptive, or false.
12. Engaging in a sexual act with a patient during the course of patient care or within six months following the termination of the professional relationship with the patient.
13. Refusing, as an attending physician, to comply with the terms of a declaration executed by a patient, and failure of the attending physician to transfer care of said patient to another physician.
14. Violation or abuse of health insurance.
15. Advertising through newspapers, magazines, circulars, direct mail, directories, radio, television, or otherwise that the licensee will perform any act prohibited by C.R.S. § 18-13-119(3).
16. Any act or omission that fails to meet generally accepted standards of medical practice.
17. Violation of any valid Board order or any rule or regulation promulgated by the Board in conformance with law.
18. Dispensing, injecting, or prescribing an anabolic steroid as defined in C.R.S. § 18-18-102(3), for the purpose of hormonal manipulation that is intended to increase muscle mass, strength, or weight without a medical necessity to do so or for the intended purpose of improving performance in any form of exercise, sport, or game.
19. Dispensing or injecting an anabolic steroid as defined in C.R.S. § 18-18-102(3), unless such anabolic steroid is dispensed from a pharmacy prescription drug outlet pursuant to a prescription order or is dispensed by any practitioner in the course of his or

her professional practice.

20. Prescribing, distributing, or giving to a family member or to oneself except on an emergency basis any controlled substance as defined in C.R.S. § 18-18-204.
21. Failing to report to the Board any adverse action taken against the licensee by another licensing agency in another state or country, etc.
22. Failing to report to the Board the surrender of a license to practice medicine in another state or jurisdiction.
23. Failing to accurately answer the questionnaire accompanying the renewal form required pursuant to C.R.S. § 12-36-123.
24. Engaging in any of the following activities and practices: (a) willful and repeated ordering or performance, without clinical justification, of demonstrably unnecessary laboratory tests or studies; (b) the administration, without clinical justification, of treatment which is demonstrably unnecessary; (c) the failure to obtain consultations or perform referrals when failing to do so is not consistent with the standard of care for the profession; or (d) ordering or performing, without clinical justification, any service, X-ray, or treatment which is contrary to recognized standards of the practice of medicine.
25. Falsifying or repeatedly making incorrect essential entries or repeatedly failing to make essential entries on patient records.
26. Committing a fraudulent insurance act in violation of C.R.S. § 10-1-128.
27. Failure to establish and maintain financial responsibility, as required by C.R.S. § 13-64-301.
28. Any violation of the provisions of C.R.S. § 12-36-202 or any rule or regulation of the Board adopted pursuant to C.R.S. § 12-36-202.
29. Failing to respond in an honest, materially responsive, and timely manner to a complaint issued pursuant to C.R.S. § 12-36-118(4).
30. Any act or omission in the practice of telemedicine that fails to meet generally accepted standards of medical practice.
31. Entering into or continuing a collaborative agreement pursuant to C.R.S. §§ 12-38-111.6(4) and 12-36-106.3 that fails to meet generally accepted standards of medical practice.

32. Entering into or continuing in a mentorship relationship with an advanced practice nurse pursuant to C.R.S. §§ 12-36-106.4 and 12-38-111.6(4.5) that fails to meet generally accepted standards of medical practice.

33. Verifying by signature the articulated plan developed by an advanced practice nurse pursuant to C.R.S. §§ 12-36-106.4 and 12-38-111.6(4.5) if the articulated plan fails to comply with the requirements of C.R.S. § 12-38-111.6(4.5).

C.R.S. § 12-36-134 provides that persons licensed to practice medicine may form professional service corporations for the practice of medicine under the Colorado Business Corporation Act, if such corporations are organized and operated in accordance with the following provisions:

1. The name of the corporation must contain the words "professional company," "professional corporation," or abbreviations thereof.
2. The corporation must be organized solely for purposes of conducting the practice of medicine by persons licensed to practice medicine in the State of Colorado.
3. All shareholders of the corporation must be persons licensed to practice medicine in the State of Colorado, and who at all times own their shares in their own right. They must be individuals who, except for illness, accident, time spent in the armed services, on vacation, and on leaves of absence not to exceed one year, are actively engaged in the practice of medicine in the offices of the corporation.
4. The articles of incorporation must provide that any shareholder who ceases to be or for any reason is ineligible to be a shareholder will dispose of all of his or her shares forthwith, either to the corporation, or to any person who is licensed to practice medicine in the State of Colorado and who, except for illness, accident, time spent in the armed services, on vacation, and on leaves of absence not to exceed one year, is actively engaged in the practice of medicine in the offices of the corporation.
5. The president must be a shareholder and a director and, to the extent possible, all other directors and officers must be persons who are licensed to practice medicine in the State of Colorado, and who, at all times, own their shares in their own right and who, except for illness, accident, time spent in the armed servic-

es, on vacation, and on leaves of absence not to exceed one year, are actively engaged in the practice of medicine in the offices of the corporation. The directors and officers must not exercise any authority whatsoever over professional matters.

6. The articles of incorporation must provide, and all shareholders of the corporation must agree, that all shareholders shall be jointly and severally liable for all acts, errors, and omissions of the employees of the corporation or that all shareholders of the corporation will be jointly and severally liable for all acts, errors, and omissions of the employees of the corporation except during periods of time when each person, licensed to practice medicine in the State of Colorado, who is a shareholder or any employee of the corporation, has a professional liability policy insuring himself or herself and all employees who are not licensed to practice medicine who act at his or her direction in the amount of $50,000 for each claim and an aggregate top limit of liability per year for all claims of $150,000, or the corporation maintains in good standing professional liability insurance which meets the following minimum standards:
    a. The insurance insures the corporation against liability imposed upon the corporation by law for damages resulting from any claim made against the corporation arising out of the performance of professional services for others by those officers and employees of the corporation who are licensed to practice medicine.
    b. Such policies insure the corporation against liability imposed upon it by law for damages rising out of the acts, errors, and omissions of all non-professional employees.
    c. The insurance is in an amount for each claim of at least $50,000, multiplied by the number of persons licensed to practice medicine employed by the corporation. The policy may provide for an aggregate top limit of liability per year for all claims of $150,000, also multiplied by the number of persons licensed to practice medicine employed by the corporation, but no firm is required to carry insurance in excess of $300,000 for each claim with an aggregate top limit of liability for claims during the year of $900,000.

6.11 Addiction Counselors

In 2011, the Colorado Legislature established a new Board to regulate certified and licensed addiction counselors: the State Board of Addiction Counselor Examiners. Like the other mental health boards, this Board will be comprised of seven members, four of whom will be certified or licensed addiction counselors. This Board will certify, license, regulate, and discipline all certified and licensed addiction counselors.

Requirements for Licensure as an Addiction Counselor. Pursuant to C.R.S. § 12-43-804, the requirements to be licensed as an addiction counselor include the following:

a. The applicant must be at least 21 years of age;

b. The applicant may not be in violation of any provision of the Mental Health Act or in violation of any rules promulgated by the Addiction Counselor Board;

c. The applicant must hold a master's or doctorate degree in the behavioral health sciences from an accredited school, college, or university or an equivalent program as determined by the Board;

d. The applicant must demonstrate professional competence by passing a national exam demonstrating special knowledge and skills in behavioral health disorders counseling as determined by the Division of Behavioral Health in the Department of Human Services and approved by the Board; and

e. The applicant must demonstrate professional competence by passing a jurisprudence examination administered by the Division of Registrations;

f. The applicant must meet the requirements for a Certificate of Addiction Counseling, Level III;

g. The applicant must have completed the number of hours of addiction-specific training, specified by the Board by Rule, including training in evidence-based treatment approaches, clinical supervision, ethics, and co-occurring disorders; and

h. The applicant must have completed at least 5,000 hours of clinically supervised work experience.

Certified Addiction Counselors. The statute establishing the Addiction Counselor Board has provided that an applicant for certification as an addiction counselor shall be certified if the individual files an application and submits evidence to the Board that he or she:

a. Is at least 18 years of age;
b. Is not in violation of any provision of the Mental Health Act or of any rules promulgated by the Addiction Counselor Board or by the State Board of Human Services;
c. Has met the requirements for certification at a particular certification level, specified in rules adopted by the State Board of Human Services in the Colorado Department of Human Services.

Addiction Counseling by Other Mental Health Professionals. The new regulatory and licensure statutes adopted by the Colorado Legislature in 2011 do not prohibit other psychotherapists or other professionals licensed under Colorado law from rendering services within their scope of practice as set forth in the statutes regulating their professional practices, so long as they do not represent themselves to be certified or licensed addiction counselors.

6.12 Psychiatric Technicians

The Colorado Legislature has declared that in order to safeguard life, health, property, and the public welfare of the people of the State of Colorado, and to protect the people against unauthorized, unqualified, and improper application of interpersonal psychiatric nursing relationships, it is necessary that a proper regulatory authority be established for licensing and reviewing persons who practice as psychiatric technicians.

C.R.S. § 12-42-102(4) defines "practice as a psychiatric technician" to mean:

> The performance for compensation of selected acts requiring interpersonal and technical skills and includes the administering of selected treatments and selected medications prescribed by a licensed physician or dentist, in the care of and in the observation and recognition of symptoms and reactions of a patient with a mental illness or developmental disability under the direction of a licensed physician and the supervision of a registered professional nurse. The selected acts in the care of a patient with a mental illness or developmental disability

shall not require the substantial specialized skill, judgment, and knowledge required in professional nursing.

C.R.S. § 12-42-113 has given the State Board of Nursing the power: (1) to revoke, suspend, withhold, or refuse to renew any license to practice as a psychiatric technician; (2) to place a licensee on probation; or (3) to issue a letter of admonition to a licensee upon proof that any such person has committed any of the following acts:

1. Has procured or attempted to procure a license by fraud, deceit, misrepresentation, misleading omission, or material misstatement of fact;
2. Has been convicted of a felony or any crime that would be a violation of Title 12, Article 43;
3. Has willfully or negligently acted in a manner inconsistent with the health or safety of persons under his or her care;
4. Has had a license to practice as a psychiatric technician or any other health care occupation suspended or revoked in any jurisdiction;
5. Has violated any provision of C.R.S. § 12-42-113 or has aided or knowingly permitted any person to violate any provision of the statute;
6. Has negligently or willfully practiced as a psychiatric technician in a manner that fails to meet generally accepted standards of practice;
7. Has negligently or willfully violated any order, rule, or regulation of the Board pertaining to practice or licensure as a psychiatric technician;
8. Has falsified or in a negligent manner made incorrect entries or failed to make essential entries on patient records;
9. Is addicted to or dependent on alcohol or habit-forming drugs, is a habitual user of a controlled substance or other drugs having similar effects, or is diverting controlled substances, except that the Board has the discretion not to discipline the licensee if he or she is participating in good faith in a program approved by the Board designed to end such addiction or dependency;
10. Has a physical or mental disability that renders him or her unable to practice as a psychiatric technician with reasonable skill and safety to the patients and that may endanger the health

or safety of persons under his or her care;

11. Has violated the confidentiality of information concerning any patient;
12. Has engaged in any conduct that would constitute a crime, and that conduct relates to such person's employment as a psychiatric technician; and
13. Willfully fails to respond in a materially factual and timely manner to a complaint issued pursuant to C.R.S. § 12-38-116.5(3).
14. Fraudulently obtains, sells, transfers, or furnishes any psychiatric technician diploma, license, renewal of license, or record, or aids or abets another in such activity;
15. Advertises, represents, or holds himself or herself out in any manner as a psychiatric technician or practices as a psychiatric technician without having a license to practice as a psychiatric technician issued under this article;
16. Uses in connection with his or her name any designation tending to imply that he or she is a licensed psychiatric technician without having a license issued under this article; or
17. Practices as a psychiatric technician during the time his or her license is suspended or revoked.

C.R.S. § 12-42-119 states that it is a class 2 misdemeanor for any person to practice or offer or attempt to practice as a psychiatric technician without an active license to practice in that capacity. Further, a person commits a class 6 felony "for the second or any subsequent offense."

6.13 Michael Skolnik Medical Transparency Act of 2010

In 2010, the Colorado Legislature extended the provisions of the Michael Skolnik Medical Transparency Act so that its requirements apply to all mental health professionals and to other healthcare professionals, as well. This statute, C.R.S. § 24-34-110, states that the people of Colorado need to be fully informed about the past practices of healthcare professionals in order to "provide transparency to the public regarding the competency of persons engaged in the practice of certain healthcare professions" so that informed decisions can be made when choosing a healthcare provider. This statute is effective July 1,

2011, and it applies to each applicant for a new license or for renewal of an existing license, as well as to persons who are registered with the Data Base of Registered Psychotherapists. All such applicants are required to provide the following information to the Director of the Division of Registrations at the Colorado Department of Regulatory Agencies (DORA):

1. The applicant's full name, including any known aliases; the current address where the applicant's practice is located; and the applicant's education and training related to his or her profession.
2. Information pertaining to any license, certification, or registration to practice the applicant's profession, issued during the preceding ten years, including any "public disciplinary action taken" against the applicant by the state board or agency that licenses or regulates the professional, as well as any agreement or stipulation entered into between the applicant and a state regulatory authority, "whereby the applicant agrees to temporarily cease or restrict his or her practice," or any board order "restricting or suspending the applicant's license, certification or registration."
3. Healthcare professionals must report "any final action of an employer that results in the applicant's loss of employment, where the grounds for termination constitute a violation of the laws governing the applicant's practice."
4. Any "criminal conviction or plea arrangement" resulting from the commission of "a felony or crime of moral turpitude in any jurisdiction at any time after the person has been issued a license, certification or registration to practice his or her healthcare profession in any state or country."
5. "Any final judgment against, settlement entered into by, or arbitration award paid on behalf of the applicant on or after September 1, 1990, for malpractice."
6. Any refusal by an insurer of professional liability insurance to issue a policy to the applicant due to past claims experience.
7. An applicant may submit information regarding awards or recognitions he or she has received or charity care he or she has provided which is related to the professional's practice.

This statute further requires that doctors, therapists, and other professionals to whom the statute applies "shall report any updated information" to the Director of Registrations within thirty days after the date of the action being reported, in order to ensure that the information provided to the public is as accurate as possible.

Penalty. For failure to comply with the Michael Skolnik Medical Transparency Act, the Director may impose an administrative fine "not to exceed five thousand dollars" against a person who fails to comply with this section. In addition, the Director of Registrations "shall notify the applicable state board that regulates the professional when the Director imposes a fine," and the professional's regulatory or licensing board may also take disciplinary action. This statute specifically provides that the failure of a professional to comply with the statute "constitutes unprofessional conduct or grounds for discipline" by the board or agency that regulates the professional.

Healthcare Professions Profiling Program. The Colorado Department of Regulatory Agencies, Division of Registrations, which is implementing the Michael Skolnik Medical Transparency Act, is establishing a "profile system" that will contain a profile of each professional containing the information that the individual is required to report to DORA. Until each professional applying for a license or for renewal of a license or a registration has provided the information required by this statute, no license, registration, or renewal will be issued by DORA. The Division of Registrations will then post the professionals' profiles on its website, containing the information needed by the people of Colorado, so that they can be fully informed when choosing a healthcare provider.

Constitutional Issues. Informed consumers and informed healthcare professionals alike may question why other licensed professionals and those who are fiduciaries, entrusted with investing money or with the authority to engage in financial transactions, are not required to make similar disclosures. Does the Michael Skolnik Medical Transparency Act violate equal protection of the law because it only applies to healthcare professionals and not to other professionals for whom integrity, honesty, and compliance with the law are vitally important? Does this statute violate the provisions of the Colorado Constitution and the U.S. Constitution, which prohibit *ex post facto* laws and which generally require statutes to be prospective in their application? This is a legitimate issue that will be determined by courts, if the issue is ever raised in an attack on this statute.

6.14 Statutory Requirement for Continuing Professional Development

In 2009, the Colorado Legislature adopted amendments to the Colorado Mental Health Act, which requires continuing professional development on the part of LMFT's, LCSW's, LPC's and Certified Addiction Counselors. Professional associations have been collaborating with DORA to adopt specific regulations and procedures for the mandatory Professional Development Activities, which these therapists must engage in.

Requirement for Professional Development. During each renewal cycle for licensure or registration with the Division of Registrations database, each therapist must complete forty Professional Development Hours (PDH). One PDH is defined as one hour of active learning. DORA has adopted a phased process for Continuing Professional Development (CPD), which consists of the following steps:

Step 1. Reflective Practice. The first step is to identify learning opportunities. DORA will have an online Professional Practice Rubric, which will identify any knowledge areas that a therapist may want to address. For example, for licensed clinical social workers, the Social Work Board has identified seven "competency dimensions" common to all social work practice settings. These seven dimension are: practice skills, communication and critical thinking, values and ethics, cultural competence, professional relationship skills, professional identity skills, and professional knowledge.

Step 2. SMART Goals. After having identified the areas of competency that a therapist wishes to pursue, the therapist then sets learning goals following the SMART principle, adopted by DORA: Specific, Measurable, Achievable, Relevant, and Timed. DORA provides on its website a worksheet to assist therapists in formulating goals.

Step 3. Learning Plan. Each therapist then develops a Learning Plan, which can be completed online through the DORA CPD Portal. The purpose of the Learning Plan is to help each therapist to achieve his or her individual goals.

Step 4. Action. To implement the Learning Plan, therapists can adopt a Professional Development Activity (PDA) as part of the therapist's strategy for accomplishing the Learning Plan and the SMART Goals formulated. Activities which may be part of the Learning Plan include volunteer service, consultation, supervision, presenting, course work, publication, and independent learning.

Step 5. Documentation. Documentation enables therapists to track their progress and to document the number of hours in which they are engaged in PDAs. Each therapist will maintain his or her own documentation of the learning process. DORA will audit selected therapists, who will be asked to provide their documentation of PDAs.

Step 6. Evaluation. Each therapist will Self-Evaluate their learning accomplishments as they meet goals that have been set. In the evaluation, a therapist will identify the outcome of PDAs, describing how learning will impact the therapist's practice. DORA will provide a Self-Evaluation form to assist in this process.

Deadlines for Continuing Professional Development. The Colorado Legislature mandated that the Continuing Professional Development Program begin on January 1, 2011. This means that participation in PDAs will be required for the renewal cycle ending on August 31, 2011. DORA has agreed to accommodate licensees, allowing them to complete program requirements in two parts. The Practice Description, Practice Rubric, and Preparation of the Learning Plan (Steps 1-2) must be completed before August 31, 2011. The implementation of the Learning Plan and all PDAs, as well as the required documentation, must be completed during the period of time from September 1, 2011 to August 31, 2013. Then, beginning on August 31, 2013, Steps 1 through 5 would all be completed during the two-year renewal cycle that runs from September 1, 2013 to August 31, 2015. In order to assist therapists in the CPD process, DORA is setting up websites to inform therapists concerning this new requirement for licensure and compliance with both the statutes and regulations adopted by DORA to implement the statute adopted in 2009. A CPD process checklist can be found at www.CPDportal.com; the Professional Development Rubric is online at www.PracticeRubric.com.

6.15 Technology in Counseling

Several states have enacted laws that prohibit therapists who are licensed out-of-state from providing counseling service to clients in-state. New York, California, Ohio, and New Jersey have adopted such laws. A therapist in Colorado whose client relocates temporarily to another state or moves out-of-state should be able to provide continuity of care by continuing to provide services to the client until that individual can establish a professional relationship with a new therapist, so long as the services provided out-of-state do not exceed 30 days. There is a caveat, however: A client who is in crisis cannot be assessed by telephone or through an internet interaction. Standards have not yet evolved that would allow an assessment of a client in crisis through the use of Skype.

The primary risk for therapists concerns the use of chatrooms, blogs, or websites where clients and others can post comments. The confidentiality of clients may be breached inadvertently, and clients or members of the public may post comments, believing that they will receive an immediate response if they are in crisis. It is impossible to monitor such sites on a 24/7 basis, and the liability that could exist is a significant risk and burden for therapists. Blogs by healthcare providers, in which they discuss their stories or their own past mental health problems or addictions can create the risk that the professional has shared too much information that clients can access, which may lead to potential embarrassment when clients begin asking questions about therapists' own histories. The experience of both therapists and medical doctors has shown that treatment providers are horrified when they learn that clients have been able to access photos of them in bathing suits, or have been able to access photos of their children and other family members on Facebook.

Experience has also demonstrated that allowing clients to email therapists with questions about clinical issues can create difficulties. In a recent disciplinary matter, a licensing board sanctioned a therapist for sending "too many emails" to her borderline client, who had initiated over 700 emails to the therapist in an 18-month period. Therefore, it is recommended that therapists adopt an email policy, disclosed to clients during the intake process, in which emails are only used for logistical purposes to schedule appointments. Therapists need to disclose to clients that if they are in crisis, they should call 911 or go to the nearest hospital emergency room, rather than sending an email or text message to their therapist regarding the situation. Establish a written policy concerning the use of emails that can be communicated to clients and strictly enforced.

Clients do use the internet to shop for therapists or to Google their therapist. Although this may seem invasive, it is a standard practice among consumers today. Is it appropriate for therapists to Google their clients? What should therapists do when they learn information about a client, either by reading a client's blog or website and learning that a client may have problems or issues that have not been shared in therapy? In general, young people in particular will try on internet personas, and they need to have the freedom to do so. Therapists generally allow clients to exercise such freedom without being confronted by a therapist with material that has been found online. Allow clients, therefore, in general, to disclose in treatment the presenting problem(s) for which the individual wants to seek counseling.

DORA'S Teletherapy Policy. In 2011, the Colorado Department of Regulatory Agencies adopted policy number 20-2, which applies to all therapists in the State of Colorado. This policy provides that mental health professionals have the discretion to determine what type of treatment modality is appropriate for the client. The teletherapy policy is as follows.

> It is recommended that the initial therapeutic contact be in person and adequate to provide a conclusive diagnosis and therapeutic treatment plan prior to implementing any psychotherapy through electronic means. The mental health professional is expected to establish an ongoing therapeutic relationship including face-to-face visits on a periodic basis thereafter.
>
> Once a mental health professional chooses to provide psychotherapy via electronic means, the mental health professional is expected to carefully identify and address issues that involve:
>
> 1) The agreed upon therapeutic means of communication between the client and the mental health professional (i.e., when will face-to-face contact be appropriate, what method(s) of electronic communication will be utilized, what is the structure of the contractual relationship);

2) Implementing written consent form(s) and proper disclosure(s) including, but not limited to the client's knowledge regarding security issues, confidentiality, structure, etc.;
3) Ensuring that the therapeutic means of communication includes confidentiality and computer/cyber security;
4) Determining the basis and ability for the mental health professional to support the rationale for the decision to choose a particular therapeutic method;
5) Ensuring that the mental health professional is practicing within his/her scope of practice;
6) Ensuring that the therapeutic means of communication that is chosen does not cause any potential harm to the client.

The mental health professional may encounter specific challenges while providing psychotherapy through electronic means. The mental health professional must realize that these challenges may include, but are not limited to:

1) Verifying the identity of the client and determining if they are a minor;
2) Providing the client with procedures for alternative modes of communication when there is possible technology failure;
3) Assessing how to cope with potential misunderstandings when the visual cues that would normally occur during face-to-face visits do not exist;
4) Assessing how to address crisis intervention when necessary;
5) Ensuring that clients are knowledgeable with regard to encryption methods, firewall, and backup systems to help secure communication and educate clients on the risk of unsecured communications;
6) Establishing a means to retain and preserve data;
7) Upon request, have the ability to capture and provide client treatment notes, summaries or other information that is received via the electronic technology;
8) Disclosing that health insurance coverage may not exist for psychotherapy service that is provided through technological means.

This teletherapy policy is similar to the provision contained in the AMHCA Code of Ethics (2010). The AMHCA provision regarding this technology-assisted counseling requires that therapists "ensure that clients are intellectually, emotionally, and physically capable of using technology-assisted counseling services, and of understanding the potential risks and/or limitations of such services." It also requires that therapists confirm that "technology-assisted counseling services are not prohibited by or otherwise violate any applicable state or local statutes, rules, regulations, or ordinances."

Use of Social Media in Marketing. Social media have proven to be an effective method for therapists to use in marketing their practice. Therapists who have created their own websites to promote themselves and their practice can link their website to professional pages on Facebook, LinkedIn, and other social media. On these professional pages, therapists can post articles of general interest to prospective clients and a list of frequently asked questions and answers concerning counseling and its benefits. Therapists can also include blogs on their professional pages containing information of interest to prospective clients. By linking all of these sites together and keeping their website and professional pages current with monthly updates, therapists can elevate their profile on Google to a great extent.

CHAPTER 7: BUSINESS ASPECTS

Psychotherapists are employed by a variety of employers. These employers include governmental bodies, corporations, nonprofit corporations, professional corporations, partnerships, and sole proprietors. The legal aspects and status of these entities are outlined in this chapter.

7.01 Government Employment

There are numerous government agencies that employ psychotherapists. These bodies include federal and state agencies, county and city governments, and school districts. A psychotherapist employed by the government is required to follow numerous policies and procedures, which are detailed and comprehensive and which encompass service requirements, documentation, and reporting. Additionally, these agencies have established certain civil service procedures and employee rights that are not generally available to non-governmental psychotherapists. Other than these requirements, there are no other unique legal or business issues associated with government employment.

Occasionally, a governmental agency will order an employee to disregard a Colorado law or rule and regulation pertaining to psychotherapy. If this occurs, a psychotherapist should immediately consult a private attorney, since the jurisdictional issues are complex.

7.02 Nonprofit Corporations

Nonprofit corporations employ a number of psychotherapists as caseworkers, counselors, therapists, or direct care staff. These organizations are generally organized solely and exclusively for charitable, educational, or eleemosynary purposes. In order to be a nonprofit corporation, no part of the corporation's income or profit may be distributed to its members, directors, or officers.

The major advantage of a nonprofit corporation is its ability to seek tax-exempt status. If such status is granted, the nonprofit corporation pays no tax on its income or profit. Additionally, charitable contributions made to such nonprofit corporations are tax deductible by the donor.

A common misperception about nonprofit corporations is that these entities may not legally make a profit. Although in reality many such organizations suffer this financial consequence, there is no such requirement. Nonprofit corporations are managed by a Board of Directors, whose members serve without compensation. These directors are responsible for the overall guidance, direction, control, and management of the nonprofit corporation's affairs. Typically, the directors are community volunteers chosen to serve because of some special interest in the organization's mission or because of some skill or expertise they bring to the Board.

The nonprofit corporation's directors elect a President or Chairman of the Board who is responsible for presiding over the Board meetings. Other officers may be elected to fulfill other Board responsibilities, such as Treasurer, Vice President, or Secretary. All of these officers serve without compensation.

The actual day-to-day affairs of the nonprofit corporation are managed by an Executive Director or Chief Executive Officer, selected by the Board of Directors. This executive officer is a salaried employee of the nonprofit corporation who hires, fires, and supervises the nonprofit corporation's other employees.

Because of the charitable nature of the nonprofit corporation's work, psychotherapists who work for such agencies are typically dedicated, competent professionals who have chosen to forego the potentially huge financial rewards that are available to those psychotherapists who have chosen to practice their profession in the for-profit world.

7.03 Business Entities

A psychotherapist who wants to establish a private practice that is not associated with a government or nonprofit agency may establish that practice as a sole proprietorship, partnership, limited liability company, or corporation. These forms of doing business are compared and contrasted in sections 7.04, 7.05, and 7.06 of this book.

7.04 Sole Proprietorship

A sole proprietorship is a business having a single owner who has chosen not to do business in the corporate form (i.e., as a corporation).

Other than procuring any licenses that may be required to engage in the particular business, there are no other legal requirements that must be met in order to establish a sole proprietorship. For example, there is no legal requirement that a separate business checking account be established. However, good accounting practice would dictate such. Hence, a person desiring to do business under this form simply commences the business without having to undertake any legal formalities.

Likewise, in order to cease doing business as a sole proprietor, one need only stop the business activity with the intent to terminate the business. A sole proprietorship, unlike a corporation, ceases to exist upon the death of the proprietor. As such, there is no continuity of the business after death.

Because of the singularity of ownership, control of the sole proprietorship remains undiluted in the hands of the owner. Because there is only one owner, the potential for capital is limited to the financial resources of the sole owner and his or her ability to borrow funds.

In the event the proprietor desires to sell or transfer the business to a third party, such transaction can occur without undue delay.

A sole proprietor may employ others to work as independent contractors or employees. A discussion of the differences between independent contractors and employees can be found in section 7.07 of this book. The reader should carefully review section 7.07, since there are important tax and liability consequences that result from each type of employment.

From a tort liability standpoint, a sole proprietor is personally liable for his or her own negligent and intentional actions, as well as the negligent actions of his or her employees when they occur within the scope of the employment relationship. Hence, not only are the business assets of the sole proprietor at risk, but the sole proprietor's personal assets (e.g., house, car, boat, bank accounts, etc.) are also available to satisfy a judgment resulting from a lawsuit filed by an injured third party.

This rule imposing personal liability upon the sole proprietor for the negligent actions of his or her employees may be avoided by choosing the corporate form of doing business. Under the corporate form of business, the corporation is the employer and is liable for its employees' actions. This protects the shareholder/owner, who enjoys limited liability in this instance. Unfortunately, the corporate shield of limited liability does nothing for the owner's own negligent or intentional actions, since a person is always personally liable for such actions. As a practical matter, if a psychotherapist who employs others in his or her practice elects to do business as a sole proprietor, adequate insurance should be carried to protect any personal wealth that would be at risk.

A sole proprietor's income is taxed at his or her ordinary tax rate. Hence, only one federal tax return is filed for an individual doing business as a sole proprietor. This is less cumbersome and complicated than the tax requirements for a partnership or corporation.

In summary, a sole proprietorship is ideal for an individual without employees. Its simplicity and lack of legal formalities and requirements make it an attractive option. However, personal liability for the actions of employees and a limited ability to raise capital make it less desirable for the proprietor who seeks the greater financial returns that are possible through the efforts of employees.

7.05 Partnerships

A partnership is defined as two or more persons who agree to carry on a business for profit with joint rights of management and control.

This is a business entity that is used frequently by professionals such as physicians, lawyers, accountants, and others who possess specialized skills and knowledge. It is also a popular entity in real estate. It is not used as much by psychotherapists, although a basic understanding of its essential features is necessary in order to select the appropriate business entity for a psychotherapist.

A partnership requires greater effort to form than a sole proprietorship. In comparison to forming a corporation, however, it requires slightly less effort. The essential requirement in formation is that two or more persons must agree to do business as a partnership. Although there is no requirement that this agreement be in writing, the better practice is to reduce the agreement to a writing that is signed by all partners.

The agreement should, at a minimum, address the following issues:

1. What will be the name of the partnership?
2. Where will the principal office be located?
3. How much will each partner contribute as an initial capital contribution?

4. What will be each partner's obligation to make future capital contributions?
5. What happens if a partner is unable to provide future capital as needed?
6. How will partnership decisions be made?
7. What will be the authority of each partner to enter into contracts for and on behalf of the partnership?
8. What happens in the event of a partner's death or disability?
9. What happens in the event a partner wants to sell his or her partnership interest or withdraw, resign, or retire?
10. How will profits and losses be distributed or handled?
11. What happens upon termination of the partnership?

These issues should be discussed and legal advice obtained prior to signing any partnership agreement. In the absence of an agreement with respect to such issues, the Colorado Uniform Partnership Law (C.R.S. §§ 7-60-101, *et seq.*) will control and provide the law that will be followed to resolve any disagreement between the parties.

Once an agreement is reached to do business as a partnership, no other formalities are required other than obtaining the appropriate business or professional licenses.

A partnership may exist for any specifically defined period of time chosen by the partners (e.g., five years). However, upon the death of a partner, the partnership ceases to exist and in the absence of an agreement to the contrary, the surviving partners are required to terminate all partnership business, sell assets, pay creditors, return to each partner his or her initial capital contributions, and distribute the profits. In most cases the surviving partners do not want to cease doing business and dismantle the partnership in this fashion. Hence, most partnership agreements will contain some provision for the surviving partners to have an option to purchase the deceased partner's interest in the partnership so that the dissolution procedure need not disrupt the partnership business. If the surviving partners elect to continue the partnership business and buy the deceased partner's interest, a new partnership consisting of the surviving partners is created and the prior partnership ceases to exist.

A partner's interest in a partnership cannot be sold or transferred to a third party without the unanimous consent of the other partners. This consequence results from the legal requirement that all partners must agree to be partners; therefore, one partner cannot simply sell his or her partnership interest to a third party if one of the other partners objects to the third party. Consequently, a partner who wants to withdraw from the partnership will trigger a process by which the partnership business is terminated and dissolved in the same manner as that which occurs when a partner dies. Here again, a provision in the partnership agreement that allows the other partners to purchase the interest of the partner desiring to leave can eliminate the disruption that is inevitable in the absence of such a clause.

Unlike a sole proprietorship, partnership decision-making is much more complicated. The Colorado Partnership Act provides that each partner has joint rights to management and control. This means that each partner is vested with the authority to make partnership decisions. In practice, most partnership agreements provide that a partner will not exercise such right without the consent of a majority of the other partners. Consequently, decision making in a partnership can be a time consuming and laborious democratic process.

One of the advantages of a partnership is that a partnership's ability to generate capital for operations is not limited to a single partner, as is the case in a sole proprietorship. Each partner brings his or her own wealth to the partnership and therefore the potential to raise capital is greater than that of a sole proprietor.

The greatest disadvantage of a partnership is that each partner is jointly and severally liable for the acts of the partnership's employees and the actions of each of the other partners, even though he or she may not have participated in the wrongful action. In other words, a psychotherapist who is a partner in a partnership is liable for the negligence or malpractice of the other partners regardless of his or her level of involvement with the particular client victim. This means that any judgment obtained against the partner committing the negligence can be satisfied or paid out of the personal wealth of the other partners.

This aspect of joint and several liability is a dangerous element of partnership law and should be carefully considered before jumping into a partnership. Although this danger can be minimized by the use of malpractice insurance, such insurance will not provide coverage for a partner who binds the partnership to purchases, contracts, or other debts. Although the innocent partner may sue the guilty partner and attempt to recover the loss, such lawsuits are successful only to the extent that the guilty partner has financial resources and is able to pay the judgment.

A partnership's income and losses are passed through to the partners in accordance with their respective agreement. This means that each partner's share of the profits and losses are reported as ordinary income on each partner's individual tax return. Consequently, a partnership itself pays no income tax on its earnings since these are passed along to the partners.

There are advantages to doing business as a partnership. The combination of resources, skills, and talents enables individuals who otherwise could not compete in the business world to do so. However, these advantages must be balanced against the management control and liability issues that are inherently present in a partnership.

7.06 Corporations For Profit

The Traditional Corporate Entity. A corporation is an artificial, fictitious person that exists by operation of law. As a legal entity, it is recognized to have certain rights, privileges, and obligations. A corporation may own and dispose of property. It may employ others and engage in business. It has certain constitutional rights such as the right to be free from unreasonable searches and seizures, although it has no right to vote, as do natural persons. It has the obligation to pay taxes and obey the law. In most respects, then, it can legally do what any natural person could do.

A corporation may be thought of as consisting of people and property.

The shareholders contribute capital or money to the corporation so that it can engage in its business. Because of these contributions, the shareholders are the owners of the corporation. Their ownership is evidenced by a stock certificate indicating how many shares are owned. Shareholders have certain rights, which exist by virtue of ownership. The most important right of shareholders is the right to elect the Board of Directors. Additionally, the shareholders have the right to receive dividends and to inspect the corporate books and records.

The Board of Directors is elected annually by the shareholders and meets periodically to review corporate activities. The Board of Directors also appoints the corporate officers who are responsible for the actual day-to-day affairs of the corporation.

There are several corporate officers. The President is the presiding officer of the corporation and is in charge of all day-to-day affairs. The President may be assisted by one or more Vice Presidents. The Secretary is responsible for the corporate books and records, as well as the corporate minutes. There may be a Treasurer who is responsible for the management of the corporation's financial activities.

The officers are assisted by employees, whom they hire and fire. The employees are considered to be agents of the corporation.

In a small, closely held corporation such as might be contemplated for a psychotherapist, the shareholders also serve as the directors, officers, and employees.

In Colorado and in most states, a corporation's legal existence commences when the Secretary of State reviews and approves a document known as Articles of Incorporation. If these articles are in proper form and contain the required information, the Secretary of State will issue a Certificate of Incorporation, which is evidence of the corporation's legal existence. In many respects, it is similar to a birth certificate, which is nothing more than evidence of the existence of a natural person.

The Articles of Incorporation are generally drafted by an attorney who acts as the incorporator. These articles must contain the following information in order to be approved by the Secretary of State:

1. The name of the corporation;
2. The period of existence;
3. The name and address of the corporation's registered agent and the corporation's principal place of business;
4. The amount of stock the corporation wants to have available for issuance;
5. The names and addresses and of the initial Board of Directors; and
6. The name and address of the incorporator.

Unlike sole proprietorships and partnerships, whose legal existence ceases upon death or transfer of ownership, a corporation's legal existence is not affected by the death of a shareholder or by his or her sale or transfer of stock. Hence, the corporation may be thought of as having perpetual existence if such is desired by the incorporator.

A corporation may issue as much stock as it desires. Thus, its ability to raise capital is potentially unlimited. There is no requirement that the shareholders consent to any new stockholders. This is one of the key advantages of the corporate form of business.

Another advantage is that the shareholders are generally not liable for the actions and conduct of the other owners, directors, officers, and employees. This legal principle is known as the shield of limited corporate liability. Under this doctrine, a shareholder's personal wealth, such as a house, boat, or car, is not subject to any judgment that might be obtained against the corporation or any other person associated with the corporation. However, a shareholder is liable for any of his or her own negligence or malpractice when it is committed as an employee or director.

The law requires that certain legal formalities be followed in order to maintain the corporate existence. For example, regular meetings of the shareholders and directors must be held and minutes recorded of the decisions of each. Corporate funds must not be commingled with the personal funds of the shareholders. Corporate documents must be signed by persons who have received authority to do so, and the signature must identify the fact that the person is signing as an agent for the corporation. If such formalities are not followed, the corporate shield will be disregarded and the shareholders will be found to be personally liable for the corporation's debts.

A corporation must file a corporate tax return and pay taxes on its earnings. If there are sufficient after-tax earnings, the Board of Directors may declare dividends for the shareholders. These dividends are taxable to the shareholders as ordinary income. This second tax on dividends is considered by many individuals to be a double taxation of corporate income. Consequently, dividends are often disfavored and ways are sought to avoid this double taxation. Accountants are best equipped to advise a psychotherapist on the best way to avoid dividends with respect to that worker's particular corporation.

The United States Tax Code permits certain corporations to elect to have their profits and losses passed through the corporation without taxation, provided all shareholders report their respective shares of such on their individual tax returns. Corporations that make this election are known Subchapter "S" corporations. Those that choose the normal form of taxation are known as "C" corporations. An accountant should be consulted with respect as to whether a "S" or "C" election is appropriate.

Corporations are also permitted to establish a variety of pension and/or profit sharing plans, which provide for the legitimate tax sheltering of income if it is for retirement purposes. Again, an accountant should be retained to determine the appropriateness of such plans.

Other Corporate-Like Entities. Colorado has enacted legislation (C.R.S. §§ 7-80-101, *et seq.*) that allows for the establishment of a type of corporation known as a Limited Liability Company (LLC). This type of corporation was created in order to allow for a greater number of companies to take advantage of "S" corporation tax treatment. A Limited Liability Company is taxed much like an "S" corporation. Many of the eligibility requirements for "S" treatment, however, have been relaxed for Limited Liability Companies. The advantage of operating as an LLC is that the owners, who are referred to as "members," are not personally liable for the alleged improper actions of the LLC or its employees.

Of more recent creation than the LLC is the Limited Liability Partnership (LLP), which provides the same advantage of limited liability that an LLC possesses. Limited liability is achieved through compliance with state laws that require both an LLC and an LLP to maintain required amounts of liability insurance. You should consult with an attorney who specializes in business transactions if you need to set up either type of limited liability business organization.

Special Requirements. A psychotherapist seeking to use the corporate form of business must comply with the particular licensing requirements for his or her particular profession. For example, psychologists, social workers, professional counselors, and marriage and family therapists must comply with the provisions of C.R.S. § 12-43-211, while psychiatrists must comply with the provisions of C.R.S. § 12-36-134. Such corporations are known as "Professional Service Corporations." The specific requirements are outlined in section 6.09

of this book for licensed psychologists, licensed clinical social workers, licensed marriage and family therapists, and licensed professional counselors, and in section 6.10 of this book for psychiatrists. A corporation or professional service corporation offers many advantages for a psychotherapist, particularly if the psychotherapist wants to be affiliated with other psychotherapists but wants to avoid the joint and several liability associated with partnerships. There are trade-offs for this protection, namely, the added costs associated with forming and maintaining the corporate existence and the procedural formalities that must continually be followed.

7.07 Employees or Independent Contractors

A psychotherapist doing business as a sole proprietor, partnership, or corporation and employing others in the practice has a financial responsibility under the Colorado Employment Security Act, Colorado Workers' Compensation Act, the United States Code, and the Colorado Tax Code to make monthly payments to fund unemployment and workers' compensation, as well as other federal and state assistance programs. Although these payments are mandatory for employers whose work is performed by employees, businesses that contract their work to independent contractors generally are not required to make such contributions. Consequently, many businesses attempt to characterize their employees as independent contractors. Unfortunately, this is easier said than done.

In a Colorado Court of Appeals case, *Dana's Housekeeping v. Butterfield*, 807 P.2d 1218 (Colo. App. 1990), an employer attempted to avoid liability under the Colorado Workers' Compensation Act by seeking independent contractor status for its employees. The employer, Dana's Housekeeping, argued that it was a referral service for domestic housekeepers that did not have or exercise control over Butterfield's work. Thus, Dana's Housekeeping contended that Butterfield was an independent contractor. When Butterfield was injured, she sought workers' compensation on the basis that she was an employee. The court held that Butterfield was an employee of Dana's Housekeeping rather than an independent contractor.

In determining that Butterfield was an employee, the court applied a "right to control" test, which provides that a person shall be considered an employee if the employer has retained the right to control the manner, method, or means of the employee's duties. Although Dana's

Housekeeping signed a contract with Butterfield that characterized their relationship as being that of an independent contractor, the court ruled that the way in which parties may refer to themselves does not determine whether a person is an independent contractor or an employee. In deciding this case, the court considered the following factors as to whether a person is an employee or independent contractor:

1. Whether the employee gives all or any part of his or her time to the work;
2. Whether the worker or the employer controls the detail;
3. Whether the employee furnishes his or her own necessary tools and equipment;
4. Whether either may terminate employment without liability to the other; and
5. Whether compensation is measured by time, piece, or lump sum for the entire task.

In 1989, the Colorado Court of Appeals considered the case of *Locke v. Longacre,* 772 P.2d 685 (Colo. App. 1989). In this case, the court considered whether a person was an independent contractor or an employee under the Colorado Employment Security Act.

The defendant, Longacre, was a licensed practical nurse who had entered into an agreement with Locke to provide substantial home care and nursing services for Locke's mother. The parties had signed an agreement purporting to create an independent contract relationship between themselves. During a three-year period, Longacre provided constant care for Locke's mother. On one occasion, she provided similar services for a neighbor for approximately one week. When Longacre sought unemployment benefits, Locke argued that Longacre was an independent contractor providing professional nursing services with the potential to provide services for other individuals, but that she chose not to do so for personal reasons. In rejecting Locke's arguments, the court noted that in order to obtain independent contractor status, the claimant must be engaged in a business venture at the same time the claimant is providing services for the employer. Thus, if a person is providing services to a *sole* employer, even if the employer does not retain the right to control the manner, method, or means of the other party, an employer-employee relationship may exist.

There is much uncertainty in the law as to whether or not a psychotherapist who employs other therapists can achieve independent contractor status for them and avoid the financial obligations associated with employee status. Certainly, if the psychotherapist-employer retains the right to control the manner, method, or means of the therapy, an employee relationship would exist and there would be liability for the unemployment, workers' compensation, and FICA contributions. This would be particularly true if the professional rendering the services was not working for any other psychotherapist.

In order to substantiate to the Colorado Division of Employment that the individual is free from direction and control, the business should have given a written document to the independent contractor, preferably prepared by legal counsel, and signed by both parties. The document and actual practice should demonstrate that the business does *not:*

1. Require the individual to work exclusively for that business;
2. Establish a quality standard, except to the extent of plans and specifications (i.e., work cannot be overseen by the person for whom the services are performed);
3. Establish a salary or hourly rate but rather pays a fixed or contract amount;
4. Terminate the work during the contract period, unless the individual fails to produce a result that meets the specifications of the contract;
5. Provide any training for the individual;
6. Provide small tools or benefits, except that materials and equipment may be supplied;
7. Dictate the time of performance (a completion schedule may be established);
8. Pay the individual personally, but rather makes checks payable to the trade or business name of the individual; and
9. Combine business operations in any way with the individual's business, but instead maintains separate and distinct operations.

The IRS has developed a 20-factor test used to characterize workers. The American Institute of Certified Public Accounts, Tax Division, has developed a guide, based on the IRS criteria, to help in determining work status. A majority of the following questions should be answered "yes" in order to indicate potential independent contractor status:

1. Have the parties signed an independent contract or agreement?
2. Does the contract state that the company has no right to control the work performed?
3. Does the contract state that the independent contractor cannot be fired as long as he or she meets contractual obligations?
4. Does the contract state that the independent contractor has a right to hire and fire assistants?
5. Does the contract provide that the independent contractor is solely responsible for providing the labor to achieve the intended result?
6. Is the independent contractor paid by the job rather than by the hour?
7. Is the company ensuring that the company provides no type of training for inexperienced workers?
8. Is the independent contractor hired for a specified time period?
9. Is the independent contractor free to work for any number of persons or firms simultaneously?
10. Does the independent contractor advertise and project himself or herself to the public as an independent contractor in business for himself or herself?
11. Does the independent contractor perform his or her job off the company premises?
12. Does the contract provide that the customer will pay the independent contractor directly rather than pay the company, which then pays the contractor?
13. Does the company refrain from sending supervisors or inspectors to the field on a regular basis to check on the work progress?
14. Does the company refrain from requesting that the independent contractor do the same type of work as its regular employees?
15. Is there evidence that the company's competitors are treating similar workers as independent contractors?

Because the delinquent taxes and penalties can be significant for non-compliance with any of the foregoing government programs, a psychotherapist is cautioned to consult an accountant prior to attempting to characterize any worker as an independent contractor.

For further information regarding employee vs. independent contractor status, and contract provisions in employment and independent contractor agreements, see *Kimberlie Ryan, Employment Law Guidebook: For Colorado Business Owners and Human Resource Professionals (Bradford Publishing Co. 2006).*

7.08 Employment Law

Prior to the evolution of modern-day service and technology-based economies, the employment relationship reflected the dominance of the employer that existed in the agricultural and industrial economies. In both of these economic states of development, the employee had no ability to influence the nature of the employment relationship. The landowner and the industrialist, by virtue of their economic power, were able to dictate working conditions, wages, and hours. The workers in such economies had no economic or political power and therefore became subservient to the landowners and capitalists. From this historical perspective, it is not surprising that the law originally characterized the employment relationship as being one of "Master-Servant."

One of the earliest laws to emerge from the Master-Servant characterization of the employment relationship was the doctrine of "employment-at-will." Under this legal doctrine, employees served at the will of the employer, who possessed the unfettered and absolute right to terminate the employee with or without cause. Hence, an employee had no recourse for the employer's decision to terminate the employment relationship, even if done in bad faith.

Modern judicial interpretations of the employment-at-will doctrine have imposed certain limitations upon the doctrine and have affirmed the right of employees to seek recourse against employers who fail to follow their own policies and procedures regarding discipline and termination. Additionally, the courts have declared that employers who terminate employees for reasons that are found to be against public policy may not invoke the employment-at-will doctrine as justification for such terminations. Hence, in many states, an employee cannot be discharged for refusing to commit an unlawful act, for reporting criminal activities, or for disclosing illegal, unethical, or unsafe business practices.

The erosion of the Master-Servant relationship and the employment-at-will doctrine may also be traced to the creation of employee rights through federal and state legislation. The following represent some of the more significant federal laws that have changed the employment relationship and eroded the employment-at-will doctrine.

The Davis-Bacon Act. Signed in 1931, this act requires the payment of "prevailing wages" to employees of contractors or subcontractors working on government construction projects. In 1936, the Walsh-Healey Act extended the Davis-Bacon Act and required a minimum wage, as well as overtime pay of time and a half, to employees of manufacturers or suppliers entering into contracts with agencies of the federal government.

The Norris-LaGuardia Act. The Norris-LaGuardia Act was passed in 1932 and removed the power of federal courts to enjoin union activity, unless such activity involved fraud or violence.

The National Labor Relations Act. In 1935, Congress enacted the National Labor Relations Act, which established the right of employees to form, join, or assist labor organizations; to bargain collectively with their employers; and to engage in concerted activity for the purpose of collective bargaining or mutual aid and protection. The Act also required employers to bargain and deal in good faith with unions and created the National Labor Relations Board to oversee union elections and prevent employers from engaging in unfair and illegal union-labor activities and unfair labor practices.

Fair Labor Standards Act (1938). This Act prohibits oppressive child labor and provides that a minimum hourly wage rate be paid to covered employees and requires individuals working over 40 hours per week to be paid overtime wages of no less than one and a half times the regular pay for hours worked beyond 40 hours a week (with some exceptions).

Equal Pay Act of 1963. In 1963, Congress enacted the Equal Pay Act as an amendment to the Fair Labor Standards Act to eliminate discrimination between employees on the basis of sex (i.e., by paying wages at a rate less than the rate at which an employer pays wages to employees of the opposite sex for equal work on jobs, the performance of which requires equal skill, effort, and responsibility and which are performed under similar working conditions).

Title VII of the Civil Rights Act of 1964. This Act prohibits discrimination by most employers on the basis of race, color, national origin, religion, or sex.

Age Discrimination in Employment Act. In 1967, the Age Discrimination in Employment Act was enacted, which prohibits discrimination against job applicants or employees falling within the 40-70 age category by those employers whose business affects interstate commerce and who employ 20 or more employees.

Rehabilitation Act of 1973. This Act prohibits discrimination in employment against handicapped persons by those who receive federal contracts or assistance. The Act requires a covered person to hire a handicapped person who can, after reasonable accommodation, perform a job at the minimum level of productivity expected of a normal person performing the job. Further, contractors with federal contracts in excess of $2,500 are required to take "affirmative action" to hire handicapped persons.

Americans with Disabilities Act. This Act provides that effective July 26, 1992 (for employers with at least 25 employees) and July 26, 1994 (for employers with at least 15 employees), employers may not discriminate on the basis of disability and must make reasonable accommodations similar to those required by the Rehabilitation Act of 1973.

Employee Polygraph Protection Act. This Act, which was passed in 1988, prohibits employers from requiring, suggesting, or causing employees or prospective employees to take lie detector tests. It also forbids discharging, disciplining, discriminating against, refusing to promote or hire, or threatening to take any action against any employees or applicants because they refuse to take lie detector tests. The Act contains exceptions for security employees, government employers, and FBI contractors, as well as employees with access to controlled substances and investigation of a specific employer's economic loss if the employee had access to the property and the employer has a reasonable suspicion of the employee's involvement.

Pregnancy Discrimination Act of 1978. This Act amended Title VII of the Civil Rights Act of 1964 to prohibit discrimination on the basis of pregnancy.

Worker Adjustment and Retraining Act. This Act requires that employers with 100 or more employees give at least 60 days' notice of a plant closing or mass layoff to each employee.

Other Laws. A variety of other federal laws impinge upon the employment relationship. These laws include the Social Security Act, Employee Retirement Income Security Act, and the Occupational Health and Safety Act. Additionally, each state has passed laws covering workers' compensation and unemployment.

Other Resources. For further information about federal and state laws affecting employers, including discrimination laws, see *Kimberlie Ryan, Employment Law Guidebook: For Colorado Business Owners and Human Resource Professionals (Bradford Publishing Co. 2006).*

7.09 Workers' Compensation

The Colorado Workers' Compensation Act is designed to provide a remedy for job-related injuries without regard to fault. Under the Act, an employer is granted immunity from common-law negligence with respect to employees, provided the employer assumes the burden of compensating workers for all job-related injuries through private insurance or through participation in the Colorado Compensation Insurance Authority. In essence, an injured employee may not sue the employer for negligence, but receives a fixed compensation for any injury that is work-related.

Compensation for injured workers is funded by premiums paid by the employer either to the Colorado Compensation Insurance Authority or to private insurance carriers. A psychotherapist should consult a competent insurance broker to determine the most economical means of fulfilling this obligation.

7.10 Employer Payroll Taxes

Employers are required to pay FICA taxes for each employee. The rates change with some regularity. A psychotherapist should consult an accountant to determine the prevailing rates, and to plan appropriately for fulfilling these obligations.

State Unemployment. The Colorado Employment Security Act sets forth a comprehensive legislative scheme for providing unemployment benefits for qualified individuals who become unemployed. The funding for this program comes from insurance taxes levied against employers. An employer's tax is based upon the employer's total payroll and unemployment history. An accountant should be consulted for planning purposes with respect to such taxes.

7.11 Employee Withholdings

Employers are currently required to withhold from each employee's wages and deposit through a bank depository the following:

1. FICA employee taxes; and
2. Federal and state income taxes, depending on the declaration of the employee on W-4 form.

Employers are required to obtain from each employee a W-4 form and an I-9 immigration form. Failure to comply with these requirements can result in civil penalties and fines.

For further information regarding employee withholdings, see *Kimberlie Ryan, Employment Law Guidebook: For Colorado Business Owners and Human Resource Professionals, Ch. 4 (Bradford Publishing Co. 2006).*

7.12 Insurance

A psychotherapist who is in private practice should seriously consider the need for the following types of insurance:

1. Professional liability insurance;
2. Health insurance for himself or herself and all employees;
3. Property casualty insurance to insure against loss and theft of property;
4. Overhead expense insurance, which will provide a source of funds to meet ongoing business expenses in the event the psychotherapist is disabled and unable to generate fees for a period of time;
5. Personal disability insurance, which will provide a stream of income for the psychotherapist in the event he or she is disabled and unable to generate fees;
6. Life insurance, particularly if the psychotherapist provides the income to pay the bills for his or her family and currently lacks personal wealth to support such family in the event of his or her death; and

7. Comprehensive general liability coverage, which insures against losses due to ordinary negligence, and covers claims for a slip and fall at the therapist's office, for automobile accidents which result from business travel, etc.

7.13 Use of Professionals

Throughout this book, references have been made to the need to obtain advice from attorneys, certified public accountants, insurance brokers, and other business advisors. These professionals generally work at an hourly rate and are compensated for time actually devoted to rendering advice. The psychotherapist is urged to seek out and retain such professionals, since their advice can result in substantial savings.

In retaining a professional, the following facts should be considered:

1. The professional's expertise in a particular area;
2. The compatibility of the professional's personality with that of the psychotherapist;
3. The professional's reputation for timeliness and accuracy; and
4. The professional's hourly rate.

The psychotherapist should not hesitate to request a written fee engagement letter that outlines the scope of the services to be rendered and the basis for calculating the fees and terms of payment.

Attorneys frequently ask for a "retainer." This term means different things to different attorneys. For example, it may mean the client pays a non-refundable amount for that attorney's availability for legal services. For others, it may mean an advance deposit against which hourly charges are billed. Most legal work for psychotherapists will be billed at hourly rates ranging from $150 to $250 per hour, depending upon the attorney's experience. Some attorneys will charge a flat fee for certain types of work, such as incorporating a business or drafting a will.

Psychotherapists should not hesitate to inquire about these matters before engaging or retaining an attorney or any other professional.

7.14 Billing Standards and Billing Practices

Because of the complexity of HIPAA standards and managed health care billing practices, therapists nationwide have had many questions regarding billing standards and billing practices. In addition, frequent questions have arisen concerning the *Current Procedural Terminology* (CPT) Codes that should be used by therapists in billing for different types of treatment. The information that follows concerning the use of CPT Codes is not meant to be a substitute for purchase of the Manual, published by the American Medical Association, entitled Current Procedural Terminology (2008 Edition). The following questions are frequently posed by psychologists, licensed clinical social workers, MFT's and professional counselors.

Q. Can a clinical supervisor, who is a licensed mental health professional and who is on insurance panels, bill for treatment or professional services provided by a supervisee or contract employee who is not on the insurance panel?

A. No, only the individual who actually provides treatment can bill for those services. It is generally considered fraud if a person other than the treatment provider bills for those services.

Q. As a licensed psychologist, I am a panel provider on most insurance panels. I am required by the contracts with insurance panels to be available in emergencies for my clients. When I provide counseling over the telephone to clients in emergencies, can I bill for this service using the 90804 CPT Code for brief psychotherapy (20-30 minutes) or the 90806 CPT Code for a 45-50 minute session with a client?

A. These CPT Codes, as well as 90808 (for psychotherapy that lasts for 75-80 minutes) all require "face-to-face" contact with the client. In addition, the HCFA billing form used for insurance billing requires you to indicate the place of service (POS). It is essential that bills for services be accurate in every respect. When you are billing for a telephone session with a client that is not conducted "face-to-face," check with the insurance company representative to see if you are allowed to use one of these CPT Codes, or if another Code can be used for telephone sessions. Confirm in writing any directions that you are given in this regard. Also check with the insurance representative to see if the place of service should be listed as your office, or if you should reference the telephone as the place of service.

Q. None of the insurance panels with which I contract will pay for missed appointments. My written policies, which every client receives, state that the client is responsible for payment for any missed appointments. However, the insurance panel contracts also prohibit me from billing their insureds directly or collecting fees from them, except for deductibles or co-pays. Under these circumstances, can I charge clients for missed appointments?

A. Any contractual provisions should be negotiable between the contracting parties. When you receive a contract from an insurance panel, you must read it thoroughly to make certain that you can agree with all of its provisions and to ensure that you have no questions concerning the agreement. Therefore, if a contract presents this dilemma, stating that you cannot collect fees directly from an insured and that you cannot bill for missed appointments, you should insert in the contract that you will collect fees for missed appointments from the insured-client.

Under no circumstances can you bill for a missed appointment as if psychotherapy occurred when it did not: This would constitute fraud.

Q. I am a marriage and family therapist who specializes in couples counseling, marital therapy, and family counseling. Can I bill insurance panels for marriage counseling? What procedural code would I use? I know that 90847 is the CPT Code for family therapy (conjoint). Can this also be used for marriage counseling?

A. First of all, not many insurance panels will pay for marriage counseling, although some do. Marriage and family therapists who bill for couples counseling do use 90847, since this Code for family therapy comes the closest to this specific type of treatment. Other MFT's bill using the more generic 90804 or 90806, depending on the length of the session. A difficulty that may arise is how to fill in the block on the HCFA bill where an ICD diagnostic code must be inserted. If the treatment is for marital problems, and not for depression, anxiety, or an adjustment disorder, can one of these three diagnoses be inserted? If the goal of treatment is not to resolve symptoms of depression, anxiety, or an adjustment disorder, can a bill be submitted which implies that a client is receiving treatment for such problems? These are difficulties inherent in insurance billing. The best practice in such a situation is to have clients pay for marital counseling the old-fashioned way: out of their own pocket. An alternative approach would be to inform an insurance company representative directly, with client consent, of the services being provided, and ask what CPT Code or Diagnostic Code should be used. If you are informed that the health insurance policy does not cover marriage counseling, abide by that decision, and do not attempt to construct a creative but fraudulent way to bill the insurance carrier.

Q. When a client cannot pay their co-pay, am I required to turn the client away, and not let them attend a treatment session? I know that I cannot waive a co-pay or a deductible, but what do I do if a client does not have the funds to pay it?

A. You should not turn the client away from an individual or group therapy session because the client lacks funds to pay a required co-pay. When clients need treatment, they need to receive treatment. Although you cannot waive a co-pay, you can carry it on your books as a balance due from the client, when he or she has the funds to pay it.

Q. Are sliding-scale fee policies required? I know that I cannot bill an insurance company more than I bill my individual clients. But I am not certain if it is ethical for me to bill some clients less than I bill others.

A. That is an excellent question. In Colorado, sliding-scale fee policies are a generally accepted practice. In fact, the Domestic Violence Offender Management Board Standards require DVOMB-approved therapists to have a sliding scale for clients, based on income. Yes, this is an ethical practice, and sliding-scale fee policies are used by therapists nationwide.

Q. I know that I cannot bill an insurance company a rate higher than that which I bill to self-pay clients. Is there anything wrong with me charging everyone the same rate: $100 per hour? If an insurance company will not pay that rate, then I am required to accept whatever the contract with insurance panels will pay. Is there anything wrong with this practice?

A. No, this is acceptable. But you may want to make an exception for any indigent clients or low-income individuals, who may need a sliding-scale fee.

Q. When clients do not pay their bills, can I turn them over to a collection agency? Can I sue them in small claims court?

A. No you cannot sue them, for two reasons. First, there is no way that you can sue without breaching confidentiality. Secondly, if you sue a client in small claims court, it is likely that the client would file a counterclaim against you for malpractice, claiming that the treatment did not provide any benefit to the client. Even if such a counterclaim could easily be defended and dismissed, you would still be required to report it to your professional liability insurance company, and to answer in the affirmative when filling out applications in the future when you are asked, "Have you ever been sued for malpractice?" Therefore, you never want to sue a client.

The use of collection agencies is a common practice for medical doctors and hospitals. Ethical Codes for mental health professionals allow psychologists and other therapists to use collection agencies, so long as informed consent is given to the client, informing that this practice will be used. Sometimes, a client's failure to pay bills becomes a clinical issue: Why isn't the client paying, when the client has a clear ability to do so? The best practice is not to allow clients to get behind by more than three sessions. It certainly is ethical for you to treat the problem as a clinical issue, find out why the client has not paid, and encourage the client to either pay any balance immediately or to institute a payment plan.

Q. Recently, I received a letter from Medicaid, requiring me to provide a copy of all client records for the last calendar year as part of an audit. I do not know if this was a quality assurance review or if some other issue was being investigated. When I called the representative from whom I received the letter, she would not inform me what the purpose is for the audit. Client records, of course, have very personal and private information. Do I need to turn over all of the client records that have been requested?

A. This is certainly a problem with our managed healthcare system, and has been for many years. You will often find that contracts for panel providers, including not only private health insurance but also government health insurance programs, contain provisions requiring panel providers to turn over copies of client records, when requested. HIPAA disclosure statements generally state that such audits constitute exceptions to the confidentiality of Private Healthcare Information (PHI).

Can you trust the government or the government contractor that administers federally funded health insurance programs?

The generally accepted standard of practice is to trust that any records provided during the audit will be kept confidential. In fact, federal law generally requires that the confidentiality of such records be protected. HIPAA standards were enacted by Congress in order to protect the confidentiality of all PHI.

The difficulty that arises if you refuse to provide the client's records in response to this request is that Medicaid will demand back from you all the payments that you received for treatment of any client(s) involved. If you refuse to pay, your name will be placed on a "hold up list" and payments from other clients' treatment will be retained by Medicaid until all funds demanded have been paid.

Private health insurers should not be engaging in such a practice, however. HIPAA standards should prevent such practices. In compliance with HIPAA, whenever a request is made for treatment information, therapists are to respond by providing the least amount of information sufficient to satisfy the request. That is an excellent Standard, and should be remembered by mental health professionals whenever they are responding to requests for treatment information.

CHAPTER 8: STANDARDS FOR DOMESTIC EVALUATIONS AND FOR DOMESTIC VIOLENCE TREATMENT PROVIDERS

Psychotherapists are increasingly being employed by the courts to assist judges with evaluation of issues relating to parental responsibilities, parenting time, and domestic violence. The legal standards and best practices for child and family investigators, parenting coordinators, and approved domestic violence treatment providers are outlined in this chapter.

8.01 Allocation of Parental Responsibilities

In the late 1990s, the Colorado Legislature made sweeping changes to the statutes regarding custody actions and custody evaluations, and changed the term "custody" to "parental responsibilities." The entire statute that provided for "joint custody" was repealed. In its place, C.R.S. § 14-10-124 provides that courts shall "determine the allocation of parental responsibilities, including parenting time and decision-making responsibilities, in accordance with the best interests of the child giving paramount consideration to the physical, mental, and emotional conditions and need of the child."

With regard to parenting time, C.R.S. § 14-10-124 requires that courts "make provisions for parenting time that the court finds are in the child's best interests unless the court finds, after a hearing, that parenting time by the party would endanger the child's physical health or significantly impair the child's emotional development," based upon various factors set forth in the statute. This statute also provides, "In order to implement an order allocating parental responsibilities, both parties may substitute a parenting plan or plans for the court's approval that shall address both parenting time and the allocation of decision-making responsibilities." In addition, the court may order mediation in order "to assist the parties in formulating or modifying a parenting time plan or in implementing a parenting plan."

The statute that previously provided for custody evaluations (C.R.S. § 14-10-127) now provides for evaluations and reports concerning the allocation of parental responsibilities. Such an evaluation may be conducted pursuant to a court order by "the court probation department, any county or district social services department, or a licensed mental health professional" who is qualified. C.R.S. § 14-10-127 further provides, "When a mental health professional performs the evaluation, the court shall appoint or approve the selection of the mental health professional."

In preparing a report concerning the allocation of parental responsibilities, the evaluator may "consult with and obtain information from medical, mental health, educational, or other expert persons who have served the child in the past *without obtaining the consent of the parent...but the child's consent must be obtained if the child has reached the age of fifteen years unless the court finds that the child lacks mental capacity to consent.*" [emphasis added] This means, for example, that a mental health professional conducting such an evaluation need not obtain the parent's consent before speaking with another mental health professional; but he or she must obtain the child's consent, if the child has reached the age of 15 years. The mental health professional consulted by the evaluator must, of course, obtain consent from his or her client before providing to the evaluator any information that was gained during the course of a professional relationship involving the child.

In order to be qualified to testify regarding an evaluation of parental responsibilities or parenting time, the court must find that the evaluator is an expert, by training and experience, in the following areas: the effects of divorce and remarriage on children, adults, and families; appropriate parenting techniques; child development, including cognitive, personality, emotional, and psychological developments; child and adult psychopathology; applicable clinical assessment techniques; and applicable legal and ethical requirements of parental responsibilities evaluation.

C.R.S. § 14-10-127 requires that the written report of the evaluator be mailed to the court, to counsel, and to any party not represented by counsel at least 20 days prior to the hearing. The evaluator must make available to counsel and to any party not represented by counsel the file of underlying data and reports, complete texts of diagnostic reports, and the names and addresses of all persons consulted for the evaluation. The written report must include, but need not be limited to, the following information:

1. A description of the procedures employed during the evaluation;
2. A report of the data collected;
3. A conclusion that explains how the resulting recommendations were reached from the data collected, with specific reference to criteria listed in the statute and their relationship to the results of the evaluation;
4. Recommendations concerning custody, parenting time, and other considerations; and
5. An explanation of any limitations in the evaluations or any reservations regarding the resulting recommendations.

The standard to be followed by courts in allocating the decision-making responsibilities between the parties is "the best interests of the child," based upon specific factors enumerated in C.R.S. § 14-10-124. In making such a determination, "the court shall *not* presume that any person is better able to serve the best interests of the child because of that person's sex."

In the past, mental health professionals who performed custody evaluations have at times become embroiled in misunderstandings regarding their role, after interviewing parents and family members. Family members have filed complaints in the past to the Grievance Board, alleging that they believed information provided to the evaluator would be confidential. Such evaluations are not confidential, since information will be shared with the court, with attorneys for the parties involved, and with guardians ad litem. In order to avoid these unfortunate misunderstandings, an evaluator should provide any person who is interviewed for purposes of such an evaluation with a statement disclosing the fact that information provided in such an interview is *not confidential*, and will be shared with the court and other appropriate professionals.

It should go without saying that a therapist who has previously provided treatment to any family members involved in a dispute regarding parenting time or allocation of parental responsibility should not accept an appointment as an evaluator, since such would constitute a dual relationship.

Decision-Making Authority. When a potential client brings his or her children to see an MFT and provides information that he or she and the children's other parent have recently divorced, careful efforts must be made to ensure that the parent has decision-making authority. Pursuant to C.R.S. § 14-10-124, courts are empowered to allocate parental responsibilities when a divorce is awarded. Parental responsibilities include the residential care of children and the authority to make decisions concerning the children's treatment providers, schools, or church.

When this statute was enacted and went into effect in 1999, its purpose was to avoid conflicts and court hearings involving disputes between the parents over therapists, schools, and church attendance. In the vast majority of cases, judges do not necessarily allocate decision-making authority to one parent or the other, choosing instead to award "joint decision-making authority."

The best practice in determining whether a parent has decision-making authority is to require the parent to provide the divorce decree or an order entered by the court. If one parent has been given exclusive decision-making authority, that is the only parent who can select a treatment provider and sign a therapist's Disclosure Statement. Where joint decision-making authority has been granted to both parents, both parents must consent to treatment by signing a therapist's Disclosure Statement. By securing the permission of both parents for treatment, both will be entitled to receive treatment information and will be involved in the treatment process, which is generally in the best interests of the children involved.

Pursuant to C.R.S. § 13-22-103, either parent may consent to treatment of a child in an emergency. This affords treatment providers the opportunity to evaluate a child and determine what treatment is needed on an emergent basis. When a therapist determines that mental health services are needed on an emergent basis, the therapist should document the facts and circumstances that justify the need for treatment, and also document the harm that would result if services are not provided.

When parents have been awarded joint decision-making authority and one of the parents refuses to consent to mental health treatment, an interesting ethical issue is posed: Is the parent who is refusing to consent to treatment committing medical neglect? Should that parent be reported to DHS for neglecting his or her child?

The public policy in the State of Colorado, established by the child abuse reporting statute contained in the Children's Code, C.R.S. § 19-3-304, requires that the basic needs of children be met by their parents. Any parent who fails to provide for a child's medical or mental health needs is potentially engaging in neglect. When domestic situations become adversarial and conflictual, children can be harmed by a parent's refusal to consent to the provision of mental health services needed by a child. In advocating for the best interests of children, MFT's should request that one parent or the other be allocated decision-making authority to avoid the disputes that can arise between warring ex-spouses.

8.02 Parenting Time

The courts are frequently asked to resolve disputes concerning parenting time. This normally arises when one parent is not complying with the visitation schedule. When presented with such a motion, the court will resolve the motion based on what is in the best interests of the child.

C.R.S. § 14-10-129(2) provides that the court must not restrict a parent's visitation rights (parenting time) unless it finds that the parenting time would endanger the child's physical health or significantly impair the child's emotional development. For example, if a non-custodial parent has been convicted of the crimes listed below or any crime in which the underlying factual basis has been found by the court on the record to include an act of domestic violence, it constitutes a potential threat or endangerment to the child.

The crimes allowing the court to restrict parenting time include the following: murder in the first degree; murder in the second degree; enticement of a child; sexual assault in the first, second, or third degree; sexual assault on a child; incest; aggravated incest; child abuse; trafficking in children; sexual exploitation of children; procurement of a child for sexual exploitation; soliciting for child prostitution; pandering of a child; procurement of child; keeping a place of child prostitution; pimping of a child; inducement of child prostitution; and patronizing a prostituted child.

8.03 Standard of Care for Testifying in Domestic Cases

Section 8.01 discusses the factors to be considered by a parental responsibilities/parenting time evaluator. It also discusses the procedures to be followed in conducting an evaluation, the factors to be considered in making recommendations to the court, and the basic qualifications that an evaluator must possess. Although the law regarding domestic evaluations changed in 1999, the practices of many attorneys who handle domestic cases have not changed. They still subpoena therapists to court, expecting them to give opinions regarding who would be the better parent. In many cases, this creates a problem for the therapist involved when the therapist has not conducted a thorough parental responsibility/parenting time evaluation and thus does not have the appropriate basis for providing recommendations to the court concerning the issues that should be addressed. If you are called to court by an attorney in a domestic case and you are asked who would be the better parent or caregiver, do not express an opinion. You may simply answer, "I have not conducted the evaluation necessary to address these issues, and therefore do not have an opinion to give you."

You must not accept a court appointment or a request by counsel to conduct an evaluation concerning allocation of parental responsibilities if you have provided treatment to the parties or the children involved in the litigation, because this would constitute a dual relationship. In addition, your professional judgment in conducting the evaluation might be impaired by your loyalty to a former client. Remember that any time you are asked to testify in court concerning your assessment of a client or your opinions concerning a client, you are entitled to an expert fee. Arrangements for payment of your fee by the attorney who requests your testimony should be made before you go to court, and you should demand payment in advance.

8.04 Standards for Child and Family Investigators

In November 2011, the Colorado Supreme Court Chief Justice, Justice Bender, amended Chief Justice Directive 04-08. In his Introduction to the revised standards, Chief Justice Bender identified the purpose of CFI investigations, in contrast to parental responsibility evaluations: "The purpose of a CFI investigation is to provide a brief assessment that is non-intrusive, efficient, and cost effective." CJD 04-08 (revised 11/11) contains procedures for complaints against CFIs, which are to be reported to the Colorado Supreme Court Administrative Office ("SCAO") and to the District Court that appointed the CFI. The SCAO will determine if a complaint is founded, or not. The Introduction to these revised standards states: "Violation of a standard should not in and of itself give rise to a cause of action nor should it create any presumption that a legal duty has been breached or that a professional ethical violation has occurred."

Revised CJD-04-08 Standards

1. **Maximum Fee for Privately Paid CFIs.** The new standards provide, "The total investigation and report fees of a privately paid CFI shall not exceed the presumptive $2,000 cap unless prior court approval is obtained in the form of a written order with specific findings concerning the extraordinary circumstances that justify the excess fees." When the testimony of a privately paid CFI is sought by a party or deemed necessary by the court, a presumptive maximum fee of $500 per appointment applies. The revised standards state that the total fees for a CFI's testimony and preparation time "shall not exceed this presumptive $500 cap unless prior court approval is obtained in the form of written order with specific findings concerning the extraordinary circumstances that justify the excess fees."
2. **Placement on Eligibility Roster.** After March 1, 2012, to be eligible for appointment, all CFIs must be listed on a state eligibility roster, which will be maintained by the SCAO, based upon the application and background check which will be conducted by the Supreme Court. After July 1, 2012, to be eligible for appointment, all CFIs must be listed on both the statewide Eligibility Roster and also the Eligibility Roster of one or more judicial districts. The eligibility list for judicial districts will be maintained by the Office of Child Representative ("OCR") for the judicial district.
3. **Complaints.** Any complaint regarding the performance of a CFI must be submitted electronically to the judicial district and to the SCAO, using the "Child and Family Investigator Formal Complaint Procedures and Form" located on the SCAO website. A paper copy of the complaint form may be submitted to the judicial district's District Administrator. The judicial district's District Administrator "shall forward the complaint to the judge presiding over the matter in which the CFI was appointed to

determine whether any immediate preventative or corrective action needs to be taken in the matter." The judicial district then shall conduct an investigation "to determine whether the complaint is founded or unfounded, and to determine whether to take any action necessary to resolve the concerns or issues raised by a founded complaint." If the judicial district determines that the complaint against an attorney CFI is founded, "the District Administrator shall inform the Colorado Supreme Court Office of Attorney Regulation Council," and notify the complainant of the action taken.

If the complaint involves a mental health professional licensed by the Department of Regulatory Agencies, and if it is determined that the complaint concerning the CFI was founded, "the District Administrator shall inform DORA and shall notify the complainant." In addition, the District Administrator shall request that DORA inform the judicial district and the SCAO of the final outcome of any investigation.

If a judicial district fails to conduct an investigation pursuant to the procedures established by CJD 04-08, then the SCAO may conduct its own investigation. Sanctions which may be imposed in the complaint process include removal of the CFI from the Statewide Eligibility Roster, from one or more of the judicial eligibility rosters, or from the OCR District List.

4. **Malpractice Insurance.** The revised CJD 04-08 requires that all attorney and non-attorney CFIs with professional liability insurance "shall notify the SCAO in writing within five days if they cease to be covered by such professional liability insurance and shall not accept court appointments until coverage is reinstated." In addition, all CFIs "shall notify the SCAO in writing within five days of any malpractice suit, grievance, formal complaint, disciplinary action or criminal charge brought or filed against them."

5. **No Psychological Testing or Referrals by the CFI.** It is clear from the revised standards that CFI investigations are to be non-intrusive. Accordingly, Standard 13 provides: "the CFI shall not conduct psychological testing. The CFI shall not routinely conduct drug and alcohol or other evaluations." Standard 13 states: "Drug and alcohol or other evaluations should only be done if specifically ordered by the court and only when such evaluation

is the sole issue for which the appointment of the CFI was made. If the CFI believes other evaluations, such as psychological testing or drug and alcohol evaluations, would be a benefit to the parties or the child/ren and would assist the court, the CFI should provide this information to the court and the parties as soon as possible and shall include this information in his or her report to the court." The Comment to Standard 4 provides that the CFI is the "investigative arm of the court," and that, it is therefore inappropriate for CFIs "to make referrals or recommendations to the parties or to the court for specific professionals to be involved in the case in any way, unless such referrals or recommendations are requested by the parties or the court."

The remaining standards for the conduct of CFI investigations have not changed. However, Chief Justice Directive 04-08 does require the parties and counsel be informed of CFI's policies and procedures, which include a disclosure of the new complaint process, the cap on fees, and the other revised standards discussed in this Section.

CJD 04-08 Standards for CFI investigations

These Standards apply to the work of both attorneys and mental health professionals, who assist judges in domestic relation cases by conducting investigations and advise the court concerning the best interests of children involved in family law matters. CFI's, appointed by the court, make recommendations regarding the allocation of parental responsibilities and parenting time. Two questions which these Standards resolve concern whether it is appropriate for CFI's to have *ex parte* contact with the judge and whether CFI's must turn over a copy of their file to the parties involved. The Standards prohibit *ex parte* contact with the judge; that is, personal communication with the judge without involving the attorneys and any *pro se* party in the case. Any communication by a CFI with a judge in writing is appropriate, so long as all attorneys and any *pro se* party (unrepresented by counsel) are copied with the written communication. Similarly, CFI's are allowed to address concerns to the court at scheduled hearings in the case.

The Standards clarify what materials from the investigator's file must be disclosed, upon request, to attorneys and *pro se* parties. They require that a copy of all data and reports upon which an investigator has relied in formulating opinions and recommendations be turned over. "Data" would undoubtably include the contemporaneous notes made by the investigator when interviewing parents, children, etc., but would not include notes made while drafting a report. In regard to raw data from psychological testing, the standards provide that the release of raw data from any psychological testing should be done in compliance with the requirements of the relevant ethical standards for the professional.

The Standards require that an investigator, in assisting the court, shall:

- Collect data and conduct an investigation to allow the investigator to provide competent opinions to the court;
- Have age-appropriate communication with the children involved;
- Report child abuse to the proper agency and the court;
- Prepare a clear and timely report;
- Provide copies of his or her files upon request;
- Request termination of the appointment when permanent or post-decree orders are entered;
- Maintain competence through training; and
- Acknowledge when an issue is beyond his or her competence.

Do child and family investigators need to worry about being sued by parents who are dissatisfied with the investigation or who seek damages in a lawsuit because they are unhappy with either the process or the court's ruling? Under existing case law, a professional appointed by the court is considered to be an agent of the court who is entitled to the same judicial immunity that the judge is entitled to receive, since the professional's function is to assist the court in the judicial process.

The Standards also answer another question, previously unresolved, concerning whether an investigator could subsequently serve in a role as a parenting coordinator. As drafted, the Standards state that this is permissible; however, before an investigator can move to the role of parenting coordinator, the appointment of the child and family investigator must be terminated by the court and both parties must consent.

The Colorado Supreme Court Standards currently provide that an investigator "shall develop written policies for the parties" and for counsel. Anyone serving as a child and family investigator needs to have a contract that explains the parties' financial obligations, deadlines for payment of fees and costs, and appropriate disclosures concerning the investigator's role, as well as the process involved. Such a contract should also disclose that a therapist is not conducting therapy, nor establishing a professional relationship with any of the parties, when serving as an investigator.

The Colorado Supreme Court's Standards specifically provide that an investigator "shall not serve dual roles," and, therefore, shall not serve as a formal mediator in the case, provide psychotherapy to any of the parties or children in the case, nor accept an appointment from the court if they have had a prior personal relationship or a prior professional role with the family.

Communication with the Court and Counsel. According to Colorado Supreme Court Standard 18, "The Special Advocate shall have no private or *ex parte* communications with the court." A child and family investigator may need to communicate with the court concerning various issues, which include the receipt of information from the court concerning the order appointing the professional; submitting information to the court concerning a party's refusal to pay or to cooperate in the investigative process; or reporting to the court concerns relating to the potential for harm to children. The Colorado Supreme Court's Standards require that an investigator communicate with the court in a process that includes the attorneys involved in the case and any *pro se* party. Suggested methods of communication include "a short written report with copies to the parties and counsel"; attendance at a status conference or hearing in court, where issues can be raised; or arranging a conference call with the court and all counsel or *pro se* parties.

Communication with counsel for the parties is meant to facilitate the investigative process, not complicate it. The drafter of the Standards, however, states in a Comment: "There should be no non-disclosed conversations with one party's counsel." This means that any matter discussed with one attorney must be disclosed to all other counsel or *pro se* parties through a written communication, which confirms and discloses any subject matter discussed. In this way, an investigator is careful to avoid any bias or the appearance of bias in the eyes of parties engaged in a high-conflict domestic relations case.

Records to be Disclosed by Child and Family Investigators Upon Request. Colorado Supreme Court Standard 12 mandates: "The Special Advocate shall, if requested, make available to counsel or to a party not represented by counsel, his or her file of underlying data or reports." The specific data to be disclosed include "the names and addresses of all persons with whom the Special Advocate has consulted and the complete text of any diagnostic reports." As stated above, the "release of raw data from any psychological testing should be done in compliance with the requirements of the relevant professional ethical standards."

8.05 Access to Treatment Information

As discussed above, under Colorado law, courts no longer grant "custody" to parents in domestic cases. The courts allocate "parental responsibilities" between the parties, granting to one parent the authority to select treatment providers, to choose the children's schools, and to choose the church that they will attend. The court also allocates parental responsibilities between the parties for payment of child support, insurance, health care expenses, etc. Only the parent who has been allocated the authority by the court to select health care providers has the legal authority to consent to treatment of the children. These days, therapists are often advised to require a parent to produce the divorce decree to demonstrate that the court granted that parent the authority to select treatment providers for their children.

C.R.S. § 14-10-123.8 contains provisions that you need to know if you provide therapy to families and children. This statute provides:

> Access to information pertaining to a minor child, including but not limited to medical, dental, and school records, shall not be denied to any party allocated parental responsibilities, unless otherwise ordered by the court for good cause shown.

Applying this statute, if you are providing treatment to the children of a mother, to whom the court granted the authority to select treatment providers, and you receive a request for records from the children's father, who has been allocated the responsibility to pay child support, you should obtain the mother's consent to provide treatment information, or a summary of it, to the father. How can you do this? One way is to provide your client with a Disclosure Statement that contains the following provision: "When parents are divorced, Colorado law allows any parent who has been assigned parental responsibilities access to medical records. Therefore, in compliance with C.R.S. § 14-10-123.8, you authorize me to provide access to treatment information to such an individual by authorizing me to provide services to a child in your custody." Of course, if it is your policy to have both parents provide you with informed consent for treatment of their children, then you can have both parents sign an authorization for release of information, allowing the other parent to have access to treatment information.

8.06 Parenting Coordinators

In 2005, the Colorado Legislature enacted C.R.S. § 14-10-128.1. This statute provides that the court may appoint a parenting coordinator to assist in the resolution of disputes between the parties concerning parental responsibilities or implementation of the court-ordered parenting plan. The duties of the parenting coordinator are listed as follows:

(a) Assisting the parties in creating an agreed-upon, structured guideline for implementation of the parenting plan;

(b) Developing guidelines for communication between the parties and suggesting appropriate resources to assist the parties in learning appropriate communication skills;

(c) Informing the parties about appropriate resources to assist them in developing improved parenting skills;

(d) Assisting the parties in realistically identifying the sources and causes of conflict between them. . . ; and

(e) Assisting the parties in developing parenting strategies to minimize conflict.

The court must appoint the parenting coordinator for a specific period of time, not to exceed two years. C.R.S. § 14-10-128.1 mandates that the court order appointing a parenting coordinator "shall include apportionment of the responsibility for payment of all of the parenting coordinator's fees between the parties."

The parenting coordinator *cannot* be compelled to testify in the domestic proceeding. In this regard, C.R.S. § 14-10-128.1(7)(c)(I) states, "[A] parenting coordinator shall not be competent to testify and may not be required to produce records as to any statement, conduct, or decision, that occurred during the parenting coordinator's appointment, to the same extent as a judge of a court of this state acting in a judicial capacity." Thus, a parenting coordinator cannot be cross-examined by either of the parties concerning recommendations made to the parties or concerning the nature of the conflicts and problems that the parenting coordinator has been attempting to resolve with the parties. There are three exceptions to this rule. The parenting coordinator can be compelled to testify when: (1) the testimony or production of records by the parenting coordinator is necessary to determine a claim of the parenting coordinator against a party; (2) the testimony or production of records by the parenting coordinator is necessary to determine a claim of a party against a parenting coordinator; or (3) both parties have agreed in writing authorizing the parenting coordinator to testify. C.R.S. § 14-10-128.1(7)(c)(II).

The procedures for communication with the court (including the prohibition on *ex parte* communication), which are discussed in Section 8.04, also apply to parenting coordinators.

The Standards issued by the Colorado Supreme Court for child and family investigators specifically state: "The Standards are not meant to apply to Parenting Coordinators by whatever name they might be known." However, the court's Standards state that an investigator may agree to serve in the "role of parenting coordinator after all of his or her duties as Special Advocate are completed and the appointment has been terminated by the court" with the parties' consent. In a Comment to the Standards, the drafters discussed the pros and cons involved in this changing of roles. A therapist who had served as an investigator would be immediately familiar with the family dynamics, which would facilitate service in the role of parenting coordinator. On the other hand, if an issue arose in the future requiring further exploration by an investigator, then the previous investigator, with a wealth of knowledge about the family, would be unavailable because, as the drafter's Comment notes, the new parenting coordinator would then be in a "prior professional role" that would prevent him or her from accepting an appointment as the investigator once again.

Because of the important work performed by a parenting coordinator, resolving disputes between parents relating to the specifics and the logistics of parenting issues and making recommendations to the court concerning permanent orders, a parenting coordinator should have the same credentials as a child and family investigator and, in the opinion of this author, should adhere to the same legal and ethical standards that have been adopted for court-appointed professionals.

New Standards for Parenting Coordinators. The Colorado Supreme Court has issued Draft Guidelines for Parenting Coordinators. Parenting coordinators are appointed by the court in divorce and family court cases pursuant to C.R.S. § 14-10-128.1. MFT's who accept appointments as parenting coordinators should adopt these Guidelines as the standards to be followed pending issuance of a Chief Justice Directive from the Colorado Supreme Court.

According to the Draft Guidelines, the objective of parenting coordination is "to assist high conflict parents in implementing court orders concerning allocation of parental responsibilities in a timely manner." The appointment of a parenting coordinator ("PC") is reserved for "high conflict parents who have demonstrated difficulty in making parenting decisions together, who are unable to comply with court-ordered parenting plans, who cannot or will not reduce their child-related conflicts, and those who are unable to protect their children from the impact of that conflict."

The role of the PC is to assist the parties in implementing the terms of a parenting plan. Pursuant to the Guidelines under consideration, the court will apportion the PC's fees between the parties, and the court will enforce its order requiring payment of the PC's fees. General principles and duties established by the Guidelines are as follows:

1. To observe all applicable statutory duties and act professionally;
2. To maintain neutrality;
3. To maintain competence through appropriate training;
4. To have no private or *ex parte* communication with the court;
5. To review court orders;
6. To maintain confidentiality;
7. To report child abuse to proper agencies;
8. To not serve dual roles; and
9. To develop written policies for the parties.

To be qualified to serve as a court-appointed PC, a therapist may not have served previously in the role of parental responsibility evaluator or as a therapist for any of the parties or children involved in a case. It is recognized that the work of a parenting coordinator does not constitute the practice of psychotherapy. Under traditional principles of immunity for judges and court-appointed professionals, a PC should be entitled to immunity from suit for serving in this role.

8.07 Decision-Makers

C.R.S. § 14-10-128.3, enacted by the Colorado Legislature in 2005, provides for the appointment of a "qualified domestic relations decision-maker." A professional serving in this role has the authority, on behalf of the court, "to resolve disputes between the parties as to implementation or clarification of existing orders concerning the parties' minor or dependent children, including but not limited to disputes concerning parenting time, specific disputed parental decisions, and child support." The statute provides that, "The decision-maker appointed pursuant to the provisions of this section may be the same person as the parenting coordinator appointed pursuant to section 14-10-128.1." The court appoints the decision-maker for a specific period of time, not to exceed two years, and may apportion "the responsibility for payment of all of the decision-maker's fees between the parties."

This statute requires the decision-maker's procedures for making determinations to be "in writing and [to] be approved by the parties prior to the time the decision-maker begins to resolve a dispute of the parties." All decisions made by the decision-maker must be in writing, dated, and signed by the decision-maker, and must be filed with the court and mailed to the parties or their counsel. The statute also provides that, "All decisions shall be effective immediately upon issuance and shall continue in effect until vacated, corrected, or modified by the decision-maker or until an order is entered by a court pursuant to a de novo hearing . . . ."

Under C.R.S. § 14-10-128.3, a decision-maker is barred from testifying in the domestic proceeding, to the same extent that a judge acting in a judicial capacity is not competent to testify. In addition, a decision-maker "may not be required to produce records as to any statement, conduct, or decision, that occurred during the decision-maker's appointment."

Immunity. The Colorado Legislature has conferred statutory immunity upon decision-makers. C.R.S. § 14-10-128.3(7) states:

> A decision-maker shall be immune from liability in any claim for injury that arises out of an act or omission of the decision-maker occurring during the performance of his or her duties or during the performance of an act that the decision-maker reasonably believed was within the scope of his or her duties unless the act or omission causing such injury was willful and wanton.

The legislature created provisions for a sanction to be imposed in the event that a litigant files suit against a decision-maker. Section 14-10-128.3 provides, "If a person commences a civil action against a decision-maker arising from the services of the decision-maker, or if a person seeks to compel a decision-maker to testify or produce records . . . the court shall award to the decision-maker reasonable attorney fees and reasonable expenses of litigation."

8.08 Recent Caselaw Concerning Domestic Evaluations

In *Ryder v. Mitchell*, 54 P. 3d 885 (Colo. 2002), the Colorado Supreme Court upheld the dismissal of a lawsuit against a therapist, which the court determined to be frivolous. This is a case where a mother (Mitchell) took her children to a therapist (Ryder) and informed Ryder that she was convinced the children were being abused by their father. Mitchell asked that Ryder evaluate the children to determine the harm done to them by their father and prepare a treatment plan to remedy the effects of the abuse.

After Ryder evaluated the children and commenced treatment, she prepared a report in which she expressed her opinion that the children's father had not been abusing them, as well as her opinion that Mitchell was engaging in parental alienation. At the time, these parents were involved in a high-conflict battle over their children.

When Mitchell sued Ryder for negligence and breach of a fiduciary duty, the trial court dismissed the claims. The dismissal was upheld by the Colorado Supreme Court, which awarded Ryder attorney fees for her defense of a lawsuit that the trial court had termed "a disturbing example of truly vexatious litigation clearly warranting the imposition of fees against both Mitchell and her counsel." *Mitchell v. Ryder*, 104 P.3d 316 (Colo. App. 2004).

8.09 Limitations on Testimony by Mental Health Clinicians in Domestic Actions: Practical and Ethical Considerations for Attorneys

Attorneys who practice in the domestic relations courts need to understand the limitations imposed by the Standards for Child and Family Investigators (CFIs) on mental health professionals who have provided counseling or treatment to family members involved in a divorce or parental responsibilities action. These Standards were adopted in Chief Justice Directive (CJD) 04-08, issued by the Chief Justice of the Colorado Supreme Court in 2004. Attorneys for family court litigants also need to know the ethical limitations imposed on therapists by their professional codes of ethics, which restrict a clinician's ability to express opinions concerning the allocation of parental responsibilities or parenting time. This section discusses the application of both CFI Standards and ethical codes for therapists, and the appropriate role for therapists subpoenaed to testify in family court cases.

The Application of CFI Standards and Ethical Codes for Therapists. Attorneys understand the bounds of legal ethics in the representation of clients, and we adhere to basic ethical principles instinctively. Mental health professionals do the same in providing treatment to clients. Attorneys are aware of the boundaries created by a professional relationship and avoid the most basic taboo—a conflict of interest. For a therapist in a professional relationship with a client, basic ethical principles prohibit a "dual relationship" or a "boundary violation." A prohibited dual relationship for a therapist, for example, would occur if a clinician were to provide counseling to a close friend, colleague, or relative. Such relationships might impair the therapist's professional judgment in providing treatment to a client or in adhering to legal duties, such as the reporting of suspected child abuse and neglect. A boundary violation would occur if a therapist were to engage in an intimate relationship with a client, or to exercise "undue influence on the client, including the promotion of the sale of services, goods, property, or drugs in such a manner as to exploit the client." These ethical principles for therapists, therefore, prohibit a clinician who has provided counseling to a family, to a couple, to individuals, or to children from conducting an evaluation and making recommendations to a court concerning the allocation of parental responsibilities and parenting time. CJD 04-08, Standard 4 also prohibits a mental health professional who has provided "psychotherapy to any of the parties or children in the case from serving in the role of CFI."

Too often, parents involved in domestic litigation engage in "therapist shopping." They will take their children to a therapist, establish trust and rapport with the professional, and try to appear as the model parent. Then they will make critical comments about their estranged spouse, emphasizing how uncaring or abusive that individual is. Finally, they make a plea to the therapist for assistance in court: "Will you testify for me at the final orders hearing? I need you to make a recommendation to the judge that I should have sole custody of my children." Or the parent may request that the therapist make a recommendation that the other parent should only have supervised parenting time. This plea is accompanied by a request from that parent's attorney for a letter to the court by the therapist, making favorable recommendations on behalf of the client.

Such pleas by parents and requests by counsel put clinicians in an untenable position. No matter how great the therapist's desire to be supportive, a therapist cannot go to court and assume the role of a CFI or other court-appointed evaluator. To do so would violate the therapist's ethical principles and the CFI Standards, referred to above. For a clinician providing therapy to make ultimate recommendations on issues relating to parental responsibilities would also violate the legal principles embodied in C.R.S. § 14-10-127(6). This statute provides for the appointment by the court in domestic cases of licensed mental health professionals who meet the qualifications specified in this statute to conduct an evaluation of issues concerning the allocation of parental responsibilities. C.R.S. § 14-10-127(6)(a) authorizes a court-appointed mental health professional to make specific recommendations to the court "when the mental health professional has interviewed and assessed all parties to the dispute, assessed the quality of the relationship, or the potential for establishing a quality relationship, between the child and each of the parties, and had access to pertinent information from outside sources." Since a clinician who has provided services to a family member is prohibited from conducting an evaluation of these issues, any recommendations by the therapist would violate the clear intent and provisions of C.R.S. § 14-10-127.

The role of a therapist, who is compelled by subpoena to appear in court for a hearing on parenting issues, is therefore limited. The

American Association for Marriage and Family Therapy (AAMFT) Code of Ethics, Principle 3.14, provides:

> To avoid a conflict of interest, marriage and family therapists who treat minors or adults involved in custody or visitation actions may not also perform forensic evaluations for custody, residence, or visitation of the minor. The marriage and family therapist who treats the minor may provide the court or mental health professional performing the evaluation with information about the minor from the marriage and family therapist's perspective . . .

While it is appropriate, then, for CFIs or other court-appointed professionals to conduct evaluations of parenting issues and to make recommendations to the court regarding them, that is their role, and not the role of a clinician who has provided treatment to a family member.

What information or input is appropriate for therapists to provide the court from their clinical perspective? The Colorado Children's Code, which mandates the reporting of suspected child abuse and neglect by all licensed and unlicensed therapists, contains statutes designed to protect children. Various provisions of the Colorado Children's Code encourage therapists to provide information to social services or law enforcement officials to promote the purposes intended by these statutes: to keep children safe from harm. Consistent with these statutory provisions, therefore, clinicians may provide input to the court or to court-appointed professionals in domestic cases that will help the court in implementing parenting plans designed to keep children safe. While it is the role of a CFI, GAL, or Child Representative to make recommendations to the court in the best interests of children, it would be appropriate for a therapist to express concerns for a child's safety from a clinical perspective by suggesting to the court that a CFI may need to be appointed to investigate problems arising from a family's history of violence, abuse, drug use, or the like, when no one has yet been appointed in one of these roles. Since therapists reporting suspected child abuse are encouraged to provide input to child protection professionals concerning safety plans to prevent the risk of harm to children, then it is reasonable for clinicians to provide the same input to the court. This has long been a "generally accepted" practice among mental health professionals. Certainly, judges and magistrate welcome such information in order to keep children safe.

What factual information or opinions might therapists provide to the court from their clinical perspective in a domestic case? To the extent that it may be admissible, and assuming that the therapist-client privilege has been waived, therapists may express opinions concerning their assessment of clients, their treatment plan, and clients' progress in treatment. For all the reasons discussed above, therapists may not express opinions or recommendations on ultimate issues regarding parental responsibilities. Such testimony would not only exceed the clinician's role, but would also lack the necessary foundation: a thorough investigation and evaluation conducted by a competent court-appointed professional in compliance with the Standards set forth in CJD 04-08 or by an evaluator appointed pursuant to C.R.S. § 14-10-127.

Practical and Ethical Considerations for Attorneys. As stated above, sometimes domestic attorneys ask therapists for letters expressing recommendations on parenting issues, in the expectation that the therapists will advocate the client's position regarding these matters. Such requests, as well as the clients' pleas for support in court, place therapists in conflict, torn between their loyalty to the client and their ethical duty. Harm to the therapeutic relationship inevitably results when therapists explain that they cannot go to court as an "advocate" for the client.

Domestic relations practitioners need to respect therapists' boundaries and comply with the Standards established by CJD 04-08 by ensuring that they not make requests of therapists that create ethical conflicts for them and undermine their clinical relationships. Since legal ethics require that our conduct as attorneys must "conform to the requirements of the law," domestic practitioners would be well advised to comply with the spirit and intent of CJD 04-08 Standard 4 and of C.R.S. § 14-10-127 by acknowledging that clinicians cannot express opinions or recommendation regarding custodial arrangements in violation of these legal provisions.

Is it practical to subpoena therapists to testify in family court matters in view of these legal and ethical limitations? Keeping in mind that a clinician who is called to provide testimony concerning treatment issues is an expert witness who must be compensated as such, attorneys may question the cost-effectiveness of such evidence. Too often, therapists subpoenaed to testify in domestic matters complain that the attorney who issued the subpoena informed them, when advised of the clinician's fee schedule for court appearances, "Oh, you're not an expert. You're just going to be called to testify concerning your treatment." It is true that on occasion a healthcare professional may be a fact witness, called to court to provide testimony concerning a statement made by a party or regarding an eye-witness account of an incident. However, mental health professionals who testify in court regarding clinical matters that require their education, training, and expertise are expert witnesses who, like attorneys, are entitled to be paid their hourly rates for the task at hand.

Conclusion. The Standards established by CJD 04-08, the Colorado statutes, and ethical principles for therapists prohibit clinicians who have treated family members from making recommendations to the court regarding parenting issues. It is the role of CFIs and other court-appointed professionals, who have conducted an appropriate investigation and evaluation, to make recommendations to the court regarding the allocation of parental responsibilities and parenting time.

Domestic relations attorneys, understanding therapists' limitations, should respect clinicians' ethical boundaries and avoid undermining their therapeutic relationships with parents, children, or families involved in domestic cases.

8.10 Approved Domestic Violence Treatment Providers

Domestic violence treatment providers are approved and regulated by the Colorado Domestic Violence Offender Management Board (DVOMB), created in July 2000 pursuant to C.R.S. § 16-11.8-103. This statute states that the consistent and comprehensive evaluation, treatment, and continued monitoring of domestic violence offenders at each stage of the criminal justice system is necessary in order to lessen the likelihood of re-offense, enhance the protection of potential victims, and to work toward the elimination of repeat offenses. The DVOMB has the authority to formulate standards for the evaluation, treatment, and monitoring of convicted domestic violence offenders, and the Board has published *Standards for Treatment with Court-Ordered Domestic Violence Offenders.*

At a minimum, the Standards require that any domestic violence offender who is convicted or pleads guilty to a domestic violence offense must complete a 36-week group treatment program. The

DVOMB has also issued standards that specify the qualifications for treatment providers, the specific education and training required for approval by the Board, and requirements for experience and supervision that must be met when an application is filed with the DVOMB for approval as a domestic violence treatment provider. In addition, the Board Standards require all approved treatment providers to complete 32 hours of CEU's every two years in topic areas relevant to treatment with court-ordered domestic violence offenders.

"Domestic violence" is defined by C.R.S. § 18-6-800.3 as "an act or threatened act of violence upon a person with whom the actor is or has been involved in an intimate relationship." It also includes any other crime against a person or property, including an animal, when the act is "used as a method of coercion, control, punishment, intimidation, or revenge directed against a person with whom the actor is or has been involved in an intimate relationship." The DVOMB has issued standards for the evaluation of a domestic violence offender who has pled guilty or been convicted of a domestic violence offense, where the offender has been ordered to undergo evaluation prior to sentencing in order to assist the court in determining an appropriate sentence. In addition, the DVOMB has set forth separate standards for an intake evaluation to assess appropriateness for treatment, treatment amenability, and the best intervention strategy. Numerous factors are considered in this assessment, including alcohol and drug abuse history, financial stability, employment stability, history of all violent behavior, previous counseling, a mental health inventory, conflicts in relationships, assessment for risk of reoffense, and an interview with the victim.

The DVOMB Standards establish treatment goals for domestic violence offenders which include: educating offenders about domestic violence and its dynamics; self-management techniques to avoid abusive behaviors; education to increase the offender's skills and problem-solving and conflict resolution; cognitive-behavioral skills to improve communication and to promote healthy relationships; and education of the offender concerning the potential for reoffending. The treatment standards require offenders to be placed in gender-specific groups generally and in a group specifically designed to address issues regarding sexual orientation.

8.11 Compliance with DVOMB Standards by Approved Treatment Providers

Treatment Evaluation. DVOMB Standard 7.2.1 requires a treatment evaluation, in compliance with C.R.S. § 18-6-801, to assess the offender and determine "the most effective containment strategy." An approved treatment provider must evaluate:

1. Client's history, including:

   (a) Alcohol and drug history; financial and employment history; history of all violent behavior; previous counseling; parent-child relationship; relationships with intimate partners; medical health issues, including current medications; relational conflicts with others; and patterns of isolation.

   (b) Information regarding the client's family of origin to include any dysfunction relating to: history of physical/emotional abuse, neglect or abandonment, or alcoholism/drug abuse by client's parents; intimate violence by a client's parent; mental health disorders; multiple primary caretakers; sibling violence; divorce; or parental loss.

   (c) Peer violence and childhood problems including school problems, juvenile arrests, school discipline problems, health problems, suicide attempts as a child, or drug/alcohol abuse as an adolescent.
2. Simple Screening Inventory (SSI).
3. Addictions Screen.
4. Assessment for risk of re-offense.
5. Assessment of suicide risk.
6. Assessment of client's "current stage of change."
7. Assessment of client's learning style.
8. Arrest, court, and probation records and reports.
9. Victim interview or, if not available, victim impact statement.
10. Collateral contacts with criminal justice agent, previous therapists, treatment providers, or offender's family.
11. Mental status exam and/or psychometric testing, if appropriate.

Practice Tips.

1. DVOMB Standard 7.2.1 provides that this treatment evaluation shall be submitted to the court or responsible criminal justice agency (CJA).
2. Prepare and use a standard evaluation form, which touches on all of the mandated factors to be considered (similar to the drug and alcohol evaluation form used by probation departments), together with other standard assessment forms for use in assessing risk of suicide, violence, etc.

Intake Evaluation in Compliance with Standard 7.2.2 and C.R.S. § 18-6-801. In the event that the offender is not appropriate for domestic violence offender treatment, "the offender shall be referred back to the court for alternative disposition." The intake evaluation must be conducted on all offenders, and includes all of the same components discussed above. However, for gay or lesbian offenders, the intake evaluation shall assess "how the offender's internalized homophobia affects his/her life, and the offender's stage in the 'coming out' process."

Treatment Plan in compliance with Standard 7.3. The treatment plan shall address mental health concerns, substance abuse issues, child abuse, and any sexual abuse concerns. The purpose of the treatment plan is to promote victim and community safety, and to identify treatment goals listed in Standard 7.5.

Offender Contract in compliance with Standard 7.4. The offender contract is a consent-to-treat form and a statement of the Approved Treatment Provider's policies, program rules, and the consequences that will be forthcoming in the event that the offender violates program rules. It is also an acknowledgment by the offender of his or her responsibilities to the program and to the criminal justice system.

The offender contract "will clearly specify that past, present and future indications of domestic violence and/or child abuse or neglect shall be reported . . . and that the victim shall be warned." Offender contract provisions must include an agreement by the offender to be free of all violence; to accept responsibility for previous violent conduct; to meet financial responsibilities for evaluation and treatment; to be alcohol- and drug-free during treatment; to sign releases of information, as needed; to cooperate in treatment; to comply with criminal statutes;

to meet court-ordered family obligations; and to have no firearms in his or her possession. The offender contract shall include disclosures by the Approved Treatment Provider regarding confidentiality and the exceptions to confidentiality, relating to the disclosure of information to the victim, to the responsible criminal justice agency, to law enforcement, and to the courts about compliance, as well as reports regarding suspected child abuse or neglect, imminent risk to the victim or other person; and reports to the victim regarding the offender's non-attendance at a group session. In addition, the Approved Treatment Provider shall disclose the costs of evaluation and treatment; the frequency of treatment sessions and their duration; grievance procedures; a response plan for offenders in crisis; information concerning referral services; reasons that an offender would be terminated from treatment; and a disclosure that the Approved Treatment Provider's program or records may be audited by the DVOMB.

> **Practice Tip.** Include a statement in the offender contract that states: "All information shared by group members in group counseling is confidential under Colorado law, and must not be disclosed outside the group. By signing this contract, you agree to comply with this law, and to maintain the confidentiality of all such information. A breach of confidentiality by any group member will be treated as a violation of this contract."

> **Practice Tip.** Offenders who are court-ordered for treatment must fill out authorizations for release of information, so that a therapist may communicate with the probation department, the court, the victim, attorneys involved in the case, allied professionals, and others whom the treatment provider may need to consult. However, the submission of reports to the probation department and to the court, required by DVOMB Standards, are mandated reports. The DVOMB Standards have the force of law. Therefore, you should consider a report mandated by the DVOMB Standards to be similar to other reports required by law, such as the reporting of suspected child abuse or the disclosure of information when a duty to warn and protect exists.

If a client enrolled in an offender management treatment, signed authorizations for release of information to probation and the court, and then revoked the authorization, the treatment provider would still be required to report treatment violations, absences, progress, etc., to the criminal justice agency and the court. Revoking an authorization for release of information to those entities would, in and of itself, constitute a violation of the offender contract.

Treatment Goals. Numerous treatment goals are outlined in Standard 7.5.1, to include educating the offender and facilitating changes in behaviors. This Standard states that a treatment plan shall be designed to meet the following goals:

1. Educate the offender about what domestic violence is and the dynamics of domestic violence, in order for an offender to be able to identify his or her own abusive behavior;
2. Teach the offender self-management techniques to avoid abusive behaviors;
3. Educate the offender on non-abusive, adaptive, and socially acceptable relationship skills, interpersonal skills, and healthy sexual relationships;
4. Increase the offender's skills and problem-solving and conflict resolution;
5. Educate the offender regarding the impact of substance abuse and its correlation with violence;
6. Educate the offender regarding the sociocultural basis for violence;
7. Educate the offender regarding the legal consequences of his or her violence;
8. Identify and address issues of gender-role socialization and its relationship to violence;
9. Increase the offender's understanding of the impact of violence on child victims and on children exposed to family violence;
10. Increase the offender's understanding of parental responsibilities, referring an offender to parenting classes, when appropriate;
11. Increase the offender's understanding of the impact of violence on adult intimate victims;
12. Educate the offender regarding the process of changing behaviors;
13. Facilitate the process whereby an offender accepts responsibility for abusive actions and the consequences of those actions;

14. Identify and offer alternatives to the offender's thoughts, emotions, attitudes, and behaviors that result in violence or abusive behaviors;
15. Identify and decrease the offender's deficits in social and relationship skills;
16. Identify and confront the offender's issues of power and control, including sexual abuse;
17. Identify and confront the offender's criminal and violent attitudes and orientations;
18. Increase the offender's empathic skills, to increase the offender's ability to empathize with the victim;
19. Identify the effects of any trauma and past victimization sustained by the offender, as factors in his or her potential for re-offending;
20. Educate the offender on the potential for re-offending, the signs of abuse escalation, and normative regressing; and
21. Aid the offender in developing a written re-offense prevention plan that will include antecedent thoughts, feelings, attitudes, and behaviors associated with abusive behaviors, and that includes alternative options to intervene in a re-offense.

Specific Offender Populations. These offenders are to receive treatment in specific groups, whether gender-specific or specific to gay/lesbian/transgendered orientation.

Treatment Discharge. Standard 7.6 mandates that an Approved Treatment Provider "shall consult with responsible criminal justice agency and the victim or victim's advocate/therapist."

Victim Advocacy. In compliance with Standard 7.7, Approved Treatment Providers shall not counsel both an offender and that person's victim, but should refer the victim to a local domestic violence victims program for support and education concerning safety issues. Approved Treatment Provider's contact with victims shall include providing information regarding the status of an offender's participation, safety planning, referrals, safety checks, and duty to warn. These contacts should be performed by a victim's advocate.

Reporting Requirements. In compliance with Standard 8.2, an Approved Treatment Provider shall report to the responsible criminal justice agency (CJA) any lack of response by the offender within one week following the initial referral; report to the responsible CJA within one week of refusal of a client; report absences within 24 hours to the CJA and to the victim; provide a monthly written summary report to the CJA, including information on attendance, payment of fees, participation, offender progress, and any violations of the treatment contract; report any violations of the offender contract to the CJA; and provide a written discharge summary to the court and the CJA, after consultation with the CJA and victim.

Supervision. In compliance with DVOMB Standard 5.4.2, Approved Treatment Providers who are not licensed therapists are required to receive a minimum of four hours of supervision per month. Both you and your supervisor should keep records concerning the number of hours of supervision received, as well as the type of supervision. Whenever you obtain a consultation or supervision concerning a specific client's case, you must thoroughly chart information concerning the discussion, including the name of the consultant or supervisor, the factual issues discussed, any advice that you receive, and any action plan that you formulate based upon the advice that you receive from the consultant or supervisor.

Approved Treatment Providers who are also licensed mental health professionals only need to receive two hours per month of peer consultation with an approved treatment provider who is licensed. For any peer group supervision, you must keep a record concerning the date and time of the consultation and the names of those who attended. Information concerning compliance with the DVOMB supervision rule will be checked by the Board in the recertification process.

8.12 Recordkeeping Practices for DVOMB Approved Treatment Providers

In compliance with Mental Health Board Rules and ethical standards for therapists, Approved Treatment Providers must keep individual notes for each group session, as well as a group session note. In each individual client's chart, mandated entries include: a note concerning each disclosure of information made, to whom information was provided, and the nature of the information disclosed. In compliance with Standard 7.7.2(c), every contact with a victim must be summarized in a chart entry, and every attempt to contact a victim must be charted. Retain all records, including intake forms, treatment contracts, evaluations, reports to probation and the court, authorization forms for releases of information, group notes, individual notes, etc., for a minimum of seven years or any longer period of time mandated by a Licensing Board Rule. Remember that any report mandated by law must be charted thoroughly, as discussed in Section 4.16.

8.13 Potential Parental Alienation and the Best Interests of Children

During the past year, I have been consulted by counselors from across the country on a new issue that seems to be arising in high-conflict domestic situations. It concerns the report of a child, communicated to the child's therapist, that the child hates one of the parents and does not want to see that parent. The context for these reports inevitably is high-conflict divorce or custody litigation. These are not situations in which the parent whom the child does not want to see has been physically abusive, or a perpetrator of sexual abuse or domestic violence. The child's therapist then communicates this information to courts or family court-appointed evaluators.

Where are these reports coming from? Are they the product of parental alienation? How should a child's therapist deal with these situations and these reports?

These are truly clinical issues for clinicians to consult upon, discuss, and address. When a child provides a therapist with a list of all the reasons that the child hates the parent and does not want to see the parent, prepared in advance of a treatment session, how should a therapist respond? Should the response include the affirmation: "I am sure that your dad/mom loves you very much, and wants to see you?" or "Can you now make up a list for me of all the reasons why you love your dad/mom?" In addition to assessing whether the child in question, who has reported animosity towards a parent, demonstrates symptoms of anxiety, stress, or fear, should the therapist ask the non-offending parent what prompted the child to write out The List? Should the therapist also inquire how the parent responded to the situation, when presented with The List? Would it be proper for the therapist in this situation to suggest to this parent: "Did you reassure your child that s/he is loved by the other parent, and that it is important that they have a relationship?"

Under Colorado law, one of the most important factors that a court considers in determining custodial arrangements is which parent will foster a relationship between children and the other parent. Parental alienation is the antithesis of this. Whether "parental alienation" is a syndrome or not, judges and court-appointed professionals who evaluate custodial issues are deeply concerned when they hear of parental behaviors which may harm children or a child's relationship with the other parent. Whose role is it to evaluate whether or not parental alienation has occurred? The judge in any domestic litigation and court-appointed professionals.

What is the role of the child's therapist in this situation where a child has expressed animosity towards a parent? To remain clinically objective and impartial, providing appropriate treatment and any referrals needed. It is not the role of the therapist to make recommendations to the court concerning the allocation of parental responsibilities, concerning who should have custody, or concerning parenting time. And, of course, a therapist must report any child abuse or neglect that a therapist suspects has occurred or is occurring.

FORMS

In this section, you will find the following forms:

Form 1. **Motion for Protective Order:** This motion discusses doctrines of confidentiality, the therapist-client privilege, and judicial decisions from both the U.S. Supreme Court and the Colorado appellate courts. The purpose of this motion is to protect against unauthorized disclosure of treatment information, where a client has not consented to any courtroom testimony regarding treatment issues or to any release of information.

Form 2. **Client Disclosure Statement:** This disclosure statement complies with the requirements of C.R.S. § 12-43-214 and provides information to the client concerning the basic exceptions to confidentiality which may apply. Keep in mind that your disclosure statement is an informed consent form. When your client or your client's representative signs it, consent is thereby given for treatment. You may, therefore, include any additional disclosures in this form which are appropriate.

HIPAA forms. These forms include:

Form 3-1. **HIPAA Privacy Statement:** This is to be given to clients at the inception of treatment in order to explain the limitations on confidentiality and the potential uses of treatment information.

Form 3-2. **HIPAA Business Associate Contract:** This is to be signed by independent contractors who provide services to mental health professionals and who may come into the possession of confidential information relating to clients' identities, their diagnosis, or other privileged information. This form may be used by billing clerks, maintenance contractors, or contract therapists working in an agency to give assurances that they will protect confidential, privileged information, and that they will not make any unauthorized disclosure of confidential information.

Form 3-3. **Accounting of Disclosures:** This form can be used by HIPAA-compliant therapists when clients exercise their right to request an accounting of any disclosures of confidential information. A form is also provided to use in responding to the client's request for an accounting. (See Section 7.01 for more information concerning the use of this form.)

Form 3-4. **Request for Confidential Treatment Information:** This form is provided for use by clients in requesting access to their treatment records.

Form 3-5. **Authorization to Disclose Protected Mental Health Information:** This form may be used by clients to authorize the release of records to treating professionals or attorneys and to authorize mental health professionals to disclose confidential information to third parties or to testify in court.

Form 4. **Form M-1:** This form is essentially a symptom checklist and report used to document a person's mental health history and information relating to either an imminent threat of physical violence made by a client; a client's homicidal or suicidal ideation, which makes a person imminently dangerous to self or others; or information which indicates that a client is gravely disabled. The Form M-1 may be signed by a licensed mental health professional or by a peace officer when a person requires a 72-hour hold pursuant to C.R.S. § 27-65-105.

Form 5. **Disclosures for Forensic Evaluation:** This form is designed for evaluations where the person being evaluated is *not* a patient and no professional relationship is being established.

Form 6. **Professional Will:** This form is designed to be used by a therapist in conjunction with the therapist's own Personal Will, to give directions to the professional executor of the therapist for closing down the therapist's practice in the event of death; or to enable a mental health professional, acting as a business associate, to transact business and handle client matters in the event of a therapist's disability.

Form 7. **Contract for Clinical Supervision.**

Form 1. Motion for Protective Order

District Court, ______________ County, Colorado ______________ Judicial District Court Address: **Plaintiff:** v. **Respondent/Co-Petitioner:** Attorney or pro se Movant (Name and Address): Phone Number: E-mail: FAX Number: Atty. Reg. #:	▲ COURT USE ONLY ▲ Case Number: Division: Courtroom:
MOTION FOR PROTECTIVE ORDER	

Pursuant to C.R.S. § 13-90-107(1)(g), ______________________ moves this Court for a Protective Order, protecting against disclosure of confidential information sought by the Board. This Motion seeks protection against disclosure of any documents sought by the Board, on grounds that any such information of the type requested in the subpoena is personal, private, privileged, and confidential pursuant to the provisions of C.R.S. § 12-43-218 and C.R.S. § 13-90-107. The grounds for issuance of a Protective Order are as follows:

1. All records in the possession of Movant, ______________________, are confidential pursuant to the provisions of C.R.S. § 12-43-218 which provides in relevant part:

> 12-43-218. Disclosure of confidential communications. (1) A licensee, licensed or certified school psychologist, registrant, or unlicensed psychotherapist shall not disclose, without the consent of the client, any confidential communications made by the client, or advice given thereon, in the course of professional employment; nor shall a licensee's, licensed or certified school psychologist's, registrant's, or unlicensed psychotherapist's employee or associate, whether clerical or professional, disclose any knowledge of such communications acquired in such capacity; nor shall any person who has participated in any therapy conducted under the supervision of a licensee, licensed or certified school psychologist, registrant, or unlicensed psychotherapist, including, but not limited to, group therapy sessions, disclose any knowledge gained during the course of such therapy without the consent of the person to whom the knowledge relates.

The legislative intent and public policy supporting confidentiality of mental health records is based upon the premise that participants in such therapy need reassurance that they can disclose information concerning emotional issues and psychological problems within the professional relationship to a psychotherapist, who will not disclose the confidential information shared by the client. See *Jaffee v. Redmond,* 518 U.S. 1, 116 S. Ct. 1923 (1996). In *Jaffee,* the U.S. Supreme Court held that a psychotherapist-client privilege exists which shall be recognized as an evidentiary privilege under Rule 501 of the Federal Rules of Evidence. The Court's rationale for recognizing such a privilege was expressed as follows:

> Effective psychotherapy ... depends upon an atmosphere of confidence and trust in which the patient is willing to make a frank and complete disclosure of facts, emotions, memories, and fears. Because

> of the sensitive nature of the problems for which individuals consult psychotherapists, disclosure of confidential communications made during counseling sessions may cause embarrassment or disgrace. For this reason, the mere possibility of disclosure may impede development of the confidential relationship necessary for successful treatment.

Jaffee v. Redmond, supra.

2. C.R.S. § 13-90-107(1)(g) provides that a testimonial and evidentiary privilege exists involving communications between psychotherapist and client. This statute provides that "it is the policy of the law to encourage confidence and to preserve it inviolate ...." This privilege provides that a mental health professional shall not be examined as a witness in the following cases:

   > (g) A licensed psychologist, professional counselor, marriage and family therapist, social worker, or unlicensed psychotherapist shall not be examined without the consent of such licensee's or unlicensed psychotherapist's client as to any communication made by the client to such licensee or unlicensed psychotherapist, or such licensee's or unlicensed psychotherapist advice given thereon in the course of professional employments ....

   See C.R.S. § 13-90-107(1)(g).

3. Because of the sensitive, personal, and private nature of mental health records, a Protective Order should be entered, protecting against production or disclosure of any documents or records in Movant's possession concerning any of his or her clients.

4. In *Dill v. People,* 927 P.2d 1315 (Colo. 1996), the Colorado Supreme Court discussed issues that are not directly related to this action; however, the court in dicta discussed the confidentiality of psychotherapy records. Citing the decision of the U.S. Supreme Court in *Pennsylvania v. Ritchie,* 480 U.S. 39 (1987), the Colorado Supreme Court observed that there is a strong public interest in protecting the type of sensitive information found in psychotherapy records of the type maintained by the Mental Health Center. In view of the magnitude of this public interest, the Colorado Supreme Court in *Dill* held that no need existed for the court to conduct an *in camera* inspection of notes and records of therapy sessions, requested by a defendant.

5. In *People v. Sisneros,* 55 P.3d 797 (Colo. 2002), the Colorado Supreme Court considered a criminal case in which charges of sexual assault on a minor had been filed and in which the defendant's attorney had issued a subpoena duces tecum to the victim's psychologist, demanding that the victim's treatment records be turned over. In its decision, the Colorado Supreme Court discussed the therapist-client privilege set forth in C.R.S. § 13-90-107(1)(g) and ruled that the trial court judge did not have the discretion to order the victim's records to be disclosed, even for the judge's *in camera* review.

6. No client of Movant's has consented to any testimony or disclosure of treatment information. Thus, the provisions of the privilege statute should be enforced, and the Motion for Protective Order submitted by Movant should be granted pursuant to the legal authority discussed above.

Respectfully submitted,

____

CERTIFICATE OF SERVICE

I hereby certify that on this ____ day of ______________, 2006, a true and correct copy of the above and foregoing was deposited in the United States mail, postage prepaid, addressed to:

____

Form 2. Client Disclosure Statement

DISCLOSURE STATEMENT

1. **INFORMATION**
   Name: ______________________________
   Address: ______________________________
   Telephone: ______________________________

2. **CREDENTIALS**
   Licensure: ______________________________
   For an unlicensed therapist, you must state: a registered psychotherapist
   Degrees: ______________________________
   Professional Experience: ______________________________
   Certifications: ______________________________

3. **REGULATION OF PSYCHOTHERAPISTS**
   The practice of licensed or registered persons in the field of psychotherapy is regulated by the Mental Health Licensing Section of the Division of Registrations. The regulatory boards can be reached at 1560 Broadway, Suite 1350, Denver, Colorado 80202, (303) 894-7800. The regulatory requirements for mental health professionals provide that a Licensed Clinical Social Worker, a Licensed Marriage and Family therapist, and a Licensed Professional Counselor must hold a masters degree in their profession and have two years of post-masters supervision. A Licensed Psychologist must hold a doctorate degree in psychology and have one year of post-doctoral supervision. A Licensed Social Worker must hold a masters degree in social work. A Psychologist Candidate, a Marriage and Family Therapist Candidate, and a Licensed Professional Counselor Candidate must hold the necessary licensing degree and be in the process of completing the required supervision for licensure. A Certified Addiction Counselor I (CAC I) must be a high school graduate, and complete required training hours and 1000 hours of supervised experience. A CAC II must complete additional required training hours and 2,000 hours of supervised experience. A CAC III must have a bachelors degree in behavioral health, and complete additional required training hours and 2,000 hours of supervised experience. A Licensed Addiction Counselor must have a clinical masters degree and meet the CAC III requirements. A Registered Psychotherapist is listed in the State's Database and is authorized by law to practice psychotherapy in Colorado, but is not licensed by the state and is not required to satisfy any standardized educational or testing requirements to obtain a registration from the state.

4. **CLIENT RIGHTS AND IMPORTANT INFORMATION**
   a. You are entitled to receive information from me about my methods of therapy, the techniques I use, and the duration of your therapy, and my fee. Please ask if you would like to receive this information.
   b. You can seek a second opinion from another therapist or terminate therapy at any time.
   c. In a professional relationship (such as ours), sexual intimacy between a therapist and a client is never appropriate. If sexual intimacy occurs, it should be reported to the Board that licenses, certifies or registers the therapist.
   d. Generally speaking, information provided by and to a client in a professional relationship with a psychotherapist is legally confidential, and the therapist cannot disclose the information without the client's consent. There are several exceptions to confidentiality which include: (1) I am required to report any suspected incident of child abuse or neglect to law enforcement; (2) I am required to report any threat of imminent physical harm by a client to law enforcement and to the person(s) threatened; (3) I am required to initiate a mental health evaluation of a client who is imminently dangerous to self or to others, or who is gravely disabled, as a result of a mental disorder; (4) I am required to report any suspected threat to national security to federal officials; and (5) I may be required by Court Order to disclose treatment information.

e. Under Colorado law, C.R.S. § 14-10-123.8, parents have the right to access mental health treatment information concerning their minor children, unless the court has restricted access to such information. If you request treatment information from me, I may provide you with a treatment summary, in compliance with Colorado law and HIPAA Standards.

5. **DISCLOSURE REGARDING DIVORCE AND CUSTODY LITIGATION**
If you are involved in divorce or custody litigation, my role as a therapist is not to make recommendations to the court concerning custody or parenting issues. By signing this Disclosure Statement, you agree not to subpoena me to court for testimony or for disclosure of treatment information in such litigation; and you agree not to request that I write any reports to the court or to your attorney, making recommendations concerning custody. The court can appoint professionals, who have no prior relationship with family members, to conduct an investigation or evaluation and to make recommendations to the court concerning parental responsibilities or parenting time in the best interests of the family's children.

I have read the preceding information, and it has been presented to me verbally. I understand the disclosures that have been made to me. I also acknowledge that I have received a copy of this Disclosure Statement.

____
Print Client's Name

____ ____
Client Signature or Responsible Party Date

If signed by the Responsible Party, identify that party's legal authority to consent to treatment:

____

Form 3-1. HIPAA Privacy Statement

HIPAA PRIVACY STATEMENT: NOTICE OF PRIVACY RIGHTS

THIS NOTICE CONTAINS INFORMATION CONCERNING HOW CONFIDENTIAL MENTAL HEALTH TREATMENT INFORMATION CONCERNING YOU MAY BE USED AND DISCLOSED AND HOW YOU CAN OBTAIN ACCESS TO THIS INFORMATION. PLEASE REVIEW IT CAREFULLY AND LET US KNOW ANY QUESTIONS THAT YOU MAY HAVE CONCERNING THIS NOTICE. During the process of providing services to you, **[NAME OF COMPANY]** will obtain and use mental health and medical information concerning you that is both confidential and privileged. Ordinarily this confidential information will be used in the manner that is described in this statement, and will not be disclosed without your consent, except for the circumstances described in this Notice.

I. USES AND DISCLOSURES OF PROTECTED INFORMATION

A. General Uses and Disclosures Not Requiring the Client's Consent. **[NAME & ADDRESS OF COMPANY]** will use and disclose protected health information in the following ways.

1. *Treatment.* Treatment refers to the provision, coordination, or management of mental health care and related services by one or more health care providers. For example, **[NAME OF COMPANY]** therapists and staff involved with your care may use your information to plan your course of treatment and consult with other health care professionals or their staff concerning services needed or provided to you.

2. *Payment.* Payment refers to the activities undertaken by a health care provider to obtain or provide reimbursement for the provision of health care. For example, **[NAME OF COMPANY]** and other health care professionals will use information that identifies you, including information concerning your diagnosis, services provided to you, dates of services, and services needed by you, and may disclose such information to insurance companies, to businesses that review bills for health care services and handle claims for payment of health care benefits in order to obtain payment for services. If you are covered by Medicaid, information may be provided to the State of Colorado's Medicaid program, including but not limited to your treatment, condition, diagnosis, and services received.

3. *Health Care Operations.* Health Care Operations means activities undertaken by health insurance companies, businesses that administer health plans, and companies that review bills for health care services in order to process claims for health care benefits. These functions include management and administrative activities. For example, such companies may use your health information in monitoring of service quality, staff training and evaluation, medical reviews, legal services, auditing functions, compliance programs, business planning and accreditation, certification, licensing, and credentialing activities.

4. *Contacting the Client.* **[NAME OF COMPANY]** may contact you to remind you of appointments and to tell you about treatments or other services that might be of benefit to you.

5. *Required by Law.* **[NAME OF COMPANY]** will disclose protected health information when required by law. This includes, but is not limited to: (a) reporting child abuse or neglect to the Department of Human Services or to law enforcement; (b) when court ordered to release information; (c) when there is a legal duty to warn of a threat that a client has made of imminent physical violence, health care professionals are required to notify the potential victim of such a threat, and report it to law enforcement; (d) when a client is imminently dangerous to herself/himself or to others, or is gravely disabled, health care professionals may have a duty to hospitalize the client in order to obtain a 72-hour evaluation of the client; and (e) when required to report a threat to the national security of the United States.

6. *Health Oversight Activities.* Your confidential, protected health information may be disclosed to health oversight agencies for oversight activities authorized by law and necessary for the oversight of

the health care system, government health care benefit programs, regulatory programs or determining compliance with program standards.

7. *Crimes on the premises or observed by* **[NAME OF COMPANY]** *personnel.* Crimes that are observed by **[NAME OF COMPANY]** staff, that are directed toward staff, or occur on **[NAME OF COMPANY]** premises will be reported to law enforcement.

8. *Business Associates.* Confidential health care information concerning you, provided to insurers or to plans for purposes or payment for services that you receive may be disclosed to business associates. For example, some administrative, clinical, quality assurance, billing, legal, auditing, and practice management services may be provided by contracting with outside entities to perform those services. In those situations, protected health information will be provided to those contractors as is needed to perform their contracted tasks. Business associates are required to enter into an agreement maintaining the privacy of the protected health information released to them.

9. *Research.* Protected health information concerning you may be used with your permission for research purposes if the relevant provisions of the federal HIPAA privacy regulations are followed.

10. *Involuntary Clients.* Information regarding clients who are being treated involuntarily, pursuant to law, will be shared with other treatment providers, legal entities, third party payors, and others, as necessary to provide the care and management coordination needed in compliance with Colorado law.

11. *Family Members.* Except for certain minors, incompetent clients, or involuntary clients, protected health information cannot be provided to family members without the client's consent. In situations where family members are present during a discussion with the client, and it can be reasonably inferred from the circumstances that the client does not object, information may be disclosed in the course of that discussion. However, if the client objects, protected health information will not be disclosed.

12. *Emergencies.* In life-threatening emergencies, **[NAME OF COMPANY]** staff will disclose information necessary to avoid serious harm or death.

B. Client Release of Information or Authorization. **[NAME OF COMPANY]** and other health care professionals may not use or disclose protected health information in any way without a signed release of information or authorization. When you sign a release of information, or an authorization, it may later be revoked, provided that the revocation is in writing. The revocation will apply, except to the extent **[NAME OF COMPANY]** has already taken action in reliance thereon.

II. YOUR RIGHTS AS A CLIENT

A. Access to Protected Health Information. You have the right to receive a summary of confidential health information concerning you with regard to mental health services needed or provided to you. There are some limitations to this right, which will be provided to you at the time of your request, if any such limitation applies. To make a request, ask **[NAME OF COMPANY]** staff for the appropriate request form.

B. Amendment of Your Record. You have the right to request that **[NAME OF COMPANY]** or your health care professionals amend your protected health information. **[NAME OF COMPANY]** is not required to amend the record if it is determined that the record is accurate and complete. There are other exceptions, which will be provided to you at the time of your request, if relevant, along with the appeal process available to you. To make a request, ask **[NAME OF COMPANY]** staff for the appropriate request form.

C. Accounting of Disclosures. You have the right to receive an accounting of certain disclosures **[NAME OF COMPANY]** has made regarding your protected health information. However, that accounting does not include disclosures that were made for the purpose of treatment, payment, or health care operations. In addition, the accounting does not include disclosures made to you, disclosures made pursuant to a signed authorization, or disclosures made prior to April 14, 2003. There are other exceptions that will be provided to you, should you request an accounting. To make a request, ask **[NAME OF COMPANY]** staff for the appropriate request form.

D. Additional Restrictions. You have the right to request additional restrictions on the use or disclosure of your health information. **[NAME OF COMPANY]** does not have to agree to that request, and there are certain limits to any restriction, which will be provided to you at the time of your request. To make a request, ask **[NAME OF COMPANY]** staff for the appropriate request form.

E. Alternative Means of Receiving Confidential Communications. You have the right to request that you receive communications of protected health information from **[NAME OF COMPANY]** by alternative means or at alternative locations. For example, if you do not want **[NAME OF COMPANY]** to mail bills or other materials to your home, you can request that this information be sent to another address. There are limitations to the granting of such requests, which will be provided to you at the time of the request process. To make a request, ask **[NAME OF COMPANY]** staff for the appropriate request form.

F. Copy of this Notice. You have a right to obtain another copy of this notice upon request.

III. ADDITIONAL INFORMATION

A. Privacy Laws. **[NAME OF COMPANY]** is required by state and federal law to maintain the privacy of protected health information. In addition, **[NAME OF COMPANY]** is required by law to provide clients with notice of its legal duties and privacy practices with respect to protected health information. That is the purpose of this notice.

B. Terms of the Notice and Changes to the Notice. **[NAME OF COMPANY]** is required to abide by the terms of this notice, or any amended notice that may follow. **[NAME OF COMPANY]** reserves the right to change the terms of its notice an to make the new notice provisions effective for all protected health information that it maintains. When the notice is revised, the revised notice will be posed in service delivery sites and will be available upon request.

C. Complaints Regarding Privacy Rights. If you believe **[NAME OF COMPANY]** has violated your privacy rights, you have the right to complain to **[NAME OF COMPANY]** management. Please submit a statement, in writing, addressed to **[NAME & ADDRESS OF COMPANY]**, concerning your complaint and the basis for it. You also have the right to complain to the United States Secretary of Health and Human Services by sending your complaint to the Office of Civil Rights, U.S. Department of Health and Human Services, 200 Independence Avenue, S.W., Room 515F, HHH Bldg., Washington, D.C. 20201. It is the policy of **[NAME OF COMPANY]** that there will be no retaliation for your filing of such complaints.

D. Additional Information. If you desire additional information about your privacy rights at **[NAME OF COMPANY]**, please ask us any questions that you may have.

IV. CONFIDENTIALITY OF ALCOHOL AND DRUG ABUSE PATIENT RECORDS

A. The confidentiality of alcohol and drug abuse patient records maintained by **[NAME OF COMPANY]** is protected by federal law and regulations. Generally, the program may not say to a person outside the program that a patient attends the program, or disclose any information identifying a patient as an alcohol or drug abuser unless:

1. The patient consents in writing;
2. The disclosure is allowed by a court order; or
3. The disclosure is made to medical personnel in a medical emergency or to qualified personnel for research, audit, or program evaluation.

B. Violation of the Federal Law and Regulations by a Program is a Crime. Suspected violations may be reported to appropriate authorities in accordance with federal regulations.

C. Federal law and regulations do not protect any information about a crime committed by a patient either at the program or against any person who works for the program or about any threat to commit such a crime. Disclosure may be made concerning any threat made by a client to commit imminent physical violence against another person to the potential victim who has been threatened and to law enforcement.

D. Federal law and regulations do not protect any information about suspected child abuse or neglect from being reported under state law to appropriate state or local authorities.

V. EFFECTIVE DATE, THIS NOTICE IS EFFECTIVE APRIL 14, 2003.

I understand these disclosures. I have received a copy of this Disclosure Statement and Notice of Privacy Rights.

____
Client Signature

Form 3-2. HIPAA Business Associate Contract

[letterhead]

HIPAA BUSINESS ASSOCIATE CONTRACT

This agreement serves as a binding, legal contract between ______________________________ (Health Care Professional) and ______________________________ (Business Associate).

1. Business Associate agrees not to use or disclose protected health information, other than as permitted by this agreement or as required by law.

2. Business Associate agrees to use appropriate safeguards to maintain the security of confidential treatment information, communicated to Associate by Professional.

3. Business Associate agrees to use confidential health information only for the specific purpose for which such information is communicated to Associate by Professional.

4. Business Associate agrees to establish internal practices and procedures to safeguard the confidentiality of protected health information. Associate acknowledges that mental health treatment information is confidential, and is privileged information. Associate understands that even the identity of the client in a therapist-client relationship is confidential.

5. Business Associate agrees not to use confidential treatment information for any purpose other than the purpose authorized by the client whom the information concerns.

6. Business Associate agrees to request specific instructions from Professional if any questions exist concerning the proper use of confidential treatment information, which is transmitted from Professional to Associate.

7. Business Associate agrees to hold harmless and indemnify Professional for any damages incurred by the client, in the event that Business Associate discloses confidential treatment information in an unauthorized manner.

8. This agreement shall be effective, beginning on the ____ day of ________, 20____, and shall terminate when all of the protected health information provided by Professional to Associate has been destroyed or returned to the Professional.

9. In the event that Professional receives information concerning a breach of this agreement by the Associate, the Professional shall either provide an opportunity for Associate to cure the breach, or Professional shall terminate this agreement and any business relationship between the parties to this agreement. In the event of termination of the business relationship between these parties, Associate agrees to the immediate return of all confidential health information in its possession to Professional.

____
Authorized Representative, Business Associate

____
Health Care Professional

Form 3-3. Accounting of Disclosures

ACCOUNTING OF DISCLOSURES

Keep the original of this form in the client record and update it each time information about the client is shared with someone outside this office/agency. When the client asks for an accounting of disclosures, copy this form and give the client the copy.

Client Name: ____
Last First Middle Initial

Client Date of Birth:________________
Month / Day / Year

Disclosures of Protected Health Information about this Client:

Date of Disclosure	Name of Recipient	Address of Recipient	Information Disclosed	Purpose of Disclosure

Form 3-4. Request for Confidential Treatment Information

REQUEST FOR CONFIDENTIAL TREATMENT INFORMATION

Client Name: ______________________________ Date of Birth: ______________

Client Number: ______________

Client Address: ____

____

Information requested:

____

____

____

Date requested: ____________________

Signature: ______________________________

For Health Care Organization Use Only:

Date received ________________. Request has been Accepted Denied

If denied, check reason for denial:

- ☐ Confidential treatment information was not created by this organization.
- ☐ Confidential treatment information is not a part of patient's designated record set.
- ☐ Confidential treatment information is not available to the patient for inspection as required by federal law.
- ☐ Confidential treatment information may be obtained from:

____

____

____

Signature: ______________________________

Form 3-5. Authorization to Disclose Protected Mental Health Information

AUTHORIZATION TO DISCLOSE PROTECTED MENTAL HEALTH INFORMATION

Patient Name:	SSN:
Address:	Birth Date:
Telephone:	Identity Code:

Health Care Information From:	Release to:

I authorize the above-named health care provider to disclose the privileged information specified below to the organization, agency, or individual named on this request:

INFORMATION REQUESTED:

Place/Dates of Service

Kind and amount of information to be disclosed

Purpose of disclosure/why information required

I understand that the information to be disclosed may include any or all information involving communicable or venereal disease, psychological or psychiatric conditions, and drug or alcohol abuse and/or alcoholism. It may also include, but is not limited to, diseases such as hepatitis, syphilis, gonorrhea, and human immunodeficiency viruses (HIV), also known as acquired immune deficiency syndrome (AIDS).

AUTHORIZATION: I certify that this request is made voluntarily and that the information given above is accurate to the best of my knowledge. I understand that I may revoke this authorization at any time in writing by sending a letter to the facility privacy officer or their designee and that it will expire at the end of litigation involving me. I understand my revocation will not be effective to the extent that action has already been taken in reliance on it. **This authorization expires six months from date of patient's or representative's signature below, unless otherwise specified:** ____________. If I have authorized disclosure of my health information to someone who is not legally required to keep it private, it may be re-disclosed and may no longer be protected. A copy or fax of this authorization will be valid as the original.

I understand that authorization disclosure of health information is voluntary. I understand that I may refuse to sign this authorization and that my refusal to sign will not affect my ability to obtain treatment, payment, or eligibility to obtain benefits. I understand that I may inspect or obtain a copy of the information to be disclosed. I understand a fee will be charged for any copy of my health record. I understand the facility will provide me a copy of the signed authorization form. If I have questions about disclosure of my health information, I can contact the facility privacy officer or their designee.

Signature: ______________________________ Date: ____________________

Patient (Parent or Guardian if patient is a minor)

Minor's signature is required for release of any records for treatment that the minor may have authorized.

RELATIONSHIP (if other than patient): ______________________________

IDENTIFICATION OF PATIENT OR DESIGNATED REPRESENTATIVE

☐ Drivers License # ____________________ ☐ Passport # ____________________

☐ State ID # ____________________ ☐ Other ID # ____________________

Form 4. Form M-1

FORM M-1
EMERGENCY MENTAL ILLNESS REPORT AND APPLICATION

Date ____________________ Time ___________

NAME ____, hereafter referred to as Respondent.

Address ____

Date of Birth ________________________________

Place of Contact ____, Colorado.

Previous Psychiatric Care ____
Where When

Who brought respondent's condition to the attention of the undersigned?

____

Nearest relative ____
Name Address Phone

APPEARANCE AND GENERAL BEHAVIOR (Circle Items That Apply):

DRESS—Neat, Untidy, Dirty, Eccentric

POSTURE—Erect, Tense, Relaxed, Lying down

FACIAL EXPRESSION—Fixed, Changing, Angry, Perplexed, Sad, Happy, Suspicious

PHYSICAL ACTIVITY—Normal, Underactive, Overactive

EMOTIONAL REACTION (Circle Items That Apply):

ATTITUDE—Composed, Polite, Cooperative, Reserved, Indifferent, Silent, Scared, Sad, Happy, Carefree, Cocky, Hilarious, Excited, Angry, Sarcastic, Antagonistic, Suspicious, Insulting, Profane, Combative, Sleepy

TALK (Circle Items That Apply):

FORM—Logical, Conversational, Illogical, Rambling, Nonsensical

RATE—Normal, Over-talkative, Under-talkative

QUALITY—Controlled, Humorous, Dramatic, Forceful, Shouting, Screaming, Mumbling

EXPRESSIONS (Circle Items That Apply):

Ideas of Being Persecuted, Feels People Are Watching Him / Talking About Him, Ideas of Grandeur, Strange or Bizarre Physical Complaints, Very Self-Critical, Hearing Voices, Seeing Things, Homicidal Thoughts, Suicidal Thoughts, Unusual Sexual Ideas

DOES PATIENT KNOW (Circle Items That Apply):

Who he is? (Yes No), Where he is? (Yes No), Date? (Yes No), How he feels? (Yes No)

Counting from 20 to 1 Backwards—Result: Good Fair Poor

GENERAL KNOWLEDGE (Circle Items That Apply):

President? (Yes No), Governor? (Yes No), Mayor? (Yes No)

Pursuant to the provisions of C.R.S. § 27-65-105, as amended, the respondent was taken into custody by the undersigned and detained for 72-hour treatment and evaluation at ______________________________ ____ (designated or approved facility).

The respondent appears to be mentally ill and, as a result of such mental illness, appears to be *an imminent danger to others or to himself or herself* *gravely disabled*. The circumstances under which the undersigned believes there is probable cause leading to the above action are as follows:

____

____

____

____

____

List any property owned by subject that may be jeopardized by his or her detention:

Location: ________________________________

____

Location: ________________________________

____

____
Signature

Ser./Colo. License No. ________________________

____
Officer/Professional Person

____
Signature

Ser./Colo. License No. ________________________

____
Officer/Professional Person

* Strike between asterisks if inapplicable.

NOTICE TO RESPONDENT

C.R.S. § 27-65-105(3), provides that if the evaluation and treatment facility to which you are admitted does not have evaluation and treatment services available on Saturdays, Sundays, or holidays, then the facility may exclude those days in calculating the 72-hour detention period.

Original to facility

Copy to respondent

Copy to records

Form 5. Disclosures for Forensic Evaluation

DISCLOSURES FOR FORENSIC EVALUATION

A. EVALUATOR

Name ________________________________

Address ________________________________

Telephone ________________________________

Fax ________________________________

E-mail ________________________________

B. EVALUATOR'S CREDENTIALS

1. Professional Education ________________________________
2. Licensure ________________________________
3. Degrees ________________________________

   Professional Experience ________________________________

   Professional Associations ________________________________

C. ROLE OF THE EVALUATOR

I have been requested to conduct an evaluation of you and to prepare a report concerning my evaluation. All information that you provide to me including sensitive, personal information will not be confidential, because it will be shared with others, including the court. This evaluation has been requested by ________________ (Requesting Authority).

Although I am a healthcare provider by training and experience, the purpose of my evaluation will *not* be to provide treatment for you. We do not have, and will not have, a professional relationship with one another. I want to make it clear that I will not be providing treatment for you, and I will have no duty to make referrals for you to healthcare providers, just as I will not have a duty to make treatment recommendations for you.

D. PROCESS

The evaluation that I will be conducting will probably include a review of records concerning you and an interview of you, and may include testing. I will then prepare a report, which will be submitted to the Requesting Authority. My report will be used by the court to make any necessary determinations. Any fees for my professional services will be paid by ______________________. If you have specific questions concerning how the information that I obtain will be used or concerning who may receive a copy of my report, please let me know, and I will try to answer your questions. You are not entitled to a copy of my report unless the court orders that it be provided to you.

E. REPORTING REQUIREMENTS

I am required to report any suspected child abuse or neglect to the local county Department of Social Services or to law enforcement, unless the suspected abuse or neglect has already been reported. If you make a threat to harm any person, I am required to notify the person threatened and also to report the threat to law enforcement.

By signing this document, you are acknowledging that you understand the disclosures that have been made in it, that you understand my role as an evaluator, and that you understand how this evaluation or my report will be used.

______________________________ ______________________________

DATE **SIGNATURE**

HEALTH INSURANCE CLAIM FORM

PLEASE DO NOT STAPLE IN THIS AREA

APPROVED OMB-0938-0008

CARRIER

PICA

HEALTH INSURANCE CLAIM FORM

PICA

1. MEDICARE (Medicare #) MEDICAID (Medicaid #) CHAMPUS (Sponsor's SSN) CHAMPVA (VA File #) GROUP HEALTH PLAN (SSN or ID) FECA BLK LUNG (SSN) OTHER (ID)

1a. INSURED'S I.D. NUMBER (FOR PROGRAM IN ITEM 1)

2. PATIENT'S NAME (Last Name, First Name, Middle Initial)

3. PATIENT'S BIRTH DATE MM DD YY SEX M F

4. INSURED'S NAME (Last Name, First Name, Middle Initial)

5. PATIENT'S ADDRESS (No., Street)

6. PATIENT RELATIONSHIP TO INSURED Self Spouse Child Other

7. INSURED'S ADDRESS (No., Street)

CITY STATE

8. PATIENT STATUS Single Married Other

CITY STATE

ZIP CODE TELEPHONE (Include Area Code) ( )

Employed Full-Time Student Part-Time Student

ZIP CODE TELEPHONE (INCLUDE AREA CODE) ( )

9. OTHER INSURED'S NAME (Last Name, First Name, Middle Initial)

10. IS PATIENT'S CONDITION RELATED TO:

11. INSURED'S POLICY GROUP OR FECA NUMBER

a. OTHER INSURED'S POLICY OR GROUP NUMBER

a. EMPLOYMENT? (CURRENT OR PREVIOUS) YES NO

a. INSURED'S DATE OF BIRTH MM DD YY SEX M F

b. OTHER INSURED'S DATE OF BIRTH MM DD YY SEX M F

b. AUTO ACCIDENT? PLACE (State) YES NO

b. EMPLOYER'S NAME OR SCHOOL NAME

c. EMPLOYER'S NAME OR SCHOOL NAME

c. OTHER ACCIDENT? YES NO

c. INSURANCE PLAN NAME OR PROGRAM NAME

d. INSURANCE PLAN NAME OR PROGRAM NAME

10d. RESERVED FOR LOCAL USE

d. IS THERE ANOTHER HEALTH BENEFIT PLAN? YES NO ***If yes***, return to and complete item 9 a-d.

READ BACK OF FORM BEFORE COMPLETING & SIGNING THIS FORM.

12. PATIENT'S OR AUTHORIZED PERSON'S SIGNATURE I authorize the release of any medical or other information necessary to process this claim. I also request payment of government benefits either to myself or to the party who accepts assignment below.

SIGNED ____ DATE ____

13. INSURED'S OR AUTHORIZED PERSON'S SIGNATURE I authorize payment of medical benefits to the undersigned physician or supplier for services described below.

SIGNED ____

PATIENT AND INSURED INFORMATION

14. DATE OF CURRENT: MM DD YY ILLNESS (First symptom) OR INJURY (Accident) OR PREGNANCY(LMP)

15. IF PATIENT HAS HAD SAME OR SIMILAR ILLNESS, GIVE FIRST DATE MM DD YY

16. DATES PATIENT UNABLE TO WORK IN CURRENT OCCUPATION FROM MM DD YY TO MM DD YY

17. NAME OF REFERRING PHYSICIAN OR OTHER SOURCE

17a. I.D. NUMBER OF REFERRING PHYSICIAN

18. HOSPITALIZATION DATES RELATED TO CURRENT SERVICES FROM MM DD YY TO MM DD YY

19. RESERVED FOR LOCAL USE

20. OUTSIDE LAB? YES NO $ CHARGES

21. DIAGNOSIS OR NATURE OF ILLNESS OR INJURY. (RELATE ITEMS 1,2,3 OR 4 TO ITEM 24E BY LINE)

1. ___ . __
2. ___ . __
3. ___ . __
4. ___ . __

22. MEDICAID RESUBMISSION CODE ORIGINAL REF. NO.

23. PRIOR AUTHORIZATION NUMBER

24. A DATE(S) OF SERVICE From MM DD YY To MM DD YY	B Place of Service	C Type of Service	D PROCEDURES, SERVICES, OR SUPPLIES (Explain Unusual Circumstances) CPT/HCPCS MODIFIER	E DIAGNOSIS CODE	F $ CHARGES	G DAYS OR UNITS	H EPSDT Family Plan	I EMG	J COB	K RESERVED FOR LOCAL USE
1										
2										
3										
4										
5										
6										

25. FEDERAL TAX I.D. NUMBER SSN EIN

26. PATIENT'S ACCOUNT NO.

27. ACCEPT ASSIGNMENT? (For govt. claims, see back) YES NO

28. TOTAL CHARGE $

29. AMOUNT PAID $

30. BALANCE DUE $

31. SIGNATURE OF PHYSICIAN OR SUPPLIER INCLUDING DEGREES OR CREDENTIALS (I certify that the statements on the reverse apply to this bill and are made a part thereof.)

SIGNED DATE

32. NAME AND ADDRESS OF FACILITY WHERE SERVICES WERE RENDERED (If other than home or office)

33. PHYSICIAN'S, SUPPLIER'S BILLING NAME, ADDRESS, ZIP CODE & PHONE #

PIN# GRP#

PHYSICIAN OR SUPPLIER INFORMATION

(APPROVED BY AMA COUNCIL ON MEDICAL SERVICE 8/88) ***PLEASE PRINT OR TYPE*** FORM HCFA-1500 (12-90), FORM RRB-1500, FORM OWCP-1500

BECAUSE THIS FORM IS USED BY VARIOUS GOVERNMENT AND PRIVATE HEALTH PROGRAMS, SEE SEPARATE INSTRUCTIONS ISSUED BY APPLICABLE PROGRAMS.

NOTICE: Any person who knowingly files a statement of claim containing any misrepresentation or any false, incomplete or misleading information may be guilty of a criminal act punishable under law and may be subject to civil penalties.

REFERS TO GOVERNMENT PROGRAMS ONLY

MEDICARE AND CHAMPUS PAYMENTS: A patient's signature requests that payment be made and authorizes release of any information necessary to process the claim and certifies that the information provided in Blocks 1 through 12 is true, accurate and complete. In the case of a Medicare claim, the patient's signature authorizes any entity to release to Medicare medical and nonmedical information, including employment status, and whether the person has employer group health insurance, liability, no-fault, worker's compensation or other insurance which is responsible to pay for the services for which the Medicare claim is made. See 42 CFR 411.24(a). If item 9 is completed, the patient's signature authorizes release of the information to the health plan or agency shown. In Medicare assigned or CHAMPUS participation cases, the physician agrees to accept the charge determination of the Medicare carrier or CHAMPUS fiscal intermediary as the full charge, and the patient is responsible only for the deductible, coinsurance and noncovered services. Coinsurance and the deductible are based upon the charge determination of the Medicare carrier or CHAMPUS fiscal intermediary if this is less than the charge submitted. CHAMPUS is not a health insurance program but makes payment for health benefits provided through certain affiliations with the Uniformed Services. Information on the patient's sponsor should be provided in those items captioned in "Insured"; i.e., items 1a, 4, 6, 7, 9, and 11.

BLACK LUNG AND FECA CLAIMS

The provider agrees to accept the amount paid by the Government as payment in full. See Black Lung and FECA instructions regarding required procedure and diagnosis coding systems.

SIGNATURE OF PHYSICIAN OR SUPPLIER (MEDICARE, CHAMPUS, FECA AND BLACK LUNG)

I certify that the services shown on this form were medically indicated and necessary for the health of the patient and were personally furnished by me or were furnished incident to my professional service by my employee under my immediate personal supervision, except as otherwise expressly permitted by Medicare or CHAMPUS regulations.

For services to be considered as "incident" to a physician's professional service, 1) they must be rendered under the physician's immediate personal supervision by his/her employee, 2) they must be an integral, although incidental part of a covered physician's service, 3) they must be of kinds commonly furnished in physician's offices, and 4) the services of nonphysicians must be included on the physician's bills.

For CHAMPUS claims, I further certify that I (or any employee) who rendered services am not an active duty member of the Uniformed Services or a civilian employee of the United States Government or a contract employee of the United States Government, either civilian or military (refer to 5 USC 5536). For Black-Lung claims, I further certify that the services performed were for a Black Lung-related disorder.

No Part B Medicare benefits may be paid unless this form is received as required by existing law and regulations (42 CFR 424.32).

NOTICE: Any one who misrepresents or falsifies essential information to receive payment from Federal funds requested by this form may upon conviction be subject to fine and imprisonment under applicable Federal laws.

NOTICE TO PATIENT ABOUT THE COLLECTION AND USE OF MEDICARE, CHAMPUS, FECA, AND BLACK LUNG INFORMATION
(PRIVACY ACT STATEMENT)

We are authorized by HCFA, CHAMPUS and OWCP to ask you for information needed in the administration of the Medicare, CHAMPUS, FECA, and Black Lung programs. Authority to collect information is in section 205(a), 1862, 1872 and 1874 of the Social Security Act as amended, 42 CFR 411.24(a) and 424.5(a) (6), and 44 USC 3101;41 CFR 101 et seq and 10 USC 1079 and 1086; 5 USC 8101 et seq; and 30 USC 901 et seq; 38 USC 613; E.O. 9397.

The information we obtain to complete claims under these programs is used to identify you and to determine your eligibility. It is also used to decide if the services and supplies you received are covered by these programs and to insure that proper payment is made.

The information may also be given to other providers of services, carriers, intermediaries, medical review boards, health plans, and other organizations or Federal agencies, for the effective administration of Federal provisions that require other third parties payers to pay primary to Federal program, and as otherwise necessary to administer these programs. For example, it may be necessary to disclose information about the benefits you have used to a hospital or doctor. Additional disclosures are made through routine uses for information contained in systems of records.

FOR MEDICARE CLAIMS: See the notice modifying system No. 09-70-0501, titled, 'Carrier Medicare Claims Record,' published in the Federal Register, Vol. 55 No. 177, page 37549, Wed. Sept. 12, 1990, or as updated and republished.

FOR OWCP CLAIMS: Department of Labor, Privacy Act of 1974, "Republication of Notice of Systems of Records," Federal Register Vol. 55 No. 40, Wed Feb. 28, 1990, See ESA-5, ESA-6, ESA-12, ESA-13, ESA-30, or as updated and republished.

FOR CHAMPUS CLAIMS: PRINCIPLE PURPOSE(S): To evaluate eligibility for medical care provided by civilian sources and to issue payment upon establishment of eligibility and determination that the services/supplies received are authorized by law.

ROUTINE USE(S): Information from claims and related documents may be given to the Dept. of Veterans Affairs, the Dept. of Health and Human Services and/or the Dept. of Transportation consistent with their statutory administrative responsibilities under CHAMPUS/CHAMPVA; to the Dept. of Justice for representation of the Secretary of Defense in civil actions; to the Internal Revenue Service, private collection agencies, and consumer reporting agencies in connection with recoupment claims; and to Congressional Offices in response to inquiries made at the request of the person to whom a record pertains. Appropriate disclosures may be made to other federal, state, local, foreign government agencies, private business entities, and individual providers of care, on matters relating to entitlement, claims adjudication, fraud, program abuse, utilization review, quality assurance, peer review, program integrity, third-party liability, coordination of benefits, and civil and criminal litigation related to the operation of CHAMPUS.

DISCLOSURES: Voluntary; however, failure to provide information will result in delay in payment or may result in denial of claim. With the one exception discussed below, there are no penalties under these programs for refusing to supply information. However, failure to furnish information regarding the medical services rendered or the amount charged would prevent payment of claims under these programs. Failure to furnish any other information, such as name or claim number, would delay payment of the claim. Failure to provide medical information under FECA could be deemed an obstruction.

It is mandatory that you tell us if you know that another party is responsible for paying for your treatment. Section 1128B of the Social Security Act and 31 USC 3801-3812 provide penalties for withholding this information.

You should be aware that P.L. 100-503, the "Computer Matching and Privacy Protection Act of 1988", permits the government to verify information by way of computer matches.

MEDICAID PAYMENTS (PROVIDER CERTIFICATION)

I hereby agree to keep such records as are necessary to disclose fully the extent of services provided to individuals under the State's Title XIX plan and to furnish information regarding any payments claimed for providing such services as the State Agency or Dept. of Health and Humans Services may request.

I further agree to accept, as payment in full, the amount paid by the Medicaid program for those claims submitted for payment under that program, with the exception of authorized deductible, coinsurance, co-payment or similar cost-sharing charge.

SIGNATURE OF PHYSICIAN (OR SUPPLIER): I certify that the services listed above were medically indicated and necessary to the health of this patient and were personally furnished by me or my employee under my personal direction.

NOTICE: This is to certify that the foregoing information is true, accurate and complete. I understand that payment and satisfaction of this claim will be from Federal and State funds, and that any false claims, statements, or documents, or concealment of a material fact, may be prosecuted under applicable Federal or State laws.

Public reporting burden for this collection of information is estimated to average 15 minutes per response, including time for reviewing instructions, searching existing date sources, gathering and maintaining data needed, and completing and reviewing the collection of information. Send comments regarding this burden estimate or any other aspect of this collection of information, including suggestions for reducing the burden, to HCFA, Office of Financial Management, P.O. Box 26684, Baltimore, MD 21207; and to the Office of Management and Budget, Paperwork Reduction Project (OMB-0938-0008), Washington, D.C. 20503.

Form 6. Professional Will

PROFESSIONAL WILL

I, ____, a resident of the County of ______________, State of _________________, being of sound and disposing mind and memory, declare this to be my Professional Will. This supersedes all prior Professional Wills, if there are any. **This is not a substitute for a Personal Last Will and Testament.** It is intended to give authority and instructions to my Professional Executor regarding my counseling practice in the event of my incapacitation or death.

FIRST

I am a therapist in independent practice. My ________________________ License # is ______________.
My office address is ____.
I also maintain an office at ____.

SECOND

In the event of my death or incapacitation, I appoint ____, whose phone number is ________________ and whose office is located at ________________________ ____ as my Professional Executor.

In the event that ____ is unavailable or unable to perform this function, I appoint ____ whose phone number is ________________ and whose office is located at ____________________________________ ____ as a backup Professional Executor.

I grant my Professional Executors full authority to:

a. Act on my behalf in making decisions about storing, releasing, and disposing of my professional records.
b. Carry out any activities deemed necessary to properly administer this Professional Will.
c. Delegate and authorize other persons to assist and carry out any activities deemed necessary to properly administer this Professional Will.

THIRD

My attorney for my Professional Will is ____, whose phone number is ________________ and whose office is located at ________________________ ____.

FOURTH

The executor of my current personal will is ____, whose phone number is ________________, and who resides at ____________________________ ____.

FIFTH

A. My current client records are located at ____.

B. My past client records are located at ____.

C. Billing and financial records related to my psychology practice are located at ____________________
____.

D. Some or all of my client, billing, and financial records are on a computer, located at ______________
____.

E. My appointment book and client phone numbers are located at ______________________________
____.

F. My email address is ________________________ and the password is ______________________.

G. My office phone number is ________________ and the voice mail access code is ______________.

H. Any necessary keys you will need for access to my office, filing cabinets, storage facilities, etc. are located at ____.

I. For assistance in locating and accessing my records you may contact ____________________
______________________________, whose phone number is ________________ and whose address is ____.
In addition, the following person(s) may be helpful in locating/accessing my records ______________
____.

SIXTH

My specific instructions for my Professional Executor are:

A. First of all, I would like to express my deep appreciation for your willingness to serve as the Professional Executor for this will.

B. There are four copies of this Professional Will. They are located as follows:
   1. One is in your possession.
   2. One is in the possession of my attorney.
   3. One is with my personal will.
   4. One is with my professional liability insurance policy.

C. A list of current and selected past clients and their phone numbers who are to be notified about my death and any planned memorial services is located with the copy of my Professional Will in my professional liability insurance file. This file is located at ____________________________________.
   1. Please use your clinical judgment and discretion in deciding how you want to notify current and past clients and whether or not to publish a notice in the newspaper notifying clients of my death and who to contact for further information.
   2. Please use your clinical judgment and discretion in deciding whether or not to arrange a special memorial service for clients only. In that eventuality you may wish to request that one or more therapists actively participate in the service.
   3. If clinically indicated, you may wish to offer a face-to-face meeting with some clients. You may also wish to provide three referral sources, which can, of course, include yourself.

D. My professional liability insurance is currently provided by ______________________________ ______________________________, whose phone number is ________________, and whose address is ____.
My policy # is ____________________.

Please notify my professional liability carrier in writing of my death as expeditiously as possible and arrange for any additional coverage that may be appropriate.

Please also notify the state Licensing Board.

E. Please arrange for copies of referred clients' records to go to their new therapists.

All remaining records should be maintained according to the Record Keeping regulations of the State Licensing Board.

When disposing of outdated records, please ensure it is done in a manner that destroys all materials that could identify the client, e.g., burning or shredding.

F. You may bill my estate for your time and any other expenses that you may incur in executing these instructions. Unless otherwise ordered by the court, the hourly rate of $75.00 per hour is acknowledged to be reasonable.

I declare under penalty of perjury and under the laws of the State of ______________________ that the foregoing is true and correct.

Executed at ____, on _________________________.
(location) (date)

____
Signature

WITNESSES:

Printed Name: ____________________________ Signature: ________________________________

Residing at: ____

Printed Name: ____________________________ Signature: ________________________________

Residing at: ____

Form 7. Contract for Clinical Supervision

CLINICAL SUPERVISION CONTRACT

The parties to this contract are ______________________, supervisor and ______________________, supervisee. The fee for clinical supervision will be $____________ per hour for an individual session and $____________ per hour for group supervision sessions. Both supervisor and supervisee agree to keep accurate records concerning the dates and times on which supervision occurs, and information concerning whether the supervision was individual or group. Supervisor and supervisee also agree as follows:

1. Supervisee will maintain a policy of professional liability insurance during the clinical supervision process, and will provide a copy of his or her Certificate of Insurance to supervisor.
2. Supervisee agrees to comply with the Code of Ethics adopted by the American Counseling Association, and hereby acknowledges receipt of a copy of the ACA ethical code. In addition, supervisee agrees to comply with the rules adopted by the Colorado Board of Licensed Professional Counselor Examiners, and acknowledges receipt of a copy of the current Rules. These Rules are posted on the Board's website.
3. Supervisee agrees to comply with the Prohibited Activities Statutes, C.R.S. § 12-43-222, and the other mental health statutes posted on the DORA website for the Mental Health Boards. Specifically, supervisee agrees to provide each of his or her counseling clients with his or her client disclosure statement in compliance with C.R.S. § 12-43-214, and agrees to name ______________________ as his or her clinical supervisor in his or her disclosure statement. Supervisee also agrees not to engage in any dual relationship with a counseling client in violation of C.R.S. § 12-43-222(1)(i) and (j).
4. Supervisor and supervisee agree in compliance with C.R.S. § 12-43-218, HIPAA Standards, and Ethical Provisions that clinical supervision is a confidential process. The limitations on confidentiality for this confidential process include: (1) waiver of the confidentiality by the counseling client; (2) reporting of suspected child abuse or neglect; (3) the duty to warn and protect (see C.R.S. § 13-21-117); (4) the duty to initiate a 72-hour hold pursuant to C.R.S. § 27-65-105; and (5) compliance with any court order for disclosure of treatment records.
5. Supervisee agrees to obtain informed consent in writing from any counseling clients whose treatment session is to be videotaped, recorded, or observed through one-way glass.
6. Frequency of clinical supervision sessions: One hour of clinical supervision will occur for every twenty hours of client counseling.
7. In compliance with Colorado Statutes and Ethical Provisions, the duty of the clinical supervisor will be to direct the therapy process and to assist the supervisee in complying with all legal and ethical standards.
8. The supervisee agrees to submit bills for his or her counseling services which accurately reflect the amount of time spent in counseling sessions.
9. As part of the supervision process, supervisee agrees to provide treatment records and billing statements to the clinical supervisor upon request. Supervisee agrees to maintain treatment records in compliance with the LPC Board's record-keeping rule.
10. Clinical supervisor agrees to keep notes concerning case consultations, issues discussed in clinical supervision, and training provided in supervision.

Dated: ______________________ ______________________________
Clinical Supervisor

Dated: ______________________ ______________________________
Supervisee

TABLES OF AUTHORITIES

Table of Statutes

C.R.S. §	Section No.
7-60-101 *et seq.*	7.05
7-80-101 *et seq.*	7.06
10-1-128	4.09, 6.07, 6.10
12-22-303	6.07
12-36-101 *et seq.*	6.10
12-36-106.3	6.10
12-36-106.4	6.10
12-36-117	6.10
12-36-118(4)	6.10
12-36-123	6.10
12-36-134	6.10, 7.06
12-36-202	6.10
12-38-111.6(4)	6.10
12-38-111.6(4.5)	6.10
12-38-116.5(3)	6.12
12-42-102(4)	6.12
12-42-113	6.12
12-42-119	6.12
12-43-101 *et seq.*	6.10
12-43-201 *et seq.*	4.01, 4.13
12-43-201(9)	2.12, 4.03, 4.18, 6.01
12-43-203	3.13
12-43-203(11)	2.02, 6.03
12-43-211	6.09, 7.06
12-43-214	4.02, 4.18, 6.02, 6.04, 6.05, Form 7
12-43-215	6.01
12-43-215(1)	4.17
12-43-215(8)	6.01
12-43-216	4.02, 6.01
12-43-218	2.01, 2.03, 2.06, 2.10, 4.18, 6.02, 6.03, Form 1, Form 7
12-43-218(1)	2.02

12-43-218(2) 2.02
12-43-218(4) 2.02, 6.03
12-43-218(5) 2.02
12-43-221.5 .... 6.07
12-43-222 .... 4.02, 4.13, 6.04, 6.05, 6.07, Form 7
12-43-222(1)(i) .... Form 7
12-43-222(1)(j) .... Form 7
12-43-222(1)(n) 6.06
12-43-222(1)(t)(IV) 6.08
12-43-224(9) 6.06
12-43-226 .... 4.02, 6.02, 6.08
12-43-226(1) 6.02
12-43-226(5) 6.02
12-43-227 .... 6.04
12-43-702.5 .... 6.01
12-43-801 .... 6.01
12-43-804 .... 6.11
13-6-107 .... 1.02
13-14-102 .... 5.03
13-21-117 .... 2.12, 4.01, 4.04, 4.16, Form 7
13-21-117.5 .... 5.07
13-22-103 .... 8.01
13-64-301 .... 6.10
13-64-502 .... 2.07
13-90-107 .... 2.03, 2.06, 2.10, 2.21, 4.18, 6.01, 6.03, Form 1
13-90-107(1)(c) 4.17
13-90-107(1)(d) 2.07
13-90-107(1)(d)(VI) 2.07
13-90-107(1)(g) .... 2.08, 4.18, Form 1
13-90-107(1)(k)(II) 2.10
13-90-107(3) 2.07, 2.08
14-10-107(4) 5.03
14-10-116 .... 1.09
14-10-116.5 .... 1.09
14-10-123.8 .... Form 2
14-10-124 .... 8.01
14-10-127 .... 8.01, 8.09

14-10-127(6) 8.09
14-10-127(6)(a) 8.09
14-10-128.1 . . . . .8.06
14-10-128.1(7)(c)(I) 8.06
14-10-128.1(7)(c)(II) 8.06
14-10-128.3 . . . . .8.07
14-10-128.3(7) 8.07
14-10-129(2) 8.02
15-14-101 *et seq.* 5.01
15-14-102(4) 5.01
15-14-203 . . . . .5.01
15-14-205 . . . . .5.01
15-14-206 . . . . .5.01
15-14-207 . . . . .5.01
15-14-208 . . . . .5.01
15-14-210 . . . . .5.01
15-14-304 . . . . .5.01
15-14-310 . . . . .5.01
15-14-311 . . . . .5.01
15-14-312 . . . . .5.01
15-14-314 . . . . .5.01
15-14-315 . . . . .5.01
15-14-316 . . . . .5.01
15-14-318 . . . . .5.01
15-14-506 . . . . .5.01
16-8-101.5(1) 5.08
16-8-103.6 . . . . .2.07, 2.08
16-8-105(1) 5.08
16-8-105.5 . . . . .5.08
16-8-109 . . . . .5.08
16-8-115(3) 5.08
16-8-120(3) 5.08
16-11.8-103 . . . . .8.10
16-22-102(9) 2.10
18-3-401(3.5) 2.10
18-3-402 . . . . .2.10
18-3-405 . . . . .2.10

18-3-405.5 .... 4.07
18-6-401(3) 2.11
18-6-401(4) 2.11
18-6-800.3 .... 5.03, 8.10
18-6-801 .... 8.11
18-6-803.5 .... 5.03
18-8-115 .... 2.13, 2.18
18-13-119 .... 4.09, 6.07
18-13-119(3) 6.10
18-18-102(3) 6.10
18-18-204 .... 6.10
19-1-103(1)(a) 2.10
19-1-103(77) 2.10
19-3-102(1)(a) 2.10
19-3-102(1)(b) 2.10
19-3-102(1)(c) 2.10
19-3-103 .... 2.10
19-3-203(2) 1.09
19-3-304 .... 4.08, 4.17, 8.01
19-3-304(1) 2.10
19-3-304(2) 2.10
19-3-304(2)(aa)(I) 4.17
19-3-304(3) 2.10
19-3-304(4) 2.10
19-3-305 .... 2.10
19-3-307 .... 2.10
19-3-309 .... 2.10
19-3-311 .... 2.10
22-60.5-210 .... 6.01
24-4-105(11) 6.05
24-34-110 .... 6.13
25-1-801 .... 2.19
25-1-802 .... 2.19, 2.22
25-1.5-103(1)(a) 6.02
25-4-1402 .... 2.09, 4.15
26-3.1-102 .... 2.14
26-6-101 .... 2.10

26-6-102 . . . . .2.10
27-10.5-101 . . . . .5.07
27-10.5-101 *et seq.* 5.01, 5.07
27-10.5-102(5) 4.14
27-10.5-110 . . . . .5.07
27-10.5-112 . . . . .5.07
27-10.5-113 . . . . .5.07
27-10.5-114 . . . . .5.07
27-10.5-114(4) 5.07
27-10.5-115 . . . . .5.07
27-10.5-115(8) 5.07
27-10.5-116 . . . . .5.07
27-10.5-117(1) 5.07
27-10.5-117(2) 5.07
27-10.5-117(3) 5.07
27-10.5-117(5) 5.07
27-10.5-117(6) 5.07
27-10.5-118 . . . . .5.07
27-10.5-119 . . . . .5.07
27-10.5-121 . . . . .5.07
27-10.5-122 . . . . .5.07
27-10.5-123 . . . . .5.07
27-10.5-124 . . . . .5.07
27-10.5-128 . . . . .5.07
27-10.5-129 . . . . .5.07
27-65-101 . . . . .Form 7
27-65-101 *et seq.* 2.16, 4.01, 5.01, 5.04
27-65-102 . . . . .2.14
27-65-102(12) 4.14
27-65-103 . . . . .2.17, 4.14, 5.05, 6.02
27-65-103(2) 2.17, 5.05
27-65-103(5) 5.05
27-65-105 . . . . .5.04, 6.02, Form 3
27-65-105(1)(a) 5.04
27-65-105(3) . . . . .Form 3
27-65-106 . . . . .5.04
27-65-107 . . . . .5.04

27-65-108 . . . . .5.04
27-65-109 . . . . .5.04, 6.02
27-65-116 . . . . .5.04
27-65-117 . . . . .5.04
27-65-120 . . . . .5.04
27-65-121 . . . . .2.16, 5.04
27-65-122 . . . . .5.04
27-65-127 . . . . .5.04
27-67-102 . . . . .5.05
27-67-104 . . . . .5.05
27-81-101 *et seq.* 5.01
27-81-111 . . . . .5.06
27-81-112 . . . . .5.06

U.S.C. § . . . . .Section No.
42 U.S.C. § 9501 . . . . .2.18, 5.04
42 U.S.C. § 10801 *et seq.* 2.16

Table of Cases

Cases **Section No.**
Awai v. Kotin, 872 P.2d 1332 (Colo. App. 1993) 3.13
Bond v. District Court of County of Denver,
682 P.2d 33 (Colo. 1984) 2.07, 2.21
Brady v. Hopper, 570 F. Supp. 1333 (D. Colo. 1983) 4.04
Briscoe v. LaHue, 460 U.S. 325 (1983) 3.13, 4.01
Dana's Housekeeping v. Butterfield, 807 P.2d 1218
(Colo. App. 1990) 7.07
Dill v. People, 927 P.2d 1315 (Colo. 1996) . . . . .Form 1
Farley v. People, 746 P.2d 956 (Colo. 1987) 3.02
Ferguson v. People, 824 P.2d 803 (Colo. 1992) 4.07
Halverson v. Pikes Peak Family Counseling & Mental Health
Ctr., Inc., 795 P.2d 1352 (Colo. App. 1990) 4.04
Jaffee v. Redmond, 518 U.S. 1 (1996) . . . . .2.03, 2.18, Form 1
Kurzawa v. Mueller, 732 F.2d 1456 (6th Cir. 1984) 3.13
Locke v. Longacre, 772 P.2d 685 (Colo. App. 1989) 7.07
Merrick v. Burns, 43 P.3d 712 (Colo. App. 2001) .3.13

Mitchell v. Ryder, 104 P.3d 316 (Colo. App. 2004) 8.08
Montoya v. Bebensee, 761 P.2d 285 (Colo. App. 1988) 2.10
Parrish v. Lamm, 758 P.2d 1356 (Colo. 1988) 4.09
Pennsylvania v. Ritchie, 480 U.S. 39 (1987) . . . . .Form 1
People v. Ashley, 687 P.2d 473 (Colo. App. 1984) 3.02
People v. Beaver, 725 P.2d 96 (Colo. App. 1986) .3.02
People v. Campbell, 785 P.2d 153 (Colo. App. 1989) 3.02
People v. Deninger, 772 P.2d 674 (Colo. App. 1989) 3.02
People v. District Court, 647 P.2d 1206 (Colo. 1982) 3.02
People v. Gillispie, 767 P.2d 778 (Colo. App. 1988) 3.02
People v. Guilbeaux, 761 P.2d 255 (Colo. App. 1988) 3.02
People v. Hampton, 746 P.2d 947 (Colo. 1987) 3.02
People v. Koon, 724 P.2d 1367 (Colo. App. 1986) 3.02
People v. Lomanaco, 802 P.2d 1143 (Colo. App. 1990) 3.02
People v. Low, 732 P.2d 622 (Colo. 1987) 5.08
People v. Mathes, 703 P.2d 608 (Colo. App. 1985) 3.02
People v. Ortega, 672 P.2d 215 (Colo. App. 1983) 3.02
People v. Rosenthal, 617 P.2d 551 Colo. 1980) 2.21
People v. Serravo, 823 P.2d 128 (Colo. 1992) 5.08
People v. Sisneros, 55 P.3d 797 (Colo. 2002) . . . . .2.21, Form 1
People v. Snook, 745 P.2d 647 (Colo. 1987) 3.02
Perreira v. State, 768 P.2d 1198 (Colo. 1989) 4.04
Ramona v. Superior Court, 57 Cal. App. 4th 107 (1997) 4.15
Ryder v. Mitchell, 54 P.3d 885 (Colo. 2002) 8.08

INDEX

References are to section numbers.

A

Abuse, child. *See* Child abuse or neglect
Accountants, 7.13
Actions against clients, 4.13
Addiction counselors. *See also* Certified Addiction Counselors licensing, 6.11
Adolescent treatment disclosures, 2.17
Age discrimination, 7.08
AIDS/HIV reporting, 2.09
Alcohol counselor licensing, 6.11
Alcoholism
- emergency commitment, 5.06
- involuntary commitment, 5.06

Americans with Disabilities Act, 7.08
Appeals
- Colorado Court of Appeals, 1.05
- Colorado Supreme Court, 1.06
- federal courts, 1.08

Arbitrators, 1.09
At-risk adult mistreatment reports, 2.14
Attorney fees, 4.13
Attorney general, 1.09
Attorneys, 1.09, 7.13
Automatic temporary divorce injunctions, 5.03

B

Bailiffs, 1.09
Billing standards and practices, 4.10, 7.14
Blogs, use of, 6.15
Bondsmen, 1.09
Business advisors, 7.13
Business entities for psychotherapists
- corporations for profit, 7.06
  - limited liability companies, 7.06
  - limited liability partnerships, 7.06
  - professional service corporations, 6.09, 6.10, 7.06
- nonprofit corporations, 7.02
- partnerships, 7.05
- sole proprietorships, 7.04

C

Candidates, 6.01
CASA volunteers, 1.09
- confidentiality, 1.09
- duties of, 1.09
- responding to requests for information, 2.21

Certification for short-term treatment, 5.04
Certified Addiction Counselors, 6.11
- Continuing Professional Development. *See* Continuing Professional Development (CPD) requirements
- licensing, 6.11
- therapist-client privilege, 2.06, 2.08
- unauthorized practice, 6.08

Certified public accountants, 7.13
Chat rooms, use of, 6.15
Child abuse or neglect
- confidentiality exceptions, 2.10, 2.11
- emotional abuse, 2.10
- mandated reporting of, 2.10
- prosecutions, 2.11
- reporting failures, 4.08
- reporting requirements for victims over age 18, 2.10
- therapist duties, 8.08

Child and Family Investigators (CFIs)
- applying to serve as CFI, 1.09
- communication with court and counsel, 8.04
- complaints, 8.04
- duties of, 1.09
- eligibility roster, 8.04
- fees, 8.04
- malpractice insurance, 8.04
- psychological testing, 8.04
- record disclosures, 8.04
- referrals, 8.04
- requests for confidential information, responding to, 2.21

role of, 1.09
Standards, 8.04, 8.09
testimony in family court, 8.09
Child Mental Health Treatment Act, 5.05
Children and minors
abuse or neglect. *See* Child abuse or neglect
child's request for no contact with parent, 8.13
custody, 8.01
decision-making authority of parent, 8.01
mental health services, 5.05
psychotherapist's role in restriction of liberties, 5.09
special advocates, 8.04
Civil Rights Act, 7.08
Clinical supervision standards, 6.06
Clinical supervisor requirements, 6.06
College counselor liability, 4.19
Colorado Court of Appeals, 1.05
Colorado Domestic Violence Offender Management Board. *See* Domestic Violence Offender Management Board
Colorado Supreme Court, 1.06
Commitment
alcoholics
emergency commitment, 5.06
involuntary commitment, 5.06
involuntary mental health commitments. *See* Mental health commitments, involuntary
Common-law confidentiality, 2.03
Confidentiality, 2.01 to 2.24
adolescent treatments, 2.17
at-risk adult mistreatment reports, 2.14
child abuse or neglect, 2.10, 2.11
child abuse prosecutions, 2.11
child sexual assault, 2.10
common law, 2.03
consultation, 6.06
crime reporting duties, 2.10, 2.13
duty of, 2.01, 2.02, 2.03, 2.04, 2.05, 2.06, 2.07, 2.08, 2.09
duty to warn, 2.12
elder abuse reports, 2.14
ethical duties, 2.04
exceptions to, 2.10 to 2.18
federal statutes, 2.05
files, releasing, 2.19
forensic evaluations, 4.18
health care facility records, 2.19
health care provider records, 2.19
HIPAA, 2.20, 2.21, 2.22, 2.23, 2.24
HIV/AIDS reporting, 2.09
licenses and licensing, 6.03
mental health commitment records, 5.04
mental illness records, 2.16
office management, 2.20
physician-patient privilege, 2.07
practice pointers, 2.19, 2.20, 2.21
privileges compared, 2.06, 2.07, 2.08
professional association addresses, 2.01
protective order motions, 2.21
records, releasing, 2.19
requests for information, responding to, 2.21
sexual assault of child, 2.10
sources of, 2.01
state statute, 2.02
subpoenas, responding to, 2.21
supervision, 6.06
therapist-client privilege, 2.08
waiver by client, 2.15
Conservators and conservatorships, 1.09, 5.01, 5.02
Continuing Professional Development (CPD) requirements, 6.14
deadlines, 6.14
effective dates, 6.14
steps required, 6.14
Corporations
for-profit, 7.06
limited liability companies, 7.06
nonprofit corporation employment for psychotherapists, 7.02
professional service corporations, 6.09, 6.10, 7.06
County courts, 1.02
Couples counseling, billing for, 4.10
Court clerks, 1.09
Court of Appeals, 1.05
Court reporters, 1.09

Court-ordered mental health evaluations, 5.04
Crime reporting duties, 2.10, 2.13
Criminal insanity, 2.07, 2.08, 5.08
  procedure, 5.08
  psychotherapist's role, 5.09
  temporary insanity, 5.08

D

Database registration requirements for licensing, 6.01
Davis-Bacon Act, 7.08
Decision-makers, 1.09, 8.01, 8.07
Declaratory orders of mental health boards, 6.05
Depositions, 3.09
Developmentally disabled, 5.07
  legal disability, imposition of, 5.07
  psychotherapist's role, 5.09
  rights of the developmentally disabled, 5.07
  service provider liability limitations, 5.07
  sterilization limitations, 5.07
Dissociative Identity Disorder, 4.15
District attorney, 1.09
District courts, 1.04
Divorce injunctions, 5.03
Divorce, high-conflict cases, 8.13
Domestic relations decision-makers, 1.09, 8.01, 8.07
Domestic violence
  definition of, 5.03
  emergency protection orders, 5.03
  restraining orders, 5.03
  treatment providers, 8.10
Domestic Violence Offender Management Board, 8.10
  record keeping for approved treatment providers, 8.12
  standards
    intake evaluations, 8.11
    offender contracts, 8.11
    practice tips, 8.11
    reports, 8.11
    specific offender populations, 8.11
    supervision, 8.11
    treatment discharge, 8.11
    treatment evaluations, 8.11
    treatment goals, 8.11
    treatment plans, 8.11
    victim advocacy, 8.11

E

Elder abuse report disclosures, 2.14
Email between counselor and client, 6.15
Emergency 72-hour hold in mental health commitments, 5.04
Emergency commitment for alcoholism, 5.06
Emergency protection orders, 5.03
Employers and employees, 7.07 to 7.11
  age discrimination, 7.08
  Americans with Disabilities Act, 7.08
  Civil Rights Act, 7.08
  Davis-Bacon Act, 7.08
  "employee" *vs.* "independent contractor" status, 7.07
  employer payroll taxes, 7.10
  Equal Pay Act, 7.08
  Fair Labor Standards Act, 7.08
  National Labor Relations Act, 7.08
  Norris-LaGuardia Act, 7.08
  Polygraph Protection Act, 7.08
  Pregnancy Discrimination Act, 7.08
  Rehabilitation Act, 7.08
  Worker Adjustment and Retraining Act, 7.08
  workers' compensation, 7.09
Employment laws, 7.08
Equal Pay Act, 7.08
Escape from mental health commitment, 5.04
Ethics
  confidentiality, 2.04
  forensic evaluations, 4.18
  malpractice and professional liability, 4.13
Expert witnesses and testimony, 1.09, 3.01 to 3.14, 8.09
  answering questions on the stand, 3.11
  basis of testimony, 3.05
  CFI Standards, 8.04, 8.09
  depositions, 3.09
  domestic relations actions, testifying in, 4.20, 8.09
  ethical limitations, 4.20, 8.09

"helpful" testimony requirement, 3.02
immunity, 3.13
nature of testimony, 3.14
oaths, 3.11
prevention of risks, 4.20
qualifying as, 3.03
report preparation, 3.08
retaining experts, 3.07
rights of witnesses, 3.12
standard of care, 8.03
standards for child and family investigations, 8.04
Standards for Child and Family Investigators, 8.04, 8.09
trial preparation, 3.10
types of testimony, 3.04
underlying facts or data, disclosure of, 3.06

F

Facebook, use for marketing purposes, 6.15
Fair Labor Standards Act, 7.08
False Memory Syndrome Foundation, 4.15
Family investigators. *See* Child and Family Investigators
Federal courts, 1.08
Forensic evaluations
confidentiality, 4.18
ethical standards, 4.18
legal standards, 4.18
model disclosures, 4.18
models, 4.18
privilege, 4.18
record keeping, 4.18
reports, 4.18
risk management, 4.18
Fraud, insurance, 4.09

G

Government employment of psychotherapists, 7.01
Grievance procedures in licensing, 6.04
Group therapy notes, 4.16
Guardians and guardianship, 1.09, 5.01
conservators and conservatorships, 5.01, 5.02
definitions, 5.01
guardians ad litem, 1.09, 5.01
of incapacitated persons, 5.01
of minors, 5.01
"protected persons," 5.01
psychotherapist's role, 5.09
"wards," 5.01

H

Health care facility record disclosures, 2.19
Health care provider record disclosures, 2.19
Health insurance fraud, 4.09
HIPAA
authorizations to disclose confidential information, 2.23
billing, 4.10, 7.14
business practices, 2.20, 2.22
death of therapist, protecting information after, 2.24
frequently asked questions, 7.14
requests for confidential information, responding to, 2.21, 2.22
subpoenas, responding to, 2.21
HIV/AIDS reporting, 2.09
Hypnosis, 4.15

I

Immunity. *See* Privileges and immunity
Incapacitated persons and guardianship, 5.01
"Independent contractor" status, 7.07
Informed consent, 4.13
record keeping, 4.16
treating adults, 4.14
treating juveniles, 4.14
Injunctions, divorce, 5.03
Insanity, criminal. *See* Criminal insanity
Insurance, 7.12
fraud, 4.09
malpractice and professional liability, 4.09, 4.10, 4.12, 4.13
Insurance brokers, 7.13
Internet, use of, 6.15
Invasion of privacy, 4.05
Investigators
child and family investigators. *See* Child and Family Investigators
defined, 1.09

Involuntary commitment of alcoholics, 5.06
Involuntary mental health commitments. *See* Mental health commitments, involuntary

J

Joint custody, 8.01
Judges, 1.09
Judicial districts, 1.01
Juries, 1.09
Jurisdiction
  Colorado Court of Appeals, 1.05
  Colorado Supreme Court, 1.06
  county courts, 1.02
  district courts, 1.04
  federal courts, 1.08
  municipal courts, 1.07
  Small Claims Division, 1.03

L

Lay witnesses, 1.09
Learning plan, 6.14
Legal aid, 1.09
Licenses and licensing, 6.01 to 6.12
  addiction counselors, 6.11
  clinical supervision standards, 6.06
  clinical supervisor requirements, 6.06
  confidentiality of communications, 6.03
  database registration requirements, 6.01
  definitions, 6.01
  grievance procedures, 6.04
  information disclosures, mandatory, 6.02
  Mental Health Act, scope of, 6.01
  Mental Health Boards. *See* Mental Health Boards
  professional service corporations, 6.09, 6.10, 7.06
  prohibited activities, 6.07
  psychiatric technicians, 6.12
  psychiatrists, 6.10
  title use restrictions, 6.01
  unauthorized practice, 6.08
Long-term care and treatment in mental health commitments, 5.04

M

M-1 process, 5.04
Magistrates, 1.09
Malpractice and professional liability, 4.01
  billing practices, 4.10
  boundaries, maintaining, 4.13
  child abuse reporting failures, 4.08
  definition of "psychotherapy," 4.03
  Dissociative Identity Disorder, 4.15
  ethical standard, following, 4.13
  False Memory Syndrome Foundation, 4.15
  forensic evaluations. *See* Forensic evaluations
  group therapy notes, 4.16
  health insurance fraud, 4.09
  hypnosis, 4.15
  informed consent, 4.13
    record keeping, 4.16
    treating adults, 4.14
    treating juveniles, 4.14
    trends and controversies, 4.15
  insurance, malpractice, 4.12, 4.13
  insurance fraud, 4.09
  invasion of privacy, 4.05
  Multiple Personality Disorder, 4.15
  negligence, 4.01
    breach of duty, 4.01
    causation, 4.01
    duty owed, 4.01
    immunity, 4.01
    injury, harm, or damage, 4.01
    types of, 4.02
  outrageous conduct, 4.06
  pastoral counseling, 4.17
  prevention of malpractice, 4.13
  protect, duty to, 4.04
  record keeping, 4.13, 4.16, 4.18
  referring clients, 4.13
  repressed memory, 4.15
  responding to a lawsuit, 4.11
  scope of liability, 4.03
  sexual orientation, 4.15
  sexual relations with clients, 4.07
  S.O.A.P. notes, 4.16
  spiritual counseling, 4.17
  standards that apply to practice, knowing, 4.13

staying current in the field, 4.13
suing clients, 4.13
taking the law into your own hands, 4.13
tape recording treatment sessions, 4.13
trends and controversies in litigation, 4.15
warn, duty to, 4.04
Marital counseling, billing for, 4.10
Marketing via social media, 6.15
Mediators, 1.09
Mental Health Act, 6.01
Mental health boards, 6.05
Rule 6 (declaratory orders), 6.05
Rule 7 (mandatory disclosure), 6.05
Rule 8 (mandatory reporting), 6.05
Rule 9 (supervision standards), 6.05
definitions, 6.05
duties, 6.05
Mental health commitments, involuntary, 5.04
certification for short-term treatment, 5.04
confidentiality of records, 5.04
court-ordered evaluations, 5.04
emergency 72-hour hold, 5.04
escape, 5.04
legal disability, imposition of, 5.04
long-term care and treatment, 5.04
M-1 process, 5.04
patient's rights, 5.04
psychotherapist's role, 5.09
right to treatment, 5.04
rights, deprivation of, 5.04
termination, 5.04
Mental health services for children, 5.05
Mental illness record disclosures, 2.15, 2.16
Michael Skolnik Medical Transparency Act, 6.13
constitutional issues, 6.13
penalty for noncompliance, 6.13
profiling program, 6.13
requirements, 6.13
Multiple Personality Disorder, 4.15
Municipal courts, 1.07

N

National Labor Relations Act, 7.08
Neglect, child. *See* Child abuse or neglect
Negligence. *See* Malpractice and professional liability
Nonprofit corporation employment for psychotherapists, 7.02
Norris-LaGuardia Act, 7.08

O

Office management confidentiality, 2.20
Outrageous conduct liability, 4.06

P

Parental alienation in divorce cases, 8.13
Parental responsibility/parenting time evaluations
allocation of responsibilities, 4.18
treatment information access, 8.05
Parenting coordinators, 1.09, 8.06
Draft Guidelines for, 8.06
Parenting time, 8.02
child's request for no contact with parent, 8.13
parental alienation, 8.13
Parole officers, 1.09
Partnerships, 7.05
Pastoral counseling liability, 4.17
Patient's rights
of the developmentally disabled, 5.07
mental health commitments, involuntary, 5.04
Payroll taxes, 7.10
Physician-patient privilege, 2.07
Police, 1.09
Polygraph Protection Act, 7.08
Pregnancy Discrimination Act, 7.08
Privacy, invasion of, 4.05
Privileges and immunity, 2.05, 2.06, 2.07, 2.08, 2.09
decision-makers, 8.07
expert witnesses and testimony, 3.13
forensic evaluations, 4.18
malpractice and professional liability, 4.01
physician-patient privilege, 2.07
therapist-client privilege, 2.08
Probation officers, 1.09
Process servers, 1.09

Professional association addresses, 2.01
Professional Development Activity (PDA), 6.14
Professional development requirements. *See* Continuing Professional Development (CPD) requirements
Professional liability. *See* Malpractice and professional liability
Professional service corporations, 6.09, 6.10, 7.06
Professional will, 2.24
Profiling program for healthcare professionals, 6.13
Protection duties, 4.04
Protection orders
  emergency protection orders, 5.03
  motions and confidentiality, 2.21
Psychiatric technician licensing, 6.12
Psychiatrist licensing, 6.10
Public defenders, 1.09

R

Record keeping
  Domestic Violence Offender Management Board, 8.12
  malpractice and professional liability, 4.13, 4.16, 4.18
Referring clients, 4.13
Reflective practice, 6.14
Rehabilitation Act, 7.08
Repressed memory, 4.15
Requests for confidential information, responding to, 2.21
Restraining orders, 5.03
  divorce injunctions, 5.03
  domestic violence protection, 5.03
  emergency protection orders, 5.03
  psychotherapist's role, 5.09
Rights of patients
  of the developmentally disabled, 5.07
  mental health commitments, involuntary, 5.04
Rights of witnesses, 3.12

S

Sexual orientation, 4.15
Sexual relations with clients, 4.07
Skype, use of, 6.15
Small Claims Division, 1.03
SMART goals, 6.14
S.O.A.P. notes, 4.16
Social media, use of, 6.15
Sole proprietorships, 7.04
Special advocates. *See* Child and Family Investigators
Spiritual counseling liability, 4.17
Standard of care for testifying, 8.03
Standards for Child and Family Investigators, 8.04, 8.09
Sterilization limitations on the developmentally disabled, 5.07
Suicide, threats of, 4.04
Subpoenas, responding to, 2.21
Supreme Court, 1.06

T

Taxes
  employee withholdings, 7.11
  employees *vs.* independent contractors, 7.07
  employer payroll taxes, 7.10
Technology-assisted counseling, 6.15
Telephone conferences, billing for, 4.10
Telephone counseling, 6.15
Teletherapy, 6.15
Temporary criminal insanity, 5.08
Temporary divorce injunctions, 5.03
Testimony of therapists. *See* Expert witnesses and testimony.
Therapist-client privilege, 2.08
Title use restrictions in licensing, 6.01
Title VII of the Civil Rights Act, 7.08
Treatment information access, 8.05

U

Unauthorized practice, 6.08
Unemployment compensation, 7.07, 7.10
University counselor liability, 4.19

V

Violence, threats of, 4.04
Visitation, 8.02

W

Waiver of confidentiality, 2.15
Warnings and threats of violence
  confidentiality exceptions, 2.12
  duties, 4.04
  zero tolerance for threats, 4.04

Websites, use of, 6.15
Will, professional, 2.24
Witnesses and testimony
  expert witnesses. *See* Expert witnesses and testimony
  lay witnesses, 1.09
  rights of witnesses, 3.12
Worker Adjustment and Retraining Act, 7.08
Workers' compensation, 7.07, 7.09